*f*ormatio
TRADITION. EXPERIENCE.
TRANSFORMATION.

Formatio books from InterVarsity Press follow the rich tradition of the church in the journey of spiritual formation. These books are not merely about being informed, but about being transformed by Christ and conformed to his image. Formatio stands in InterVarsity Press's evangelical publishing tradition by integrating God's Word with spiritual practice and by prompting readers to move from inward change to outward witness. InterVarsity Press uses the chambered nautilus for Formatio, a symbol of spiritual formation because of its continual spiral journey outward as it moves from its center. We believe that each of us is made with a deep desire to be in God's presence. Formatio books help us to fulfill our deepest desires and to become our true selves in light of God's grace.

ANCIENT CHRISTIAN Devotional

A Year of Weekly Readings

LECTIONARY CYCLE

B

General Editor Thomas C. Oden

Edited by Cindy Crosby

IVP Books

An imprint of InterVarsity Press
Downers Grove, Illinois

InterVarsity Press
P.O. Box 1400, Downers Grove, IL 60515-1426
World Wide Web: www.ivpress.com
E-mail: email@ivpress.com

InterVarsity Press® is the book-publishing division of InterVarsity Christian Fellowship/USA®, a movement of students and faculty active on campus at hundreds of universities, colleges and schools of nursing in the United States of America, and a member movement of the International Fellowship of Evangelical Students. For information about local and regional activities, write Public Relations Dept., InterVarsity Christian Fellowship/USA, 6400 Schroeder Rd., P.O. Box 7895, Madison, WI 53707-7895, or visit the IVCF website at <www.intervarsity.org>.

Design: Cindy Kiple
Images: Scala/Art Resource, NY

ISBN 978-0-8308-3556-0

Printed in the United States of America ∞

Library of Congress Cataloging-in-Publication Data

Ancient Christian devotional: a year of weekly readings / edited by
Cindy Crosby; general editor, Thomas C. Oden.
    p. cm.
Includes bibliographical references and index.
ISBN 978-0-8308-3431-0 (pbk.: alk. paper)
1. Bible—Devotional literature. I. Crosby, Cindy, 1961- II. Oden,
Thomas C.
BS491.5.A52 2007
242'.3—dc22

    2006101569

P	18	17	16	15	14	13	12	11	10	9	8	7	6	5	4	3	2	1
Y	26	25	24	23	22	21	20	19	18	17	16	15	14	13	12	11		

CONTENTS

Welcome to the
ANCIENT CHRISTIAN
DEVOTIONAL

Listen carefully to me. Procure books [of the Bible]
that will be medicines for the soul. . . . Don't simply dive into them.
Swim in them. Keep them constantly in your mind.

JOHN CHRYSOSTOM,
HOMILIES ON COLOSSIANS 9

Many Christians today lack grounding in the riches of church history. We may find ourselves "rootless and drifting in a barren secular and ecclesiastical landscape."* The church fathers offer us context and tradition that will help us establish the roots we need. They do so by taking us deeper into the rich resources of Scripture, helping us to read holy writings with ancient eyes.

This devotional combines excerpts from the writings of the church fathers as found in the twenty-nine-volume Ancient Christian Commentary on Scripture with a simple structure of daily reading and prayer. It is designed to allow you to work through the material at your own pace. You can read a little each day, or, if you like to have a longer time of prayer once a week, it would work nicely in that format as well.

For centuries, these moving classic biblical texts have called the intergenerational church to the life of prayer. Each week you will be praying with believers of all cultures, stretching over two thousand years of shared common prayer. Each of the fifty-two weeks has one Old and two New Testament readings, one from an Epistle and the other from a Gospel passage. So keep the Bible close. Remember that the promises of the Old Testament are always seen in light of their fulfillment in the New.

How are these themes organized, and in what sequence? They arise out of centuries of the church's practice of daily prayer in the worldwide worshiping community. Each text fits into the seasons of celebration of the Christian year (from Advent to Christmas to Epiphany to Lent to Easter to Pentecost). This basic order is easily found in the sixteenth-century Book of Common Prayer, but that book itself depends heavily upon the previous centuries of the orders of common prayer. Altogether these seasons annually rehearse the expectation, coming, death, resurrection and coming again of our Lord. When the word *proper* is used for a prayer, it refers to a classic prayer of the ancient church befitting (hence "proper" to) the theme of the season being celebrated.

The date range with each week indicates the Sunday associated with the reading. The year begins with the readings for the first Sunday in Advent, four Sundays before Christmas. Depending on where Easter falls in a given year, you may need to adjust your reading. The readings for the first Sunday of Lent begin in Week 13 and go through Week 18. Easter is in Week 19. Six weeks of Easter readings then follow. If Easter was early and you skipped some readings, you might at this point go back and pick them up. Pentecost is in Week 26. In Week 27 we then pick up the dating of the entries. You will also find a special week of readings in Week 48 for All Saints' Day, which is celebrated November first or the first Sunday in November.

Each week you will find the following elements.

THEME

An overview of the week's theme, drawing together the texts of the week. (The texts follow the Revised Common Lectionary Cycle B.)

OPENING PRAYER

A simple prayer taken from early church sources, which you can pray daily.

READINGS

Each week you will find an Old Testament, Epistle and Gospel reading, in keeping with the long tradition of the church lectionary cycles (depending on the liturgical cycle, some readings may differ slightly).

PSALM OF RESPONSE

The psalm can be used for prayer and meditation. It is there to help you offer words of petition and praise to God. You may want to pray through it daily.

REFLECTIONS FROM THE CHURCH FATHERS

The Latin and Greek sentences which these ancient Christian commentators were writing are sometimes longer than those normally used in English. A single Greek sentence that might take two or three English sentences is sometimes tightly packed into a single extended sentence. Give yourself time to absorb the meaning of each phrase.

CLOSING PRAYER

This simple prayer drawn from ancient sources is designed to be used daily to close your time with God.

If you want to spend ten or fifteen minutes with this material each day, a suggested structure for your time would be to read the opening prayer, the psalm, one of the Scripture texts, two or three of the Reflections from the church fathers, and the closing prayer. Feel free to write in the book to note the sections you have completed as you go.

Don't worry about getting through the material on any particular schedule. Allow God to speak to you. Listen. Rest. This book should not be a source of guilt but a resource of grace. May your reading draw you to dig deep into the riches of God's Word.

> The Word of God is in your heart. The Word digs in this soil so that the spring may gush out. (Origen)

---

*Robert Wilken, as quoted in Christopher Hall, *Reading Scripture with the Church Fathers* (Downers Grove, Ill.: InterVarsity Press, 1998).

God Is Faithful

THEME

Our awe-inspiring heavenly Father knows our sins (Is 64:1-9). Restore us, O Lord God, that we may be saved (Ps 80:1-7, 17-19). God is faithful (1 Cor 1:3-9). We must keep an ever-present watch, for Jesus is coming again (Mk 13:24-37).

OPENING PRAYER: *First Sunday in Advent*

We beseech you, Almighty God, to behold our prayers and to pour out on us your loving tenderness that we who are afflicted by reason of our sins may be refreshed by the coming of our Savior; through the same Jesus Christ our Lord. Amen. *The Gelasian Sacramentary*

OLD TESTAMENT READING: *Isaiah 64:1-9*

REFLECTIONS FROM THE CHURCH FATHERS

The Need for Righteousness. LEO THE GREAT: The brightness of the true light will not be able to be seen by the unclean sight, and that which will be happiness to minds that are bright and clean will be a punishment to those that are stained. Therefore, let the mists of earth's vanities be shunned, and let your inward eyes be purged from all the filth of wickedness, that the sight may be free to feed on this great manifestation of God. For to the attainment of this we understand what follows to lead. *Sermon 95.8.*

The Blessings of Heaven. CHRYSOSTOM: Let us scrutinize those who enjoy the good things of the world in this present life, I mean wealth and power and glory. Exulting with delight, they reckon themselves as no longer being on the earth. They act this way even though the things that they are enjoying are acknowledged not to be really good and do not abide with them but take to flight more quickly than a dream. And even if these things should even last for a little time, their favor is displayed within the limits of this present life and cannot accompany us further. Now if these things uplift those who possess them to such a pitch of joy, what do you suppose is the condition of those souls that are invited to enjoy the countless blessings in heaven, blessings that are always securely fixed and stable? And not only this, but also in their quantity and quality heaven's blessings excel present things to such an extent as never entered even the heart of the human being. *Letter to the Fallen Theodore* 1.13.

Human Sin Comes Before Divine Anger. JEROME: It is not because you are angry that we sinned, but rather it is because we sinned that you are angry. Because we sinned, you are angry with us, O Lord, for we strayed and abandoned the right path, or, according to the Hebrew text, we, who always lived in sin and are unclean in ourselves, will be saved only by your mercy. *Commentary on Isaiah* 17.35.

PSALM OF RESPONSE: *Psalm 80:1-7, 17-19*

NEW TESTAMENT READING: *1 Corinthians 1:3-9*

REFLECTIONS FROM THE CHURCH FATHERS

Still of the Flesh. CHRYSOSTOM: Here Paul talks about the particular problem that made the Corinthians carnal. There were other matters, like fornication and uncleanness, which he would deal with later, but first he wants to tackle something which he has clearly been trying to put right for some time. If jealousy makes people carnal, every one of us ought to be crying out because of our sin and covering ourselves in sackcloth and ashes. Who is not tainted with this? I say this of others only because I know how true it is of me. *Homilies on the Epistles of Paul to the Corinthians* 8.3.

God the Spirit Gives Growth. AMBROSIASTER: To plant is to evangelize and to bring to faith, to water is to baptize with the approved form of words. To forgive sins, however, and to give the Spirit belongs to God alone. We know that the Holy Spirit is given by God without the laying on of hands, and it has happened that an unbaptized person has received the forgiveness of his sins. Was such a person invisibly baptized, considering that he received the gift that belongs to baptism? *Commentary on Paul's Epistles.*

Planted in the House of the Lord. JEROME: I have been planted in the house of the Lord, I mean in the church; not in the walls but in its doctrines. Everyone who has been planted in the house of the Lord, who has put down roots there, brings forth flowers. *Homily.*

Only God Gives Increase. AUGUSTINE: Since the apostles would not have accomplished anything if God had not given the increase, how much more true is this of you or me, or anyone else of our time, who fancies himself as a teacher. *Letter* 193.

Sustained Forever. ORIGEN: Who sustains us? Christ Jesus, the Word and Wisdom of God. Moreover, he sustains us not merely for a day or two, but forever. *Commentary on 1 Corinthians* 1.2.52-54.

GOSPEL READING: *Mark 13:24-37*

REFLECTIONS FROM THE CHURCH FATHERS

The Coming of the Son. TERTULLIAN: If you examine this whole passage of Scripture from the inquiry of the disciples down to the parable of the fig tree, you will find that it makes sense at every point in connection with the coming of the Son of man. He will bring both sorrow and joy. The Son of man is coming in the midst of both calamities and promises, both the grief of nations and the longing of the saints. He is the common element in both. He who is common to both will end the one by inflicting judgment on the nations, and will commence the other by fulfilling the longings of the saints. *Against Marcion* 4.39.

The Gathering of Fruits. HIPPOLYTUS: *The summer* signifies the end of the world, because at that time fruits are gathered up and stored. *On Matthew.*

Sober Hearts. PRUDENTIUS:
"Away," he cries, "with dull repose,
The sleep of death and sinful sloth;
With hearts now sober, just and pure,
Keep watch, for I am very near."
A Hymn for Cock-Crow.

His Second Coming. AUGUSTINE: The first coming of Christ the Lord, God's Son and our God, was in obscurity. The second will be in sight of the whole world. When he came in obscurity no one recognized him but his own servants. When he comes openly he will be known by both the good and the bad. When he came in obscurity, it was to be judged. When he comes openly it will be to judge. He was silent at his trial, as the prophet foretold. . . . Silent when accused, he will not be silent as judge. Even now he does not keep silent, if there is anyone to listen. But it says he will not keep silent then, because his voice will be acknowledged even by those who despise it. *Sermon* 18.1-2.

CLOSING PRAYER

Almighty God, who sees that we have no power of ourselves to help ourselves, keep us both outwardly in our bodies and inwardly in our souls, that we may be defended from all adversities that may happen to the body and from all evil thoughts that may assault and hurt the soul; through Jesus Christ our Lord. Amen. *The Gregorian Sacramentary*

Eternal Word

THEME

God forgives us; we look to his steadfast love and faithfulness (Ps 85:1-2, 8-13). The grass withers, the flower fades, but the Word of God is eternal (Is 40:1-11). Prepare the way of the Lord (Mk 1:1-8), who will bring new heavens and a new earth in which righteousness dwells (2 Pet 3:8-15a).

OPENING PRAYER: *Second Sunday in Advent*

I pray you, merciful Jesus, that as you graciously granted me to drink down sweetly from the Word that tells of you, so will you kindly grant that I may come at length to you, the fount of all wisdom, and stand before your face forever. *Bede*

OLD TESTAMENT READING: *Isaiah 40:1-11*

REFLECTIONS FROM THE CHURCH FATHERS

On Behalf of Hezekiah's Descendants. EPHREM THE SYRIAN: Hezekiah offered prayers to God because he had been told that death was imminent, but he failed to pray that evil should be averted from his descendants. Hence Isaiah says, "Comfort, comfort my people, you priests." *Commentary on Isaiah* 40.1.

Making a Path in the Heart for God to Find. ORIGEN: The Lord wants to find in you a path by which he can enter into your souls and make his journey. Prepare for him the path of which it is said, "Make straight his path." "The voice of one crying in the desert"—the voice cries, "prepare the way." *Homilies on the Gospel of Luke* 21.5.

Clear Reminders of the Creator. BASIL THE GREAT: I want the marvel of creation to gain such complete acceptance from you that, wherever you may be found and whatever kind of plants you may chance on, you may receive a clear reminder of the Creator. First, then, whenever you see a grassy plant or a flower, think of human nature, remembering the comparison of the wise Isaiah, that "all flesh is as grass, and all the glory of humanity as the flower of the grass." For the short span of life and the briefly enduring pleasure and joy of human happiness have found a most apt comparison in the words of the prophet. Today he is vigorous in body, grown fleshy from delicacies, with a flowerlike complexion, in the prime of life, fresh and eager, and irresistible in attack. Tomorrow that same one is piteous or wasted with age or weakened by disease. *Homilies on the Hexameron* 5.2.

The Unchangeable Nature of the Divine Word. AUGUSTINE: Both what is being thought of by intelligence and what is sounding out loud in speech is changeable and dissimilar. The first will not remain when you have forgotten it, nor will the second when you stop speaking. But "the Word of the Lord remains forever" and abides unchanged and unchangeable. *Sermon* 187.3.

PSALM OF RESPONSE: *Psalm 85:1-2, 8-13*

NEW TESTAMENT READING: *2 Peter 3:8-15a*

REFLECTIONS FROM THE CHURCH FATHERS

Whether Judgment Day Will Last a Thousand Years. BEDE: There are some people who think that this means that the day of judgment will last for a thousand years, but the context from which it is taken makes such an interpretation impossible. Psalm 90:4 says clearly that the thousand years refer to what is already past and that it is a way of describing the shortness of our life here on earth. What we regard as long or short is all the same to God. *On 2 Peter.*

His Promises Not Delayed. AUGUSTINE: The Lord does not delay the promise. A little while and we shall see him, where we shall no more ask anything. We will no more ask anything because nothing will remain to be desired, nothing will be hidden to be inquired about. *Tractates* 101.6.2.

Like a Thief. OECUMENIUS: The day of the Lord will come without notice and unexpectedly, just as the flood did in the days of Noah. People will be eating and drinking and will not realize what is happening to them until the flood overtakes them. *Commentary on 2 Peter.*

Creation Will Share in Our Glory. ANDREAS: It is not just we, says Peter, but the whole creation around us also, which will be changed for the better. For the creation will share in our glory, just as it has been subjected to destruction and corruption because of us. Either way it shares our fate. *Catena.*

The Friend of Truth. GREGORY THE GREAT: Look how Peter says that there is much to be admired in Paul's writings. Yet in his letters, Paul criticized Peter. Peter could hardly have said what he did if he had not read Paul, but when he read him he would have discovered criticism of himself in them. Thus the friend of truth was able to praise even the fact that he had been criticized, and he was happy to do so because he realized that he had been wrong. *Lessons in Job* 2.6.9.

GOSPEL READING: *Mark 1:1-8*

REFLECTIONS FROM THE CHURCH FATHERS

Preparing the Heart. ORIGEN: The way of the Lord must be prepared within the heart; for great and spacious is the heart of man, as if it were a whole world. But see its greatness, not in bodily quantity but in the power of the mind that enables it to encompass so great a knowledge of the truth. Prepare, therefore, in your hearts the way of the Lord, by a worthy manner of life. Keep straight the path of your life, so that the words of the Lord may enter in without hindrance. *Homily* 21.

His Sudden Appearance. EUSEBIUS OF CAESAREA: He emerged from the desert clothed in a strange garment, refusing all ordinary social intercourse. He did not even share their common food. For it is written that from childhood John was in the deserts until the day of his public appearance to Israel. Indeed, his clothing was made of camel's hair! His food locusts and wild honey! . . . It is understandable that they should have been alarmed when they saw a man with the hair of a Nazarite of God, and a divine face, suddenly appearing from the lonely wilderness dressed in bizarre clothing, who after preaching to them, disappeared again into the wilderness, without eating or drinking or mingling with the people. Must they not have suspected that he was a little more than human? For how could a human being go without food? And so they understood him to be a divine messenger, the very angel foretold by the prophet. *Proof of the Gospel* 9.5.

Through a Narrow Passage. CYRIL OF JERUSALEM: He fed on locusts to make his soul grow wings. Sated with honey, the words he spoke were sweeter than honey and of more profit. Clothed in a garment of camel's hair, he exemplified in his own person the holy life. . . . For every snake puts off its signs of age by pushing through some narrow place, and gets rid of its old apparel by squeezing it off. From then on it is young again in body. So "enter in at the straight and narrow gate," squeeze yourself through by fasting, break yourself away from perishing, "put off the old nature with its deeds." *Catechetical Lectures* 3.6.

CLOSING PRAYER

O God, who looked on us when we had fallen down into death and resolved to redeem us by the Advent of your only begotten Son; grant, we beg you, that those who confess his glorious incarnation may also be admitted to the fellowship of their Redeemer, through the same Jesus Christ our Lord. *Ambrose*

Hold Fast to Good

THEME

John prepared the way for Jesus Christ (Jn 1:6-8, 19-28). God has done great things for us (Ps 126); he brings good tidings to the afflicted and loves justice (Is 61:1-4, 8-11). Rejoice always, pray constantly, hold fast to that which is good (1 Thess 5:16-24).

OPENING PRAYER: *Third Sunday in Advent*

Grant me the dew of your grace, Lord. Forgive my sins. But above all, may the glory belong to you. *Rabbula of Edessa*

OLD TESTAMENT READING: *Isaiah 61:1-4, 8-11*

REFLECTIONS FROM THE CHURCH FATHERS

The Anointing of Jesus. EPHREM THE SYRIAN: "The Spirit of the Lord God is on me, because the Lord has anointed me to bring good tidings to the afflicted," that is, God anointed him with the Holy Spirit. Therefore, after being incarnated and clothed with a human body, as is said, he has received the Spirit and has been anointed with the Spirit, because he has received the Spirit for us and has anointed us with it. *Commentary on Isaiah* 61.1.

The Anointing Spirit. AMBROSE: We have shown by the clear evidence of the Scripture that the apostles and prophets were appointed, the latter to prophesy, the former to preach the gospel, by the Holy Spirit in the same way as by the Father and the Son. Now we add what all will rightly wonder at and not be able to doubt, that the Spirit was on Christ; and that as he sent the Spirit, so the Spirit sent the Son of God. For the Son of God says, "The Spirit of the Lord is on me, because he has appointed me, he has sent me to preach the gospel." And having read this from the book of Isaiah, he says in the Gospel, "Today has this Scripture been fulfilled in your ears," that he might point out that it was said of himself. *On the Holy Spirit* 3.1.1.

Do Not Despair. ISAAC OF NINEVEH: Do not fall into despair because of stumbling. I do not mean that you should not feel contrition for your sins but that you should not think them incurable. For it is more expedient to be bruised than dead. There is, indeed, a Healer for the person who has stumbled, even he who on the cross asked that mercy be shown to his crucifiers, he who pardoned his murderer while he hung on the cross. . . . Christ came in behalf of sinners to heal the broken of heart and to bandage their wounds. "The Spirit of the Lord," he says, "is on me, to preach good tidings to the poor." And the apostle says in his epistle, "Jesus Christ came into the world to save sinners." *Ascetical Homilies* 64.

⊰ **PSALM OF RESPONSE:** *Psalm 126*

⊰ **NEW TESTAMENT READING:** *1 Thessalonians 5:16-24*

REFLECTIONS FROM THE CHURCH FATHERS

Keep the Feast. ATHANASIUS: For no one is going to turn away from sin and start behaving righteously unless he thinks about what he is doing. Not until he has been straightened out by practicing godly behavior will he actually possess the regard of faith: the crown of righteousness that Paul possessed, having fought the good fight. That crown is laid up not just for Paul but for all who are like him in this respect. This sort of meditation and exercise in godliness should be familiar to us, as it was to the saints of old. It should be especially so in the season when the divine word calls upon us to keep the feast. For what, after all, is the feast but continual worship of God, recognition of godliness and unceasing prayer all done from the heart in full agreement with each other? St. Paul, wanting us to be so inclined, urges us, "Always rejoice, pray without ceasing, give thanks in all things." *Festal Letters* 9.

Perfect Devotion. CASSIODORUS: "Sing with jubilation to God, all the earth." The prophet was troubled for the faithful people in case they believe they are to serve the Lord with gloomy anxiety, so he began at once with jubilation, for ministering to the Lord with happiness of mind constitutes the perfect devotion of the just man. As Paul warns you, "Always rejoice: pray without ceasing: in all things give thanks." *Commentary on the Psalms* 99.2.

The Recollected Heart. BASIL THE GREAT: For prayer and psalmody, however, as also, indeed, for some other duties, every hour is suitable, that, while our hands are busy at their tasks, we may praise God sometimes with the tongues (when this is possible, or, rather, when it is conducive to edification); or, if not, with the heart. . . . Thus we acquire a recollected spirit when in every action we beg from God the success of our labors and satisfy our debt of gratitude to him who gave us the power to do the work, and when, as has been said, we keep before our minds the aim of pleasing him. If this is not the case, how can there be consistency in the words of the apostle bidding us to "pray without ceasing," with those other words, "we worked night and day." *The Long Rules* Q37.R.

Fire and Fuel. CHRYSOSTOM: On this account Paul says, "Do not quench the Spirit," that is, the gift of grace. . . . But an impure life extinguishes the gift of grace. For as anyone who has sprinkled both wa-

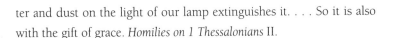
ter and dust on the light of our lamp extinguishes it. . . . So it is also with the gift of grace. *Homilies on 1 Thessalonians* II.

GOSPEL READING: *John 1:6-8, 19-28*

REFLECTIONS FROM THE CHURCH FATHERS

Prophecies and Miracles Testify to Christ. ORIGEN: Some try to undo the testimonies of the prophets to Christ by saying that the Son of God has no need of such witnesses. . . . To this we may reply that where there are a number of reasons to make people believe, persons are often impressed by one kind of proof and not by another. And with respect to the doctrine of the incarnation, it is certain that some have been forced by the prophetical writings into an admiration of Christ by the fact of so many prophets having, before his advent, fixed the place of his birth. . . . It is to be remembered too, that, though the display of miraculous powers might stimulate the faith of those who lived in the same age with Christ, they might, in the lapse of time, fail to do so; as some of them might even get to be regarded as fabulous. Prophecy and miracles together are more convincing than simply past miracles by themselves. . . . He, therefore, who maintains that there is no need for the prophetic witness to Christ deprives the choir of prophets of their greatest gift. For what would prophecy, which is inspired by the Holy Spirit, have that is so great, if one exclude from it those matters related to the dispensation of our Lord? . . . John, too, therefore came to bear witness concerning the light. *Commentary on the Gospel of John* 2.199, 202-4, 206, 208, 212.

Sympathy Toward John As the More Deserving. CHRYSOSTOM: [The Jews] were influenced by a kind of human sympathy for John [the Baptist], whom they were reluctant to see made subordinate to Christ because of the many marks of greatness about him. [For example], there was in the first place his illustrious descent, since he was the son of a chief priest. There was also his hard training and his contempt for the world. . . . In Christ, however, the contrary was apparent. He was of humble birth, for which they reproach him by asking, "Is not this the carpenter's son?" . . . When John then was constantly sending them to Christ . . . therefore, they send someone to him, thinking by their flattery that they will induce him to confess that he was the Christ. They do not therefore send inferior people to him . . . servants and Herodians, as they did to Christ, but priests and Levites . . . of Jerusalem, that is, the more honorable ones. . . . They send them to ask, "Who are you?" . . . They send them not because they want to be informed but in order to induce him to do what I have said. . . . John replies then to their intention, not to their interrogation. . . . "And he confessed, 'I am not the Christ.' " *Homilies on the Gospel of John* 16.1-2.

Footprints on Our Souls. AMBROSE: For Christ alone walks in the souls and makes his path in the minds of his saints, in which, as on bases of gold and foundations of precious stone the heavenly Word has left his footprints ineffaceably impressed. *On the Christian Faith* 3.10.71-74.

CLOSING PRAYER

As each day passes, the end of my life becomes ever nearer, and my sins increase in number. You, Lord, my creator, know how feeble I am, and in my weakness, strengthen me; when I suffer, uphold me, and I will glorify you, my Lord and my God. *Ephrem the Syrian*

Nothing Is Impossible for God

⊰ THEME

The Lord was with David (2 Sam 7:1-11, 16); through his lineage and
the virgin Mary, the Son of God was born. Nothing is impossible for
God (Lk 1:26-38). Glory to his name (Rom 16:25-27), the Rock of our
salvation (Ps 89:1-4, 19-26).

⊰ OPENING PRAYER: *Fourth Sunday in Advent*

Almighty God, Father of our Lord Jesus Christ, establish and confirm
us in your truth by your Holy Spirit. Reveal to us what we do not know;
perfect in us what is lacking; strengthen us in what we know; and keep
us faultless in your service; through the same Jesus Christ our Lord.
Clement of Rome

⊰ OLD TESTAMENT READING: *2 Samuel 7:1-11, 16*

REFLECTIONS FROM THE CHURCH FATHERS

God the Spirit Moves Where He Pleases. GREGORY THE GREAT:
The spirit of prophecy does not enlighten the minds of the prophets
constantly. . . . We read in sacred Scripture that the Holy Spirit breathes
where he pleases, and we should also realize that he breathes when he
pleases. For example, when King David asked whether he could build
a temple, the prophet Nathan gave his consent but later had to with-
draw it. *Dialogue 2.21.*

Christ the Temple of God. CYPRIAN: That Christ should be the house and temple of God, and that the old temple should cease, and the new one should begin. In the second book of Kings [Samuel]: "And the word of the Lord came to Nathan, saying, 'Go and tell my servant David, Thus says the Lord, You shall not build me a house to dwell in; but it shall be, when your days are fulfilled, and you sleep with your fathers, that I will raise up your seed after you, which shall come from your body, and I will prepare his kingdom. He shall build me a house in my name, and I will raise up his throne forever; and I will be a father to him, and he shall be a son to me, and his house shall obtain faith, and his kingdom [will be] forever in my sight.' " Also in the Gospel the Lord says, "There shall not be left in the temple one stone upon another that shall not be thrown down." And "After three days another shall be raised up without hands." *To Quirinus: Testimonies Against the Jews* 1.15.

PSALM OF RESPONSE: *Psalm 89:1-4, 19-26*

NEW TESTAMENT READING: *Romans 16:25-27*

REFLECTIONS FROM THE CHURCH FATHERS

The Revelation of the Mystery. ORIGEN: Paul wants to show that there are two ways in which those who believe in the gospel are strengthened. One is by his preaching, which is the preaching of Christ. The other is by the revelation of the mystery which was kept secret for long ages and which has now been revealed in Christ . . . not without suitable witnesses but with the backing of the prophetic Scriptures. *Commentary on the Epistle to the Romans.*

The Limits of Human Wisdom. ORIGEN: God cannot be called wise in the way that human beings are wise, because a wise man merely has a share in wisdom, whereas God is its author and source. *Commentary on the Epistle to the Romans.*

Glory to the Father Through the Son in the Spirit. **CHRYSOSTOM:**
Do not think that Paul said this in disparagement of the Son. For if all
the things whereby his wisdom was made apparent were done by
Christ and nothing was done without him, it is quite plain that the Son
is equal to the Father in wisdom also. The word *only* is used in order to
contrast God with every created being. *Homilies on Romans 27.*

Glory to the Father Through the Son in the Spirit. **AMBROSIASTER:**
Without Christ nothing is complete, because all things are through
him. It is acknowledged that praise is given to God the Father through
him, because it is understood that "through Christ" means "through his
wisdom," in whom he has saved believers. Therefore glory to the Father
through the Son is glory to both in the Holy Spirit, because both are in
the one glory. *Commentary on Paul's Epistles.*

GOSPEL READING: *Luke 1:26-38*

REFLECTIONS FROM THE CHURCH FATHERS

Why Mary Must Be Betrothed to Joseph. **BEDE:** As to why he wished
to be conceived and born not of a simple virgin but of one who was betrothed to a man, several of the Fathers have put forward reasonable
answers. The best of these is to prevent her from being condemned as
guilty of defilement if she were to bear a son when she had no husband.
Then too, in the things the care of a home naturally demands, the
woman in labor would be sustained by a husband's care. Therefore
blessed Mary had to have a husband who would be both a perfectly
sure witness to her integrity and a completely trustworthy foster father
for our Lord and Savior, who was born of her. He was a husband who
would, in accordance with the law, make sacrificial offerings to the temple for him when he was an infant. He would take him, along with his
mother, to Egypt when persecution threatened. He would bring him
back and would minister to the many other needs consequent on the

weakness of the humanity that he had assumed. It did no great harm if, for a time, some believed that he was Joseph's son, since from the apostles' preaching after his ascension it would be plainly evident to all believers that he had been born of a virgin. *Homilies on the Gospels* 1.3.

Mother Yet Virgin. PRUDENTIUS:
A heavenly fire engenders him, not flesh
Nor blood of father, nor impure desire.
By power of God a spotless maid conceives
As in her virgin womb the Spirit breathes.
The mystery of this birth confirms
That Christ is God; a maiden by the Spirit
Is wed, unstained by love; her purity
Remains intact; with child within, untouched
Without, bright in her chaste fertility,
Mother, yet virgin, mother that knew not man.
Why, doubter, do you shake your silly head?
An angel makes this known with holy lips.
Will you not hearken to angelic words?
The Virgin blest, the shining messenger
Believed, and by her faith she Christ conceived.
Christ comes to men of faith and spurns the heart
Irresolute in trust and reverence.
The Virgin's instant faith attracted
Christ into her womb and hid him there
Till birth.
The Divinity of Christ 566-84.

The Mystery of the Timeless Entering Time. JOHN THE MONK:
Wonder! God is come among humanity; he who cannot be contained is contained in a womb; the timeless enters time, and great mystery: his conception is without seed, his emptying past telling! So great is this mystery! For God empties himself, takes flesh and is fashioned as a

creature, when the angel tells the pure Virgin of her conception: "Rejoice, you who are full of grace; the Lord who has great mercy is with you!" *Stichera of Annunciation.*

Exceeding All Understanding. LEO THE GREAT: But the birth of our Lord Jesus Christ exceeds all understanding and goes beyond any precedent. *Sermon 30.4.2.*

Jesus' Birth Prefigures Our Birth to New Life. PETER CHRYSOLOGUS: "Who was born from the Holy Spirit." Precisely thus is Christ born for you, in such a way that he may change your own manner of birth. . . . Formerly, death awaited you as the setting sun of your life; he wants you to have a new birth of life. "Who was born from the Holy Spirit of the Virgin Mary." Where the Spirit is begetting, and a virgin giving birth, everything carried on is divine; nothing of it is merely human. *Sermon 57.*

CLOSING PRAYER

We thank you, O God, through your child, Jesus Christ our Lord, because you have enlightened us and revealed to us the light that is incorruptible. The day's allotted span is over; we have reached the beginning of the night. We have had our fill of that daylight that you created for our pleasure. And now that evening has come and again we have no lack of light, we praise your holiness and glory, through your only Son, our Lord Jesus Christ. Through him the glory and power that are his and the honor that is the Holy Spirit's are also yours, as they will be throughout the unending succession of ages. Amen. *Hippolytus*

Christ Is Born!

THEME

Let the heavens be glad, and let the earth rejoice (Ps 96), for Jesus Christ redeems us from all of our sins (Tit 2:11-14). The people who walked in darkness have seen a great light (Is 9:2-7). Jesus Christ is born (Lk 2:1-20)!

OPENING PRAYER: *Christmas*

Almighty and everliving God, in your tender love for the human race you sent your Son our Savior Jesus Christ to take on him our nature and to suffer death on the cross, giving us the example of his great humility: Mercifully grant that we may walk in the way of his suffering and also share in his resurrection; through Jesus Christ our Lord, who lives and reigns with you and the Holy Spirit, one God, forever and ever. Amen. *The Gregorian Sacramentary*

OLD TESTAMENT READING: *Isaiah 9:2-7*

REFLECTIONS FROM THE CHURCH FATHERS

A Child Is Born. AMBROSE: So we have in another place: "A child is born to us, and a son is given to us." In the term *child* there is an indication of age; in the term *son* a reference to the fullness of Godhead. He was made of his mother and born of the Father, but as the same person he was born and given. Do not think of two but of one. For the Son of

God is one person, born of the Father and sprung from the virgin. The names differ in order but unite in one, just as the scriptural lesson just read teaches: "Man was made in her, and the Highest himself has founded her." He was man indeed in body, but the Highest in power. And while he is God and man through diversity of nature, he is the same person, not two persons, though being God and man. He has, therefore, something peculiar to his own nature and something in common with us, but in both cases he is one, and in both he is perfect. *On His Brother Satyrus* 1.12.

The Son Reveals the Father. CHRYSOSTOM: The Son of God is said to be the angel of great counsel because of his many other teachings, but especially because he revealed his Father to humankind. *Homilies on the Gospel of John* 81.

Peace to the World. BEDE: And indeed, just as in his divinity the Mediator between God and human beings foresaw the mother of whom he willed to be born when he should so will, so also in his humanity he chose the time that he wished for his nativity. Moreover, he himself granted that that time should be such as he willed, namely, that in a calm among the storm of wars a singular tranquility of unusual peace should cover the whole world. . . . He chose a time of utmost peace as the time when he would be born because this was the reason for his being born in the world, that he might lead the human race back to the gifts of heavenly peace. *Homilies on the Gospels* 1.6.

PSALM OF RESPONSE: *Psalm 96*

NEW TESTAMENT READING: *Titus 2:11-14*

REFLECTIONS FROM THE CHURCH FATHERS

Two Comings. CYRIL OF JERUSALEM: For Paul has also shown us that there are these two comings, in his epistle to Titus where he says,

"The grace of God our Savior has appeared unto all men, teaching us that, denying ungodliness and worldly lusts, we should live soberly, righteously and godly in this present world; looking for that blessed hope and the glorious appearing of the great God and our Savior Jesus Christ." You note how he acknowledges with thanksgiving the first coming and that we look for a second. . . . So our Lord Jesus Christ comes from heaven and comes with glory at the last day to bring this world to its close. *Catechetical Lectures* 15.2-3.

Only by Grace. FULGENTIUS OF RUSPE: The apostle Paul exclaims in a similar way: "Be imitators of God as his dear children." What will we reply to these words, brethren, or what excuse will we be able to have? If someone tells you that you should imitate the powers that our Lord exercised, there is a reasonable excuse for you, because not everyone is given the grace to exercise those powers and to work miracles. But to live piously and chastely, to preserve charity with all men, with God's help is possible for everyone. *Sermon* 223.2.

Church Within the Church. AUGUSTINE: The faithful who are holy and good may be few in comparison with the larger number of the wicked, but . . . "many shall come from the east and the west and shall sit down with Abraham and Isaac and Jacob in the kingdom of heaven." God shows to himself "a numerous people, zealous for good works." . . . Even when sometimes darkened and, as it were, clouded over by a great number of scandals . . . still this people shines forth in her strongest members. *Letter* 93.9.30.

GOSPEL READING: *Luke 2:1-20*

REFLECTIONS FROM THE CHURCH FATHERS

Firstborn in Grace. BEDE: He is the only-begotten of the substance of the divinity, firstborn in the assuming of humanity; firstborn in grace, only-begotten in nature. *Exposition of the Gospel of Luke* 2.7.

Swaddling Clothes and Manger Signal a Human Birth. CHRYSOS-
TOM: To prevent you from thinking that his coming to earth was
merely an accommodation, and to give you solid grounds for truly believing that his was real flesh, he was conceived, born and nurtured.
That his birth might be made manifest and become common knowledge, he was laid in a manger, not in some small room but in a lodging
place before numerous people. This was the reason for the swaddling
clothes and also for the prophecies spoken long before. The prophecies
showed not only that he was going to be a man but also that he would
be conceived, born and nurtured as any child would be. *Against the
Anomoeans* 7.49.

Shepherds Need the Presence of Christ. ORIGEN: Listen, shepherds
of the churches! Listen, God's shepherds! His angel always comes down
from heaven and proclaims to you, "Today a Savior is born for you, who
is Christ the Lord." For, unless that Shepherd comes, the shepherds of
the churches will be unable to guard the flock well. Their custody is
weak, unless Christ pastures and guards along with them. We read in
the apostle: "We are coworkers with God." A good shepherd, who im-
itates the good Shepherd, is a coworker with God and Christ. He is a
good shepherd precisely because he has the best Shepherd with him,
pasturing his sheep along with him. For "God established in his church
apostles, prophets, evangelists, shepherds and teachers. He established
everything for the perfection of the saints." *Homilies on the Gospel of
Luke* 12.2.

Swaddling Bands. GREGORY OF NAZIANZUS: He was wrapped in
swaddling bands, but at the resurrection he released the swaddling
bands of the grave. He was laid in a manger but was praised by angels,
disclosed by a star and adored by magi. *Oration* 29.19, On the Son.

The Christ child Makes for Us Peace and Goodwill. CYRIL OF ALEX-
ANDRIA: Look not on him who was laid in the manger as a babe

merely, but in our poverty see him who as God is rich, and in the measure of our humanity him who prospers those in heaven and who therefore is glorified even by the angels. And how noble was the hymn, "Glory to God in the highest, and on earth peace, and among men good will!" The angels and archangels, thrones and lordships, and the seraphim are at peace with God. Never in any way do they oppose his good pleasure but are firmly established in righteousness and holiness. But we wretched beings, by having set up our own lusts in opposition to the will of our Lord, had put ourselves into the position of his enemies. Christ has abolished this. "For he is our peace" and has united us by himself to God the Father. He has taken away from the middle the cause of the enmity and so justifies us by faith, makes us holy and without blame, and calls near to him those who were far off. Besides this, he has created the two people into one new man, so making peace and reconciling both in one body to the Father. For it pleased God the Father to form into one new whole all things in him, and to bind together things below and things above, and to make those in heaven and those on earth into one flock. Christ therefore has been made for us both peace and goodwill. *Commentary on Luke,* Homily 2.

CLOSING PRAYER

Almighty God, we give you thanks for surrounding us, as daylight fades, with the brightness of the vesper light, and we implore you of your great mercy that, as you enfold us with the radiance of this light, so you would shine into our hearts the brightness of your Holy Spirit; through Jesus Christ our Lord. Amen. *The Ambrosian Sacramentary*

The Light Has Come!

☙ THEME

The Light has come (Is 60:1-6)! As the wise men followed the star to find Jesus, let us also search for you (Mt 2:1-12). The Lord will bring justice, defend the cause of the poor and give deliverance to the needy. May peace (Ps 72:1-7, 10-14) and grace abound (Eph 3:1-12).

☙ OPENING PRAYER: *The Epiphany*

Almighty and everlasting God, who is always more ready to hear than we to pray, and is wont to give more than either we desire or deserve, pour down on us the abundance of your mercy, forgiving us those things whereof our conscience is afraid and giving us those good things that we are not worthy to ask, but through the merits and mediation of Jesus Christ, your Son, our Lord. Amen. *The Gelasian Sacramentary*

☙ OLD TESTAMENT READING: *Isaiah 60:1-6*

REFLECTIONS FROM THE CHURCH FATHERS

Christian Illumination Makes a Difference to Lifestyle. ORIGEN: And the Logos, exhorting us to come to this light, says, in the prophecies of Isaiah, "Enlighten yourself, enlighten yourself, O Jerusalem, for your light is come, and the glory of the Lord is risen on you." Observe now the difference between the fine phrases of Plato respecting the chief good and the declarations of our prophets regarding the light of the blessed; and notice that the truth as it is contained in Plato concerning this subject did not at all help his readers to attain to a pure worship of God, or even himself, who could philosophize so grandly about the chief good, whereas the simple language of the Scriptures led to their honest readers being filled with a divine spirit; and this light is nourished within them by the oil, which as a certain parable is said to have preserved the light of the torches of the five wise virgins. *Against Celsus* 6.5.

Christ as God Is the Light Himself. METHODIUS: Hail and shine, you Jerusalem, for your light is come, the Light eternal, the Light forever enduring, the Light supreme, the Light immaterial, the Light of same substance with God and the Father, the Light that is in the Spirit, and that is the Father; the Light that illumines the ages; the Light that gives light to mundane and superamundane things, Christ our very God. *Oration Concerning Simeon and Anna* 13.

Sketch and Painting. THEODORET OF CYR: This prophecy has three subjects. One subject, presented as in a sketch, is the rebuilding of Jerusalem that took place at the time of Cyrus and Darius. Another is like an icon "written" or drawn with many colors as it shows more precisely the lines of truth—the shining brightness of the holy church. The third is the archetype of the icon, that is, the life to come and our citizenship in heaven. The divine Paul taught this distinction: "The law contained the shadow of things to come and not the image of the realities." And he calls the things to come the immortal and pain-free existence, the lie unsullied by worry; whereas the image of the realities is the ecclesiastical commonwealth and its existence, which is like a model of the things to come. . . . For the painters have the reality that they copy to make their picture, drawing a sketch first before filling in the shadow with colors . . . the prophetic words apply to the church of God, which has received the light of the knowledge of God and is encircled by the glory of the Savior. *Commentary on Isaiah* 19.60.1.

◁ PSALM OF RESPONSE: *Psalm 72:1-7, 10-14*

◁ NEW TESTAMENT READING: *Ephesians 3:1-12*

REFLECTIONS FROM THE CHURCH FATHERS

Members of the Same Body. JEROME: Now the meaning of fellow heirs is this: Just as there are many members in one body . . . and these, though in one body, have their differences and feel their own joy and grief in turn, so those who have believed in Christ, even if they have different gifts, are bonded together in the one body of Christ. *Epistle to the Ephesians* 2.3.5.

Grace, Preparation and Prudent Understanding. CHRYSOSTOM: The gift was not sufficient if he did not provide power along with it. And, great as the power was, human zeal was not sufficient either. For Paul brought three things to the task of proclamation: ready and boiling fervor, a soul prepared to bear anything whatever, and prudent understanding. *Homily on Ephesians* 6.3.7.

The Grace to Work. MARIUS VICTORINUS: Was work given before grace? Or did grace come before any works? That which is working is God's power. So grace had already been given. When it is said that Paul was made a minister according to the gift of God, we understand that the gift of being a minister was given before his working to make him a minister, and his being a minister is the gift and grace of God. *Epistle to the Ephesians* 1.3.7-8.

◁ GOSPEL READING: *Matthew 2:1-12*

REFLECTIONS FROM THE CHURCH FATHERS

What They Saw. ANONYMOUS: "And on entering the house they saw the boy and his mother." Do we understand why, on seeing such a glorious sight, they delighted in the boy, the boy whom they sought as King and for whom they undertook the labor of so great a journey? Did they see a palace splendid in its marble? Did they see his mother crowned with a diadem or reclining on a gilded couch? Did they see a boy swaddled in purple and gold, a royal hallway thronged with various peoples? What did they see? A dark and lowly stable, more fit for animals than people, in which no one would be content to hide unless compelled by the necessity of the journey. . . . Their eyes could not see an unworthy boy, because the spirit in their hearts was revealing him to them as an awesome thing. If, moreover, they had sought him as a king of this world, they would have stayed with him, as is often the case when people abandon one king and transfer their allegiance to another. Instead they adored him and returned home that they might have Jesus as the just, heavenly king over their souls and the king of their home country as ruler over their bodies. *Incomplete Work on Matthew*, Homily 2.

Offering of the Hallowed Mind, Speech and Will. GREGORY THE GREAT: There is something more that must be understood about the gold, incense and myrrh. Solomon testifies that gold symbolizes wisdom when he says, "A pleasing treasure lies in the mouth of the wise." The psalmist bears witness to that incense which prayer offers to God when he says, "Let my prayer ascend as incense in your sight." The myrrh indicates the mortification of our bodies, of which the holy church speaks of its workmen who strive even unto death on behalf of God, "My hands dripped with myrrh." And so do we too offer gold to the newborn king if we shine in his sight with the brightness of the wisdom from on high. We too offer him incense if we enkindle on the altar of our hearts the thoughts of our human minds by our holy pursuit of prayer, so as to give forth a sweet smell to God by our heavenly desire. And we offer him myrrh if we mortify the vices of our bodies by our self-denial. *Forty Gospel Homilies* 10.6.

The Wiles of the Tyrant Overcome. CHROMATIUS: This is an example to us of modesty and faith, that once we have come to know and adore Christ as King, we may abandon the path we were traveling before, which was the path of error. We may now proceed by the other path, on which Christ is our guide. We may return to our place, paradise, from which Adam was driven out. *Tractate on Matthew 5.2.*

CLOSING PRAYER

We beseech you, O Lord, let our hearts be graciously enlightened by your holy radiance, that we may serve you without fear in holiness and righteousness all the days of our life; that so we may survive the storms of this world, and with you for our pilot attain the haven of eternal brightness; through your mercy, O blessed Lord, who lives and governs all things, world without end. Amen. *The Leonine Sacramentary*

God, the Creator

THEME

God is the creator of all things and the author of light (Gen 1:1-5). He sent John the Baptizer to prepare the way for the Light (Mk 1:4-11). We praise God, who has given us the Holy Spirit (Acts 19:1-7). May the Lord give strength to his people! May the Lord bless his people with peace (Ps 29).

OPENING PRAYER: *First Sunday After Epiphany*

Almighty God, who shows to them who are in error the light of your truth, to the intent that they may return into the way of righteousness; grant unto all them who are admitted into the fellowship of Christ's religion that they may eschew those things that are contrary to their profession and follow all such things as are agreeable to the same; through our Lord Jesus Christ. Amen. *The Leonine Sacramentary*

OLD TESTAMENT READING: *Genesis 1:1-5*

REFLECTIONS FROM THE CHURCH FATHERS

Creating Precedes Ordering. AMBROSE: The good architect lays the foundation first and afterward, when the foundation has been laid, plots the various parts of the building, one after the others, and then adds to it the ornamentation. . . . Scripture points out that things were first created and afterward put in order lest it be supposed that they

ANCIENT CHRISTIAN DEVOTIONAL

were not actually created and that they had no beginning, just as if the nature of things had been, as it were, generated from the beginning and did not appear to be something added afterward. *Hexaemeron* 1.7.

Creation Initiated Through the Spirit. EPHREM THE SYRIAN: The Holy Spirit warmed the waters with a kind of vital warmth, even bringing them to a boil through intense heat in order to make them fertile. The action of a hen is similar. It sits on its eggs, making them fertile through the warmth of incubation. Here then, the Holy Spirit foreshadows the sacrament of holy baptism, prefiguring its arrival, so that the waters made fertile by the hovering of that same divine Spirit might give birth to the children of God. *Commentary on Genesis* 1.

Distinction Between Light and Darkness. AUGUSTINE: "And God divided the light and the darkness, and God called the light day and he called the darkness night." It did not say here "God made the darkness," because darkness is merely the absence of light. Yet God made a division between light and darkness. So too we make a sound by crying out, and we make a silence by not making a sound, because silence is the cessation of sound. Still in some sense we distinguish between sound and silence and call the one sound and the other silence. . . . "He called the light day, and he called the darkness night" was said in the sense that he made them to be called, because he separated and ordered all things so that they could be distinguished and receive names. *Two Books on Genesis Against the Manichaeans* 1.9.15.

PSALM OF RESPONSE: *Psalm 29*

NEW TESTAMENT READING: *Acts 19:1-7*

REFLECTIONS FROM THE CHURCH FATHERS

Christ Gives Baptism Its Power. CHRYSOSTOM: Christ, then, did not need baptism—not John's or any other's; rather, baptism was needful of the power of Christ. In fact, that which was lacking was the chief of all blessings, namely, for the baptized to be deemed worthy of the Spirit. Therefore Paul added this valuable gift of the Spirit when he came. *Homilies on the Gospel of John* 17.

The True Baptism Is Christ's. AUGUSTINE: Did he baptize after a heretic had baptized? Or, if perhaps you dare to say that the friend of the bridegroom was a heretic and was not in the unity of the church, I wish you would write that also. But, if it is complete madness either to think or to say that, then it is the duty of your prudence to reflect on the reason why the apostle Paul baptized after John. *Letter* 93.

Twelve Men. BEDE: Truly, "the judgments of God are like mighty depths." Behold, Asia, which not long before was unworthy to be visited by the apostles, now consecrated by the apostolic number [i.e., twelve] and exalted by the prophetic gift! And it should be noted that the Holy Spirit showed signs of his coming, both here in the twelve disciples, and earlier in the hundred and twenty (which is the number twelve multiplied ten times). I believe that the former manifestation occurred in Jerusalem, and this one in Ephesus, which is a Greek city, to show that whether the one who believes is from the Jews or the Gentiles, the Spirit fills only those who share in the unity of the catholic and apostolic church. *Commentary on the Acts of the Apostles* 10.7.

GOSPEL READING: *Mark 1:4-11*

REFLECTIONS FROM THE CHURCH FATHERS

Types of Baptism. GREGORY OF NAZIANZUS: Let us here treat briefly of the different kinds of baptism. Moses baptized, but in water, in the cloud and in the sea; but this he did figuratively. John also baptized, not indeed in the rite of the Jews, not solely in water but also for the remission of sins; yet not in an entirely spiritual manner, for he had not added: "in the spirit." Jesus baptized, but in the Spirit; and this is perfection. There is also a fourth baptism, which is wrought by martyrdom and blood, in which Christ himself was also baptized, which is far more venerable than the others, in as much as it is not soiled by repeated contagion. There is yet a fifth, but more laborious, by tears: with which David each night bedewed his bed, washing his couch with tears. *Oration 39.*

John's Baptism and Christ's. **AUGUSTINE:** Those who receive the baptism of Christ need not seek the baptism of John. Those who received the baptism of John did indeed seek the baptism of Christ. . . . No baptism was necessary for Christ, but he freely received the baptism of a servant [John] to draw us toward his baptism. *Tractate on John 5.5.3, 4.*

A Stranger to Malice. **BEDE:** The image of a dove is placed before us by God so that we may learn the simplicity favored by him. So let us meditate on the nature of the dove, that from each one of its features of innocence we may learn the principles of a more becoming life. The dove is a stranger to malice. So may all bitterness, anger and indignation be taken away from us, together with all malice. The dove injures nothing with its mouth or talons, nor does it nourish itself or its young on tiny mice or grubs, as do almost all smaller birds. Let us see that our teeth are not weapons and arrows. *Homilies on the Gospels 1.12.*

CLOSING PRAYER

When the dawn appears, when the light grows, when midday burns, when has ceased the holy light, when the clear night comes; I sing your praises, O Father, healer of hearts, healer of bodies, Giver of wisdom, remedy of evil, O Giver also of a life without evil, a life not troubled by earthly fear—mother of distress, mother of sorrows—keep my heart in purity, let my songs speak of the hidden source of created things; and, far from God, never let me drawn into sin. *Synesius*

He Knows Us

THEME

O Lord, you knew me before I was born! Nothing I do escapes your notice (Ps 139:1-6, 13-18). Here am I, Lord. I am listening for your voice (1 Sam 3:1-10, 11-20). Jesus told his disciples, "You will see greater things than these" (Jn 1:43-51). Our bodies are the temple of the Holy Spirit, so we should shun sin (1 Cor 6:12-20).

OPENING PRAYER: *Second Sunday After Epiphany*

Pour out, O Lord, we beseech you, the Spirit of grace on your family, and cast out from them whatever evil they have incurred by the fraud of the devil or by earthly corruption; that being cleansed within and without, they may ever render unto you a pure worship and may they more readily obtain what they fitly and reasonably ask; through Jesus Christ our Lord. *The Leonine Sacramentary*

OLD TESTAMENT READING: *1 Samuel 3:1-10, 11-20*

REFLECTIONS FROM THE CHURCH FATHERS

Mistaken Kindness. BASIL THE GREAT: Benevolence to such persons is like that mistaken kindness of Eli that he was accused of showing his sons, contrary to the good pleasure of God. A feigned kindness to the wicked is a betrayal of truth, an act of treachery to the community and a means of habituating oneself to indifference to evil. *The Long Rules 28.*

Zealousness for God's Laws. CHRYSOSTOM: For no one of those who are now rich will stand up for me there when I am called to account and accused, as not having thoroughly vindicated the laws of God with all due earnestness. For this is what ruined that admirable old man, though the way he lived his life provided no reason for blame: yet for all that, because he overlooked the treading under foot of God's laws he was chastised with his children and paid that grievous penalty. And if, where the absolute authority of nature was so great, he who failed to treat his own children with due firmness endured so grievous a punishment, what indulgence shall we have, freed as we are from that dominion and yet ruining all by flattery? *Homilies on the Gospel of Matthew* 17.6.

Love for the Lord's Statutes. ISAAC OF NINEVEH: For what reason did wrath and death come on the house of the priest Eli, the righteous elder who was eminent for forty years in his priesthood? Was it not because of the iniquity of his sons Hophni and Phinehas? For neither did he sin, nor did they with his assent, but it was because he did not have the zeal to demand from them the Lord's vindication and he loved them more than the statues of the Lord. Lest someone surmise that the Lord manifests his wrath only on those who pass all the days of their life in iniquities, behold how for this unseemly sin he manifests his zeal against his genuine servants, against priests, judges, rulers, people consecrated to him, to whom he entrusted the working of miracles, and he does not overlook their transgression of his statues. *Ascetical Homilies* 10.

PSALM OF RESPONSE: *Psalm 139:1-6, 13-18*

NEW TESTAMENT READING: *1 Corinthians 6:12-20*

REFLECTIONS FROM THE CHURCH FATHERS

Premised on Self-Discipline. CLEMENT OF ALEXANDRIA: All things are lawful, but that is obviously premised on self-discipline. *Stromateis* 3.40.5.

Some Choices Are Flatly Wrong. THEODORET OF CYR: Now that we are no longer under the law, we have the freedom to make choices, but we need to realize that some choices are right and others wrong. *Commentary on the First Epistle to the Corinthians* 19-7.

Pretending the Belly Is God. NOVATIAN: One who worships God through food is almost like one who has God for his belly. *Jewish Foods* 5.9.

Do Not Demean Your Body. CHRYSOSTOM: Paul seeks to shame the fornicator by saying that if he really belongs to Christ he ought to know better than to indulge in such demeaning behavior. He speaks in graphic terms about the prostitute in order to startle his hearers and fill them with alarm. Nothing could be better suited to strike them with horror than this expression. *Homilies on the Epistles of Paul to the Corinthians* 17.1.

One Spirit with Him. ORIGEN: The soul of Jesus clung to God from the beginning of the creation in a union inseparable and indissoluble, as the soul of the wisdom and word of God, and of the truth and the true light. Receiving him wholly and itself entering into his light and splendor, it was made one spirit with him in a preeminent degree. This is what the apostle promises to those who imitate Jesus. *On First Principles* 2.9.3.

Bought with a Price. AMBROSIASTER: Someone who has been bought does not have the power to make decisions, but the person who bought him does. And because we were bought for a very high price, we ought to serve our master all the more, so that the offense from which he has bought our release may not turn us back over to death. *Commentary on Paul's Epistles.*

GOSPEL READING: *John 1:43-51*

REFLECTIONS FROM THE CHURCH FATHERS

The Best Disciples Chosen from the Worst Place. CHRYSOSTOM: Having then taken Peter and the other disciple, Jesus next goes to the capture of the others and draws to him Philip and Nathanael. Now in the case of Nathanael this was not so amazing because the fame of Jesus had gone all over Syria. But it is truly remarkable concerning Peter, James and Philip, that they believed not only before the miracles, but that they did so being from Galilee, out of which "arises no prophet," nor "can any good thing come." The Galileans were somehow of a more boorish and dull disposition than others. But even in this Christ displayed his power. He selected his choicest disciples from a land that bore no fruit. *Homilies on the Gospel of John* 20.1.

"Amen, Amen" Means You Have Been Found Trustworthy. AMMO-NIUS: Sometimes our Savior said "amen" once, at other times twice, when he wished to confirm what he was saying. This is a Hebrew manner of speaking, revealing that which was taking place, such as that "you have been found trustworthy" so as to see "the heavens opened," and so on. He says that it is possible to see the heavens opened not in a manner open to the senses but only by a mind observing the angels coming to serve Jesus. The word *amen* is used instead of "really and truthfully" and is more fitting here. *Fragments on John* 53.

The Fig Tree and Worldliness. AMBROSE: Would that Jesus would cast a glance on me still lying under that barren fig tree, and that my fig tree might also after three years bear fruit. But how can sinners have that kind of hope? If only that gospel dresser of the vineyard, perhaps already bidden to cut down my fig tree, would at least let it alone this year also, until he digs around it and fertilizes it so that he may by some chance lift the helpless out of the dust and lift the poor out of the mire. . . . The fig tree, that is, the tempting attraction of the pleasures of the world, still overshadows me, low in height, brittle for working, soft for use and barren of fruit. *Concerning Virgins* 1.1.3-4.

A Hint of Jesus' Real Nature. THEODORE OF MOPSUESTIA: The Lord shows that nothing he had said was so great or sufficient enough to demonstrate all of what he really was. So then he declares what greater things are that Nathanael would have seen. . . . He spoke of angels ascending and descending on him, because they assist him in dealing with the whole of creation. *Commentary on John* 1.1.50-51.

CLOSING PRAYER

Lord, you know me. Let me know you. Let me come to know you even as I am known. You are the strength of my soul; enter it and make it a place suitable for your dwelling, a possession "without spot or blemish." This is my hope and the reason I speak. In this hope I rejoice, when I rejoice rightly. *Augustine*

Our Hope Is in God

⊰ THEME

Our hope is in God; we trust Him. He is our rock and our refuge (Ps 62:5-12). God is aware of our attempts to turn from evil and honors them (Jon 3:1-5, 10). Repent of your sins (Mk 1:14-20), for this world as we know it is passing away, and Christ is coming again (1 Cor 7:29-31).

⊰ OPENING PRAYER: *Third Sunday After Epiphany*

Unto you will I offer up an offering of praise. Late have I loved you, O Beauty ever old and ever new. You were within me and I without, and there I sought you. You were with me when I was not with you. You called and cried to me, and pierced my deafness. You shone and glowed, and dispelled my blindness. You touched me, and I burned for your peace. *Augustine*

⊰ OLD TESTAMENT READING: *Jonah 3:1-5, 10*

REFLECTIONS FROM THE CHURCH FATHERS

The Ninevites Repent. AUGUSTINE: In uncertainty they repented and obtained certain mercy. *Explanation of the Psalms* 50.

Learning from Nineveh About Prayer. CLEMENT OF ROME: These things, dearly beloved, we are writing, not only to warn you but also to remind ourselves; for we are in the same arena, and the same contest lies before us. For this reason let us abandon empty and silly concerns and come to the glorious and holy rule of our tradition. Let us see what is good and pleasing and acceptable in the sight of our Maker. Let us fix our gaze on the blood of Christ and realize how precious it is to his Father, seeing that it was poured out for our salvation and brought the grace of conversion to the whole world. Let us look back over all the generations and learn that from generation to generation the Lord has given an opportunity of repentance to all who would return to him. Noah preached penance, and those who heeded were saved. Then Jonah announced destruction to the Ninevites, and they repented of their sins, besought God in prayer and, estranged though they were from God, obtained salvation. *1 Clement 7.*

Nineveh: *Example of Repentance.* CHRYSOSTOM: Yet, nevertheless, these barbarians, foolish people, who had not yet heard anyone teaching them wisdom, who had never received such precepts from others, when they heard the prophet saying, "Yet three days, and Nineveh shall be overthrown," laid aside, within three days, the whole of their evil customs. The fornicator became chaste; the bold man meek; the grasping and extortionate moderate and kind; the slothful industrious. They did not, indeed, reform one or two or three or four vices by way of remedy, but the whole of their iniquity. . . . After this are we not ashamed, must we not blush, if it turns out that in three days only the barbarians laid aside all their wickedness, but that we, who have been urged and taught during so many days, have not got the better of one bad habit? *Homilies Concerning the Statues* 20.21.

PSALM OF RESPONSE: *Psalm 62:5-12*

NEW TESTAMENT READING: *1 Corinthians 7:29-31*

REFLECTIONS FROM THE CHURCH FATHERS

Marriage in the End Time. SEVERIAN OF GABALA: If married people are supposed to live as if they were single, how is it possible not to prefer virginity? *Pauline Commentary from the Greek Church.*

Beget Spiritual Children. CAESARIUS OF ARLES: Those who practice physical sterility should observe fruitfulness in souls, and those who cannot have earthly children should try to begin spiritual ones. All our deeds are children. If we perform good works every day, we shall not lack spiritual offspring. *Sermon 51.3.*

Those Who Mourn Live as Though Not Mourning. AMBROSIASTER: Those who know that the end of the world is near realize that they will soon be consoled, and they comfort each other with this hope. *Commentary on Paul's Epistles.*

The Form of This World Is Passing Away. AMBROSIASTER: Note that Paul says that the form of this world is passing away, not the substance of it. Therefore if the form of the world is going to perish, there is no doubt that everything in the world will vanish. It will all pass away. Every day the world gets older. *Commentary on Paul's Epistles.*

GOSPEL READING: *Mark 1:14-20*

REFLECTIONS FROM THE CHURCH FATHERS

The Mingling of Joy and Sorrow. JEROME: The sweetness of the apple makes up for the bitterness of the root. The hope of gain makes pleasant the perils of the sea. The expectation of health mitigates the nauseousness of medicine. One who desires the kernel breaks the nut. So one who desires the joy of a holy conscience swallows down the bitterness of penance. *Commentary on the Gospels.*

Common Men on an Uncommon Mission. EUSEBIUS OF CAESAREA: Reflect on the nature and grandeur of the one Almighty God who could associate himself with the poor of the lowly fisherman's class. To use them to carry out God's mission baffles all rationality. For having conceived the intention, which no one ever before had done, of spreading his own commands and teachings to all nations, and of revealing himself as the teacher of the religion of the one Almighty God to all humanity, he thought it good to use the most unsophisticated and common people as ministers of his own design. Maybe God just wanted to work in the most unlikely way. For how could inarticulate folk be made able to teach, even if they were appointed teachers to only one person, much less to a multitude? How should those who were themselves without education instruct the nations? . . . When he had thus called them as his followers, he breathed into them his divine power and filled them with strength and courage. As God himself he spoke God's true word to them in his own way, enabling them to do great wonders, and made them pursuers of rational and thinking souls by empowering them to come after him, saying: "Come, follow me, and I will make you fish for people." With this empowerment God sent them forth to be workers and teachers of holiness to all the nations, declaring them heralds of his own teaching. *Proof of the Gospel* 3-7.

Making a Place for Him. AUGUSTINE: And from that day they adhered to him so resolutely that they did not depart. . . . Let us, also, ourselves build a house in our heart and make a place where he may come and teach us. *Tractate on John* 7.9.2, 3.

CLOSING PRAYER

Take away from us, we beseech you, O Lord, all our iniquities, and the spirit of pride and arrogance, which you resist, and fill us with the spirit of fear, and give us a contrite and humbled heart, which you do not despise, that we may be enabled with pure minds to enter into the Holy of Holies; through Jesus Christ our Lord. Amen. *The Leonine Sacramentary*

Love Builds Us Up

THEME

The fear of the Lord is the beginning of wisdom (Ps 111). The Lord raised up prophets to speak in his name (Deut 18:15-20). While Jesus was on earth, he taught with authority and did many miracles (Mk 1:21-28). Knowledge puffs us up, but love builds up (1 Cor 8:1-13).

OPENING PRAYER: *Fourth Sunday After Epiphany*

O God, who knows us to be set in the midst of so many and great dangers that by reason of the frailty of our nature we cannot always stand upright: Grant to us such strength and protection as may support us in all dangers, and carry us through all temptations; through Jesus Christ our Lord. *The Gregorian Sacramentary*

OLD TESTAMENT READING: *Deuteronomy 18:15-20*

REFLECTIONS FROM THE CHURCH FATHERS

Israel Did Not Find the Prophet Like Moses. ORIGEN: It is written in Deuteronomy, "The Lord your God will raise up a prophet like me for you from your brothers. You shall hear him; and it shall be that every soul that will not hear that prophet shall be destroyed from his people." Therefore some prophet was specially expected who would be similar to Moses in some respect, to mediate between God and humanity, and who would receive the covenant from God and give the new covenant to those who became disciples. And the people of Israel knew so far as each of the prophets was concerned that no one of them was the special one announced by Moses. *Commentary on the Gospel of John* 6.90.

Christ Like Moses in the Flesh. AUGUSTINE: "Like me," says Moses. This means according to the form of the flesh, not to the eminence of majesty. Therefore we find the Lord Jesus called a prophet. Accordingly that woman is no longer greatly in error when she says, "I see that you are a prophet." She begins to call her husband, to exclude the adulterer. "I see that you are a prophet." And she begins to ask about a thing that constantly disturbs her. *Tractate on the Gospel of John* 15.23.1.

Beware of False Prophets. ORIGEN: We can be prepared to find some prophet even of impiety—and perhaps not just one but several—who will tell us of a word of the Lord, which the Lord has not at all commanded, or a "word of wisdom" which has nothing whatever to do with wisdom. His purpose is to slay us by the word of his mouth. *Exhortation to Martyrdom* 8.

PSALM OF RESPONSE: *Psalm 111*

NEW TESTAMENT READING: *1 Corinthians 8:1-13*

REFLECTIONS FROM THE CHURCH FATHERS

Love Builds Up. CLEMENT OF ALEXANDRIA: Love builds up. It moves in the realm of truth, not of opinion. *Stromateis* 1.54.4.

Knowledge Without Love. CHRYSOSTOM: Paul rebukes those who think they are wiser than the rest by saying that everybody possesses knowledge—the self-appointed wise people are nothing special in this respect. If anyone has knowledge but lacks love, not only will he gain nothing more, but also he will be cast down from what he already has. Knowledge is not productive of love, but rather it prevents the unwary from acquiring it by puffing him up and elating him. Arrogance causes divisions, but love draws people together and leads to true knowledge. *Homilies on the Epistles of Paul to the Corinthians* 20.2.

He Does Not Yet Know. AMBROSIASTER: Only when a person has love can he be said to know as he ought to know. *Commentary on Paul's Epistles.*

One Name. AMBROSE: It is written: "Go baptize the nations in the name of the Father, and of the Son and of the Holy Spirit." "In the name," he said, not "in the names." So there is not one name for the Father, another name for the Son, and another name for the Holy Spirit, because there is one God, not several names, because there are not two gods, not three gods. *The Holy Spirit* 13.132.

The Son Is No Less God Than the Father. SEVERIAN OF GABALA: The Father is one, just as the Son is one. If the Son is called Lord, that does not make the Father any less Lord, just as when it is said that God the Father is one, the Son is no less God. *Pauline Commentary from the Greek Church.*

Consider Who Died for Him. AUGUSTINE: If you love the weak person less because of the moral failing that makes him weak, consider the One who died on his behalf. *Questions* 71.

GOSPEL READING: *Mark 1:21-28*

REFLECTIONS FROM THE CHURCH FATHERS

The Earliest Intimation of His Identity. BEDE: It was appropriate, since death first entered into the world through the devil's envy, that the healing medicine of salvation should first operate against him. . . . The presence of the Savior is the torment of the devils. *Homilies on the Gospels* 1.13.

Demonic Recognition. IRENAEUS: Even the demons cried out, on beholding the Son: "I know who you are, the Holy One of God." Later, the devil looking at him and tempting him, would say: "If you are the Son of God." All of these thus recognized the Son and the Father, yet without believing. So it was fitting that the truth should receive testimony from all, and should become a means of judgment for the salvation not only of those who believe, but also for the condemnation of those who do not believe. The result is that all should be fairly judged, and that faith in the Father and Son should be established for all, receiving testimony from all, both from those belonging to it who were its friends, and by those having no connection with it who were its enemies. For that evidence is most trustworthy and true which elicits even from its adversaries striking testimonies on its behalf. *Against Heresies* 4.6.6-7.

Forced Notice. CHRYSOSTOM: Does no demon call on God's name? Did not the demons say, "We know who you are, O Holy One of God"? Did they not say to Paul: "these men are the servants of the Most High God"? They did, but only on scourging, only on compulsion, never of their own will, never without being trounced. *Homilies on First Corinthians* 29.3.

When Demons Speak Truth. EUTHYMIUS: He has taught us never to believe the demons, even when they say what is ostensibly true. For since they love falsehood and are most hostile to us, they never speak the truth except to deceive. They make use of the truth as a kind of bait. *Fragments.*

The Confession That Lacked Love. AUGUSTINE: Faith is mighty, but without love it profits nothing. The devils confessed Christ, but lacking charity it availed nothing. They said, "What have we to do with you?" They confessed a sort of faith, but without love. Hence they were devils. Do not boast of that faith that puts you on the same level with the devils. *On the Gospel of St. John* 6.21.

Bridling the Mouth. ATHANASIUS: He put a bridle in the mouths of the demons that cried after him from the tombs. For although what they said was true, and they did not lie when they said, "You are the Son of God" and "the Holy One of God," yet he did not wish that the truth should proceed from an unclean mouth, and especially from such as those who under pretense of truth might mingle with it their own malicious devices. *To the Bishops of Egypt* 3.

CLOSING PRAYER

Assist us mercifully, O Lord, in these our supplications and prayers, and dispose the way of your servants toward the attainment of everlasting salvation; that among all the changes and chances of this mortal life, they may ever be defended by your most gracious and ready help; through Jesus Christ our Lord. Amen. *The Gelasian Sacramentary*

God Is Great

THEME

Thanks be to God, the creator of the world (Ps 147:1-11), who renews our strength (Is 40:21-31). Jesus worked great miracles while he was on earth (Mk 1:29-39). Like Paul, we should do everything for the sake of the gospel (1 Cor 9:16-23).

OPENING PRAYER: *Fifth Sunday After Epiphany*

O God, whose never-failing providence orders all things both in heaven and earth; we humbly beseech you to put away from us all hurtful things and to give us those things that are profitable for us; through Jesus Christ our Lord. Amen. *The Gelasian Sacramentary*

OLD TESTAMENT READING: *Isaiah 40:21-31*

REFLECTIONS FROM THE CHURCH FATHERS

God's Ease in Making Creation. CHRYSOSTOM: When he spoke of the heavens, Isaiah said, "It is he who set up the heaven as a vaulted chamber and stretched it out as a tent over the earth." And he said of the earth, "It is he that comprehends the circle of the earth and made the earth as if it were nothing," even though the earth is so great and vast. . . . Despite the fact that the earth is so great and so vast, God made it with such ease that the prophet could find no fitting example. So he said that God made the earth "as if it were nothing." *Against the Anomoeans,* Homily 2.24-25.

How Can One Compare? THEODORET OF CYR: To him who has performed works, to him who has accomplished these works and who continually goes on performing them, to whom do you compare him? What mark of respect do you offer to him that is worthy of him? *Commentary on Isaiah* 12.40.25.

Think of Higher Things. ORIGEN: "Lift up your eyes" occurs in many places in Scripture when the divine Word admonishes us to exalt and lift up our thoughts, to elevate the insight that lies below in a rather sickly condition and is stooped and completely incapable of looking up, as it is written, for instance, in Isaiah: "Lift up your eyes on high and see. Who has made all these things known?" *Commentary on the Gospel of John* 13.274.

PSALM OF RESPONSE: *Psalm 147:1-11*

NEW TESTAMENT READING: *1 Corinthians 9:16-23*

REFLECTIONS FROM THE CHURCH FATHERS

The Dispensation of the Word. ORIGEN: What then shall I do, to whom the dispensation of the Word is committed? Although I am an "unprofitable servant," I have, nevertheless, received from the Lord the commission "to distribute the measure of wheat to the master's servants." *Genesis,* Homily 10.

Not a Pretense. AMBROSIASTER: Did Paul merely pretend to be all things to all men, in the way that flatterers do? No. He was a man of God and a doctor of the spirit who could diagnose every pain, and with great diligence he tended them and sympathized with them all. We all have something or other in common with everyone. This empathy is what Paul embodied in dealing with each particular person. *Commentary on Paul's Epistles.*

Not a Deception. AUGUSTINE: Paul was not pretending to be what he is not but showing compassion. *Letter* 82, to Jerome.

Under the Law of Christ. THEODORE OF MOPSUESTIA: Paul states, somewhat surprisingly, that he is under the law of Christ, lest anyone think that he is under the law of Moses. *Pauline Commentary from the Greek Church.*

Christ as Pattern of Empathy. CYRIL OF JERUSALEM: Everywhere the Savior becomes "all things to all men." To the hungry, bread; to the thirsty, water; to the dead, resurrection; to the sick, a physician; to sinners, redemption. *Sermon on the Paralytic* 10.

Paul the Imitator of Christ. AMBROSE: He who did not think it robbery to be equal with God took the nature of a slave. He became all things to all men to bring salvation to all. Paul, an imitator of him, lived as if outside the law while remaining accountable to the law. He spent his life for the advantage of those he wished to win. He willingly became weak for the weak in order to strengthen them. He ran the race to overtake them. *Letters to Priests* 54.

GOSPEL READING: *Mark 1:29-39*

REFLECTIONS FROM THE CHURCH FATHERS

The Rotten Odor of Sin Becomes the Perfume of Repentance. JEROME: Can you imagine Jesus standing before your bed and you continue sleeping? It is absurd that you would remain in bed in his presence. Where is Jesus? He is already here offering himself to us. "In the middle," he says, "among you he stands, whom you do not recognize." "The kingdom of God is in your midst." Faith beholds Jesus among us. If we are unable to seize his hand, let us prostrate ourselves at his feet. If we are unable to reach his head, let us wash his feet with our tears. Our repentance is the perfume of the Savior. See how costly is the compassion of the Savior. Our sins give off a terrible odor; they are rottenness. Nevertheless, if we repent of our sins, they will be transformed into perfume by the Lord. Therefore, let us ask the Lord to grasp our hand. "And at once," he says, "the fever left her." Immediately as her hand is grasped, the fever flees. *Tractate on Mark's Gospel* 2.

The Habit of Prayer. ORIGEN: Jesus prayed and did not pray in vain, since he received what he asked for in prayer when he might have done so without prayer. If so, who among us would neglect to pray? Mark says that "in the morning, a great while before day, he rose and went out to a lonely place, and there he prayed." And Luke says, "He was praying in a certain place, and when he ceased, one of his disciples said to him, 'Lord, teach us to pray,' " and elsewhere, "And all night he continued in prayer to God." And John records his prayer, saying, "When Jesus had spoken these words, he lifted up his eyes to heaven and said, 'Father, the hour has come; glorify your Son that the Son may glorify you.' " The same Evangelist writes that the Lord said that he knew "you hear me always." All this shows that the one who prays always is always heard. *On Prayer* 13.1.

CLOSING PRAYER

To those who rule and lead us on the earth, you, sovereign Master, have given their authority and kingship—so marvelous that power of yours words fail to express—that seeing the glory and honor you have provided for them, we should be subject to their rule, not resisting your will. Grant them, Lord, the health, peace, concord and stability to use rightly the sovereignty you have bestowed on them. For you, King of heaven, you it is that give mortals glory, honor and power over what is on earth. Lord, make their counsels conform to what is good and pleasing to you, that using with reverence, peacefully, gently the power you have given them, they might find favor with you. *Clement of Rome*

Share the Light

THEME

The heavens declare the righteousness, power and beauty of the Lord
(Ps 50:1-6). Let the strong faith of the prophets be an example to us (2
Kings 2:1-12) and the hope of the resurrection (Mk 9:2-9) encourage
us as we share the light of the gospel (2 Cor 4:3-6).

OPENING PRAYER: *Sixth Sunday After Epiphany*

Almighty God, who through your only-begotten Son Jesus Christ has
overcome death and opened unto us the gate of everlasting life; we
humbly beseech you, that as by your special grace preventing us, you
put into our minds good desires, so by your continual help we may
bring the same to good effect; through Jesus Christ our Lord, who lives
and reigns with you and the Holy Spirit, ever one God, world without
end. Amen. *The Gregorian Sacramentary*

OLD TESTAMENT READING: *2 Kings 2:1-12*

REFLECTIONS FROM THE CHURCH FATHERS

Elijah and Elisha Were Baptized in the Jordan. ORIGEN: We must
note in addition that when Elijah was about to be taken up in a whirl-
wind as into heaven, he took his sheepskin and rolled it up and struck
the water, and it was divided on this side and that, and both crossed,
that is to say, himself and Elisha. He was better prepared to be taken up

after he was baptized in the Jordan, since Paul, as we explained previously, called the more incredible passage through water a baptism. It is because of this same Jordan that Elisha is capable of receiving the gift that he has desired through Elijah, for he said, "Let a double portion come on me in your spirit." Perhaps he received the gift in the spirit of Elijah in a double measure on himself because he crossed the Jordan twice, once with Elijah and a second time when he took the sheepskin of Elijah and struck the water and said, "Where is the Lord, the God of Elijah? And he struck the waters, and they divided on this side and that." *Commentary on the Gospel of John* 6.238-39.

God Is Everywhere Wholly Present in Himself. AUGUSTINE: Therefore, he who is everywhere does not dwell in all, and he does not even dwell equally in those in whom he does dwell. Otherwise, what is the meaning of the request made by Elisha that there might be in him double the Spirit of God that was in Elijah? And how is it that among the saints some are more holy than others, except that they have a more abundant indwelling in God? How, then, did we speak the truth when we said above that God is everywhere wholly present if he is more amply present in some, less in others? But it should be noticed with care that we said he is everywhere wholly present in himself, not in things of which some have a greater capacity for him, others less. *Letter* 187.17.

PSALM OF RESPONSE: *Psalm 50:1-6*

NEW TESTAMENT READING: *2 Corinthians 4:3-6*

REFLECTIONS FROM THE CHURCH FATHERS

The Truth Will Be Plain. THEODORET OF CYR: Paul is saying that unbelief is limited to this world, because in the next life the truth will be plain to everyone. *Commentary on the Second Epistle to the Corinthians* 308.

The Call to Resemble Christ. CLEMENT OF ALEXANDRIA: Our Educator, O children, resembles his Father, God, whose Son he is. He is without sin, without blame. . . . God immaculate in human form, accomplishing his Father's will. He is God the Word, who is in the bosom of the Father and also at the right hand of the Father, with even the nature of God. He it is who is the spotless image. We must try, then, to resemble Him in spirit as far as we are able. . . . Yet we must strive to the best of our ability to be as sinless as we can. There is nothing more important for us than first to be rid of sin and weakness and then to uproot any habitual sinful inclination. The highest perfection, of course, is never to sin in any least way, but this can be said of God alone. The next highest is never deliberately to commit wrong; this is the state proper to the man who possesses wisdom. In the third place comes not sinning except on rare occasions; this marks a man who is well educated. Finally, in the lowest degree we must place delaying in sin for a brief moment, but even this, for those who are called to recover their loss and repent, is a step on the path to salvation. *Christ the Educator* 2.4.

We Preach Christ. AMBROSIASTER: In expressing himself humbly, Paul spoke in a way that was designed to show that he was not preaching the gospel for his own advantage but for the glory of the Lord Christ, to whom he is obedient. *Commentary on Paul's Epistles.*

Dawning of Divine Wisdom. ISAAC OF NINEVEH: When the apostle said, "God, who commanded the light to shine out of the darkness, has shined in our hearts," he referred to the resurrection. He showed this resurrection to be the exodus from the old state which in the likeness of Sheol incarcerates a person where the light of the gospel will not shine mystically on him. This breath of life shines through hope in the resurrection. By it the dawning of divine wisdom shines in the heart, so that a person should become new, having nothing of the old. *Ascetical Homilies* 37.

The Spirit's Fire. SAHDONA: We should accordingly worship and glorify him who raised our dust to such state, recounting ceaselessly the holiness of him who mingled our spirit with his Spirit and mixed into our bodies the gift of his grace, causing the fire of his Holy Spirit to burst into flame in us. For "he has shone out in our hearts" which had been submerged in darkness. *Book of Perfection.*

GOSPEL READING: *Mark 9:2-9*

REFLECTIONS FROM THE CHURCH FATHERS

The Reckoning of Days. AUGUSTINE: Leaving out of their calculation the day on which Jesus spoke these words, and the day on which he exhibited that memorable spectacle on the mount, they have regarded simply the intermediate days and have used the expression "after six days." But Luke, reckoning in the extreme day at either end, that is to say, the first day and the last day, has made it "after eight days," in accordance with that mode of speech in which the part is put for the whole. *Harmony of the Gospels* 2.56.

Manifested to the Children of Light. ORIGEN: But when he is transfigured, his face also shines as the sun that he may be manifested to the children of light who have put off the works of darkness and put on the armor of light, and are no longer the children of darkness or night but have become the children of day, and walk honestly as in the day. Being manifested, he will shine unto them not simply as the sun, but as demonstrated to be the sun of righteousness. *Commentary on Matthew* 12.37.

The Tent of the Spirit. JEROME: It seems to me that this cloud is the grace of the Holy Spirit. Naturally, a tent gives shelter and overshadows those who are within; the cloud, therefore, serves the purpose of the tents. O Peter, you who want to set up three tents, have regard for the one tent of the Holy Spirit who shelters us equally. *Homily* 80.

His Sonship Declared. **AMBROSE:** In his baptism he identified him, saying, "You are my beloved Son, in whom I am well pleased." He declared him on the mount, saying, "This is my beloved Son, hear him." He declared him in his passion, when the sun hid itself and sea and earth trembled. He declared him in the centurion, who said, "Truly this was the Son of God." *On the Holy Spirit* 2.6.

Until He Shall Have Risen. **CHRYSOSTOM:** So he bound them to silence. Furthermore, he spoke of his passion as though it were the reason why he asked them to be silent. Note that he did not tell them that they must never tell this to anyone. Instead they should not tell it until he had risen from the dead. In this respect he was silent as to what was painful, and spoke only of what was joyful. *Homilies on the Transfiguration* 57.

CLOSING PRAYER

O God, by your mercy strengthen us who lie exposed to the rough storms of troubles and temptations. Help us against our own negligence and cowardice, and defend us from the treachery of our unfaithful hearts. Succor us, we beseech you, and bring us to your safe haven of peace and felicity. *Augustine*

God's Covenant

⸎ THEME

Help us to know your ways, Lord; teach us your paths (Ps 25:1-10).
God has made a covenant with us (Gen 9:8-17) and sent the Holy Spirit
to guide us (Mk 1:9-15). We follow Jesus' example and are baptized for
the repentance of our sins and the promise of eternal life (1 Pet 3:18-
22).

⸎ OPENING PRAYER: *First Sunday in Lent*

Grant, we beseech you, O Lord, that by the observance of this Lent we
may advance in the knowledge of the mystery of Christ and show forth
his mind in conduct worthy of our calling; through Jesus Christ our
Lord. *The Gelasian Sacramentary*

⸎ OLD TESTAMENT READING: *Genesis 9:8-17*

REFLECTIONS FROM THE CHURCH FATHERS

God Makes His Covenant with Noah Out of Love. CHRYSOSTOM:
God's purpose, therefore, was to eliminate all apprehension from
Noah's thinking and for him to be quite assured that this would not
happen again. He said, remember, "Just as I brought on the deluge out
of love, so as to put a stop to their wickedness and prevent their going
to further extremes, so in this case too it is out of my love that I promise
never to do it again, so that you may live free of all dread and in this

way see your present life to its close." Hence he said, "Behold, I make my covenant," that is, I form an agreement. Just as in human affairs when someone makes a promise he forms an agreement and gives a firm guarantee, so too the good Lord said, "Behold, I make my covenant." God did not say that this massive disaster might come again to those who sin. Rather, he said, "Behold, I make my covenant with you *and your offspring after you.*" See the Lord's loving kindness: not only with your generation, he says, do I form my agreement, but also in regard to all those coming after you I give this firm guarantee. *Homilies on Genesis* 28.4.

God Will Never Bring a New Deluge on Earth. EPHREM THE SYRIAN: And his Lord spoke to Noah, as he desired that Noah hear, "Because of your righteousness, a remnant was preserved and did not perish in that flood that took place. And because of your sacrifice that was from all flesh and on behalf of all flesh, I will never again bring a flood on the earth." God thus bound himself beforehand by this promise so that even if humankind were constantly to follow the evil thoughts of their inclination, he would never again bring a flood on them. *Commentary on Genesis* 6.13.2.

God Will Never Forget His Covenant. GREGORY OF NAZIANZUS: Who "binds up the water in the clouds"? The miracle of it— that he sets something whose nature is to flow, on clouds, that he fixes it there by his word! Yet he pours out some of it on the face of the whole earth, sprinkling it to all alike in due season. He does not unleash the entire stock of water—the cleansing of Noah's era was enough, and God most true does not forget his own covenant. *Theological Orations* 28.28.

◢ PSALM OF RESPONSE: *Psalm 25:1-10*

◢ NEW TESTAMENT READING: *1 Peter 3:18-22*

REFLECTIONS FROM THE CHURCH FATHERS

Saving All Who Would Believe. CYRIL OF ALEXANDRIA: Here Peter answers the question that some objectors have raised, namely, if the incarnation was so beneficial, why was Christ not incarnated for such a long time, given that he went to the spirits who were in prison and preached to them also? In order to deliver all those who would believe, Christ taught those who were alive on earth at the time of his incarnation, and these others acknowledged him when he appeared to them in the lower regions, and thus they too benefited from his coming. Going in his soul, he preached to those who were in hell, appearing to them as one soul to other souls. When the gatekeepers of hell saw him, they fled; the bronze gates were broken open, and the iron chains were undone. And the only-begotten Son shouted with authority to the suffering souls, according to the word of the new covenant, saying to those in chains: "Come out!" and to those in darkness: "Be enlightened." In other words, he preached to those who were in hell also, so that he might save all those who would believe in him. For both those who were alive on earth during the time of his incarnation and those who were in hell had a chance to acknowledge him. The greater part of the new covenant is beyond nature and tradition, so that while Christ was able to preach to all those who were alive at the time of his appearing and those who believed in him were blessed, so too he was able to liberate those in hell who believed and acknowledged him, by his descent there. However, the souls of those who practiced idolatry and outrageous ungodliness, as well as those who were blinded by fleshly lusts, did not have the power to see him, and they were not delivered. *Catena.*

The Meaning of Baptism. CYPRIAN: Peter showed and vindicated the unity of the church by commanding and warning that we can be saved only through the baptism of the one church. Just as in that baptism of the world by which the ancient iniquity was purged, the one who was not in the ark could not be saved through water, so now anyone who has not been baptized in the church cannot be saved, for the church has been founded in the unity of the Lord, as the sacrament of the one ark. *Letter* 74.11.

A Clear Conscience. AUGUSTINE: If some people have the worst consciences, full of every fault and crime, unchanged by penance for their evil deeds, baptism nevertheless saves them, for on the basis of the foundation that is laid in baptism they will be saved, even if it is through fire. *Eight Questions of Dulcitius* 1.

GOSPEL READING: *Mark 1:9-15*

REFLECTIONS FROM THE CHURCH FATHERS

One Without Beginning. ORIGEN: This is spoken to him by God, with whom all time is today. For there is no evening with God, as I see it, and there is no morning—nothing but time that stretches out, along with his unbeginning and unseen life. The day is today with him in which the Son was begotten. Thus the beginning of his birth is not to be found, as neither is the day of it. *Commentary on John* 1.32.

The Wilderness Setting. CHRYSOSTOM: You see how the Spirit led him, not into a city or public arena, but into a wilderness. In this desolate place, the Spirit extended the devil an occasion to test him, not only by hunger, but also by loneliness, for it is there most especially that the devil assails us, when he sees us left alone and by ourselves. In this same way did he also confront Eve in the beginning, having caught her alone and apart from her husband. *The Gospel of St. Matthew,* Homily 13.1.

Suggestion, Delight, Consent. GREGORY THE GREAT: Temptation is brought to fulfillment by three stages: suggestion, delight, consent. And we in temptation eternally fall through delight and then through consent; for being begotten of the sin of the flesh we bear within us that through which we suffer conflict. But God, incarnate in the womb of a virgin, came into the world without sin and so suffers no conflict within himself. He could therefore be tempted by suggestion, but the delight of sin could never touch his mind. So all these temptations of the devil were from without, not from within him. *On the Gospel of the Sunday Sermon* 16.

The Succession of Temptations. BEDE: Let us be wary that we do not relight the fires of old obsessions which would wreck us on our new voyage. Whatever sort of flaming sword it is that guards the doorway of paradise has been already effectively extinguished for each of the faithful in the font of baptism. For the unfaithful, however, the gate remains always formidable, and also for those falsely called *faithful* though they have not been chosen, since they have no fear of entangling themselves in sins after baptism. It is as though the same fire put out in baptism has been rekindled after it had been once extinguished. *Homilies on the Gospels* 1.12.

❧ CLOSING PRAYER

Remember, O Lord, what you wrought in us, and not what we deserve; and as you called us to your service, make us worthy of our calling; through Jesus Christ our Lord. Amen. *The Leonine Sacramentary*

God's Promises

THEME

When we cry out to you, we remember your power, your ability to deliver us (Ps 22:23-31) and your promises (Gen 17:1-7, 15-16). We cling to them, as we give God glory (Rom 4:13-25). As we grow in faith, help us to order our lives with good judgment (Mk 8:31-38).

OPENING PRAYER: *Second Sunday in Lent*

O Lord, let your Spirit check in us whatever is contrary to your good will. Suffer us not to be deceived by the follies or seduced by the customs of the world, but enable us always and in all places to live as befits our citizenship which is in heaven. Grant us therefore, O Lord, we beseech you, always to seek your kingdom and righteousness; and of whatsoever you see us to stand in need, mercifully grant us an abundant portion; through Jesus Christ our Lord. Amen. *The Gelasian Sacramentary*

OLD TESTAMENT READING: *Genesis 17:1-7, 15-16*

REFLECTIONS FROM THE CHURCH FATHERS

A Slave for an Heir. CHRYSOSTOM: These words reveal the extreme degree of the pain in his soul. [It is if he were saying] to God, Far from being granted what my slave was, I am to pass away without child or heir, whereas my slave will inherit the gifts granted me by you, despite the promise received from you more than once in the words "to your descendants I will give this land." Consider, I ask you, the just man's virtue in this case also in the fact that while entertaining these thoughts in his mind he did not protest nor say any harsh words. Instead, driven on in this case by the words spoken to him, he spoke boldly to the Lord, revealed the tumult of his interior thoughts and made no secret of the wound to his spirit. Hence in turn he received instant healing. *Homilies on Genesis* 36.11.

He Believed with Promptness of Spirit. AMBROSE: And how did Abraham's progeny spread? Only through the inheritance he transmitted in virtue of faith. On this basis the faithful are assimilated to heaven, made comparable to the angels, equal to the stars. This is why he said, "So will your descendants be. And Abraham," the text says, "believed in God." What exactly did he believe? Prefiguratively he believed that Christ through the incarnation would become his heir. In order that you may know that this was what he believed, the Lord says, "Abraham saw my day and rejoiced." For this reason "he reckoned it to him as righteousness," because he did not seek the rational explanation but believed with great promptness of spirit. *On Abraham* 1.3.21.

That Evening Signified the End of the World. CAESARIUS OF ARLES: Notice, brothers, that what is called a fiery torch passing between those pieces is also not said to have touched the turtledove and pigeon. That evening signified the end of the world. Those animals, as we already said, showed a type of all the nations who believe in Christ. *Sermon* 82.3.

PSALM OF RESPONSE: *Psalm 22:23-31*

NEW TESTAMENT READING: *Romans 4:13-25*

REFLECTIONS FROM THE CHURCH FATHERS

The Promise Rests on Grace. ORIGEN: It might appear from this that faith is not a free gift of God but that it must first be offered to him by man in order for grace to be given in return. But consider what the apostle teaches about this elsewhere. For when he lists the gifts of the Spirit, which he says are given to believers according to the measure of faith, there among the rest he asserts that the gift of faith is also given. Therefore faith is given by grace. . . .

If the promise rested on works, it would not be guaranteed. But now it is guaranteed because it rests on grace, not on works. I think this can be understood to mean that the things of the law are external to us, but the things of grace are internal . . . and therefore they have a firmer foundation. *Commentary on the Epistle to the Romans.*

The Obstacle to Inheritance Removed. CHRYSOSTOM: The law works wrath and makes those who are under it liable for their transgressions, which is a curse, not a promise! . . . But when faith comes it brings grace with it, and so the promise takes effect. For where there is grace there is forgiveness, and where there is forgiveness there is no punishment. Once punishment is removed and righteousness takes hold from faith, there is no obstacle to our becoming heirs of the promise. *Homilies on Romans 8.*

The Resurrection Hope. ORIGEN: As always, when the apostle Paul talks about faith, he adds hope as well, and rightly so, for hope and faith are inseparable. . . . Just as Abraham believed against hope, so all believers do the same, for we all believe in the resurrection of the dead and the inheritance of the kingdom of heaven. These appear to go against hope as far as human nature is concerned, but when we take the power of God into consideration, there is no problem. *Commentary on the Epistle to the Romans.*

GOSPEL READING: *Mark 8:31-38*

REFLECTIONS FROM THE CHURCH FATHERS

What Seems Hard, Love Makes Easy. AUGUSTINE: How hard and painful does this appear! The Lord has required that "whoever will come after him must deny himself." But what he commands is neither hard nor painful when he himself helps us in such a way so that the very thing he requires may be accomplished. . . . For whatever seems hard in what is enjoined, love makes easy. *Sermons on New Testament Lessons* 46.1.

Body as Cross. TERTULLIAN: "Your cross" means your own anxieties and your sufferings in your own body, which itself is shaped in a way already like a cross. *On Idolatry* 12.

Walking Requires Two Feet. CAESARIUS OF ARLES: When the Lord tells us in the Gospel that anyone who wants to be his follower must renounce himself, the injunction seems harsh; we think he is imposing a burden on us. But an order is no burden when it is given by one who helps in carrying it out. To what place are we to follow Christ if not where he has already gone? We know that he has risen and ascended into heaven; there, then, we must follow him. There is no cause for despair—by ourselves we can do nothing, but we have Christ's promise. . . . One who claims to abide in Christ ought to walk as he walked. Would you follow Christ? Then be humble as he was humble. Do not scorn his lowliness if you want to reach his exaltation. Human sin made the road rough. Christ's resurrection leveled it. By passing over it himself he transformed the narrowest of tracks into a royal highway. Two feet are needed to run along this highway; they are humility and charity. Everyone wants to get to the top—well, the first step to take is humility. Why take strides that are too big for you—do you want to fall instead of going up? Begin with the first step, humility, and you will already be climbing. *Sermon* 159, 1.4-6.

⁂ CLOSING PRAYER

Give concord and peace to us and all living on the earth, as you gave them to our fathers when they prayed to you, believing truly, ready to obey the All Powerful, the All Holy. *Clement of Rome*

Obedience

⊰ THEME

Let the words of our mouths and the meditations of our hearts be acceptable in your sight (Ps 19). Help us to follow your commandments (Ex 20:1-17) and fully believe and embrace the teachings of Jesus (Jn 2:13-22). Help us to remember that God makes foolish the wisdom of the world (1 Cor 1:18-25).

⊰ OPENING PRAYER: *Third Sunday in Lent*

Hear, Lord, my prayer; let not my soul faint under your discipline, nor let me faint in confessing unto you all your mercies, whereby you have drawn me out of all my most evil ways, that you might become a delight to me above all the allurements that I once pursued; that I may most entirely love you, and clasp your hand with all my affections, and you may yet rescue me from every temptation, even unto the end. *Augustine*

⊰ OLD TESTAMENT READING: *Exodus 20:1-17*

REFLECTIONS FROM THE CHURCH FATHERS

The Two Tablets of the Law. CAESARIUS OF ARLES: We should also know that the ten commandments of the law are also fulfilled by the two gospel precepts, love of God and love of neighbor. For the three commandments that were written on the first tablet pertain to the love of God, while on the second tablet seven commandments were inscribed, one of which is "Honor your father and your mother." Doubtless all of the latter are recognized as pertaining to love of neighbor. The Lord said in the Gospel: "On these two commandments depend the whole Law and the Prophets." Likewise we read what the apostle James said: "But whoever offends in one point has become guilty in all." What does it mean to offend in one point and lose all, except to have fallen from the precept of charity and so to have offended in all the other commands? According to the apostle, without charity nothing in our virtues can be shown to avail at all. *Sermon* 100A.12.

The Honor Due to Parents. AMBROSE: The formation of the children is then the prerogative of the parents. Therefore honor your father, that he may bless you. Let the godly man honor his father out of gratitude and the ingrate do so on account of fear. Even if the father is poor and does not have plenty of resources to leave to his sons, still he has the heritage of his final blessing with which he may bestow the wealth of sanctification on his descendants. And it is a far greater thing to be blessed than it is to be rich. *The Patriarchs* 1.1.

The Standard of Morals. AUGUSTINE: Therefore whatsoever things God commands (and one of these is "You shall not commit adultery") and whatsoever things are not positively ordered but are strongly advised as good spiritual counsel (and one of these is, "It is a good thing for a man to not touch a woman")—all of these imperatives are rightly obeyed only when they are measured by the standard of our love of God and our love of our neighbor in God. *A Handbook on Faith, Hope and Love* 32.121.

PSALM OF RESPONSE: *Psalm 19*

NEW TESTAMENT READING: *1 Corinthians 1:18-25*

REFLECTIONS FROM THE CHURCH FATHERS

The Humbling of Greek Wisdom and Jewish Law. AMBROSIASTER: Here Paul attacks the Jews as much as the Gentiles, because their scribes and doctors of the law think that it is foolish to believe that God has a Son. Gentiles also laugh at this, but the Jews' unbelief is based on the fact that the matter is not openly stated in the law, whereas the Gentiles think it is silly because the reasoning of the world does not accept it, claiming that nothing can be made without sexual union. The debater of this age is one who thinks the world is governed by the conjunction of the stars and that births and deaths are brought about by the twelve signs of the zodiac. Is there anything more foolish than the belief that the Creator does not care about the world he has made? What would be the point of making it in that case? It is because they see some people enjoying life and others not, because they see the righteous suffering while the wicked boast, that they have come to believe that God does not care. But to say this is to say that God is malevolent and unjust. *Commentary on Paul's Epistles.*

Human Wisdom Does Not Convert. CHRYSOSTOM: To believe in the one who was crucified and buried and to be fully convinced that he rose again does not need more reasoning but faith alone. The apostles themselves were converted not by wisdom but by faith. Once they had that, they surpassed the heathen wise men in both wisdom and intellectual depth. . . . Plato was cast out not by another philosopher of more skill but by unlearned fishers. *Homilies on the Epistles of Paul to the Corinthians* 4.4.

The Offense and the Call. CHRYSOSTOM: The gospel produces the exact opposite of what people want and expect, but it is that very fact that persuades them to accept it in the end. The apostles won their case, not simply without a sign, but by something that appeared to go against all the known signs. The cross seems to be a cause of offense, but far from simply offending, it attracts and calls believers to itself. *Homilies on the Epistles of Paul to the Corinthians* 4-5.

GOSPEL READING: *John 2:13-22*

REFLECTIONS FROM THE CHURCH FATHERS

Why Such Violence? CHRYSOSTOM: But why did Christ use such violence? He was about to heal on the sabbath day and to do many things that appeared to them transgressions of the law. However, so that he might not appear to be acting as a rival to God and an opponent of his Father, he takes occasion to correct any such suspicion of theirs. . . . He did not merely "cast them out" but also "overturned the tables" and "poured out the money," so that they could see how someone who threw himself into such danger for the good order of the house could never despise his master. If he had acted out of hypocrisy, he would have only advised them, but to place himself in such danger was very daring. It was no small thing to offer himself to the anger of so many market people or to excite against himself a most brutal mob of petty dealers by his reproaches and the disruption he caused. This was not, in other words, the action of a pretender but of one choosing to suffer everything for the order of the house. For the same reason, to show his agreement with the Father, he did not say "the holy house" but "my Father's house." See how he even calls him "Father," and they are not angry with him. They thought he spoke in a more general way, but when he went on and spoke more plainly of his equality, this is when they become angry. *Homilies on the Gospel of John* 23.2.

Jesus Abolishes the Sacrificial System. THEODORE OF MOPSUESTIA: Having a symbolic purpose in mind, Jesus obscured his intent with allusions instead of stating plainly what he was doing. He thought that his hearers could not understand yet what he said. The disciples themselves did not understand either, as the Evangelist observes. They believed that by driving away the sellers of cattle and sheep, he abolished the market, but in truth what he meant was that the sacrifices of animals would be abolished. *Commentary on John* 1.2.13-18, 19.

CLOSING PRAYER

Almighty God, bestow on us the meaning of words, the light of understanding, nobility of diction and faith in the truth. And grant that what we believe we may also speak. Amen. *Hilary of Poitiers*

He Gave His Son

THEME

Give thanks to the Lord (Ps 107:1-3, 17-22), for the power of sin was broken on the cross (Num 21:4-9). For God so loved the world that he gave his Son (Jn 3:14-21); by his grace and mercy we are saved (Eph 2:1-10).

OPENING PRAYER: *Fourth Sunday in Lent*

O almighty God, who alone can order the unruly wills and affections of sinful men; grant unto your people that they may love the thing that you command, and desire that which you do promise, that so among the sundry and manifold changes of the world, our hearts may surely there be fixed, where true joys are to be found, through Jesus Christ our Lord. Amen. *The Gelasian Sacramentary*

OLD TESTAMENT READING: *Numbers 21:4-9*

REFLECTIONS FROM THE CHURCH FATHERS

Serpents in the Scriptures. BEDE: The wounds caused by the fiery serpent are the poisonous enticements of the vices, which afflict the soul and bring about its spiritual death. The people were murmuring against the Lord. They were stricken by the serpents' bites. This provides an excellent instance of how one may recognize from the results of an external scourge what a great calamity a person might suffer inwardly by murmuring. In the raising up of the bronze serpent (when those who were stricken beheld it, they were cured) is prefigured our Redeemer's suffering on the cross, for only by faith in him is the kingdom of death and sin overcome. The sins that drag down soul and body to destruction at the same time are appropriately represented by the serpents, not only because they were fiery and poisonous and artful at bringing about death but also because our first parents were led into sin by a serpent, and from being immortal they became mortal by sinning. The Lord is aptly made known by the bronze serpent, since he came in the likeness of sinful flesh. Just as the bronze serpent had the likeness of a fiery serpent but had absolutely none of the strength of harmful poison in its members—rather by being lifted up it cured those who had been stricken by the live serpents—so the Redeemer of the human race did not merely clothe himself in sinful flesh but entered bodily into the likeness of sinful flesh, in order that by suffering death on the cross in this likeness he might free those who believed in him from all sin and even from death itself. *Homilies on the Gospels* 2.18.

Contrast Between the Serpent and Christ. GREGORY OF NAZIAN-ZUS: That brazen serpent was hung up as a remedy for the biting serpents, not as a type of him who suffered for us but as a contrast. It saved those who looked on it, not because they believed it to live but because it was killed, and killed with it were the powers that were subject to it, being destroyed as it deserved. And what is the fitting epitaph for it from us? "O death, where is your sting? O grave, where is your victory?" You are overthrown by the cross. You are slain by him who is the giver of life. You are without breath, dead, without motion, even though you keep the form of a serpent lifted up high on a pole. *Oration* 45.22.

PSALM OF RESPONSE: *Psalm 107:1-3, 17-22*

NEW TESTAMENT READING: *Ephesians 2:1-10*

Dead in Sin. MARIUS VICTORINUS: Death is understood in two ways. The first is the familiar definition—when the soul is separated from the body at the end of life. The second is that, while abiding in that same body, the soul pursues the desires of the flesh and lives in sin. *Epistle to the Ephesians* 1.2.1-2.

The Corruption of Our Nature. AUGUSTINE: What then is meant by this wickedness of the natural man and those who . . . *by nature* are children of wrath? Could this possibly be the nature created in Adam? That created nature was debased in him. It has run and is running its course now through everyone by nature, so that nothing frees us from condemnation except the grace of God through Jesus Christ our Lord. *On Marriage and Concupiscence* 2.20.

How Grace Saves. THEODORET: Since he rose we hope that we too shall rise. He himself has paid our debt. Then Paul explains more plainly how great the gift is: *You are saved by grace.* For it is not because of the excellence of our lives that we have been called but because of the love of our Savior. *Epistle to the Ephesians* 2.4-5.

Dare We Claim This Promise? AMBROSE: Do not rely on your own efforts but on the grace of Christ. "You are," says the apostle, "saved by grace. Therefore it is not a matter of arrogance here but faith when we celebrate: We are accepted! This is not pride but devotion." *On the Sacraments* 5.4.19.

Whether God Has Forbidden Works. CHRYSOSTOM: God's mission was not to save people in order that they may remain barren or inert. . . . Now in what case, tell me, does faith save without itself doing anything at all? Faith's workings themselves are a gift of God, lest anyone should boast. What then is Paul saying? Not that God has forbidden works but that he has forbidden us to be justified by works. No one, Paul says, is justified by works, precisely in order that the grace and benevolence of God may become apparent! *Homily on Ephesians* 4.2.9.

GOSPEL READING: *John 3:14-21*

REFLECTIONS FROM THE CHURCH FATHERS

The Intensity of God's Love and Our Response. CHRYSOSTOM: The text, "God so loved the world," shows such an intensity of love. For great indeed and infinite is the distance between the two. The immortal, the infinite majesty without beginning or end loved those who were but dust and ashes, who were loaded with ten thousand sins but remained ungrateful even as they constantly offended him. This is who he "loved." For God did not give a servant or an angel or even an archangel "but his only-begotten Son." And yet no one would show such anxiety even for his own child as God did for his ungrateful servants. . . . He laid down his life for us and poured forth his precious blood for our sakes—even though there is nothing good in us—while we do not even pour out our money for our own sake and neglect him who died for us when he is naked and a stranger. . . . We put gold necklaces on ourselves and even on our pets but neglect our Lord who goes about naked and passes from door to door. . . . He gladly goes hungry so that you may be fed; naked so that he may provide you with the materials for a garment of incorruption, yet we will not even give up any of our own food or clothing for him. . . . These things I say continually, and I will not cease to say them, not so much because I care for the poor but because I care for your souls. *Homilies on the Gospel of John* 27:2-3.

The Great Physician Stoops to Heal My Festering Wounds. GREGORY OF NAZIANZUS: Let us praise the Son first of all, venerating the blood that expiated our sins. He lost nothing of his divinity when he saved me, when like a good physician he stooped to my festering wounds. He was a mortal man, but he was also God. He was of the race of David but Adam's creator. He who has no body clothed himself with flesh. He had a mother who, nonetheless, was a virgin. He who is without bounds bound himself with the cords of our humanity. He was victim and high priest—yet he was God. He offered up his blood and cleansed the whole world. He was lifted up on the cross, but it was sin that was nailed to it. He became as one among the dead, but he rose from the dead, raising to life also many who had died before him. On the one hand, there was the poverty of his humanity; on the other, the riches of his divinity. Do not let what is human in the Son permit you wrongfully to detract from what is divine. For the sake of the divine, hold in the greatest honor the humanity, which the immortal Son took on himself for love of you. *Poem* 2.

Love-Hate Relationship with the Truth. AUGUSTINE: People love truth when it shines on them and hate it when it rebukes them. For, because they are not willing to be deceived but definitely want to practice the art of deception, they love truth when it reveals itself and hate it when it reveals them. *Confessions* 10.23.34.

CLOSING PRAYER

We give you thanks, yes, more than thanks, O Lord our God, for all your goodness at all times and in all places, because you have shielded, rescued, helped and led us all the days of our life, and brought us unto this hour. *The Liturgy of St. Mark*

A Clean Heart

THEME

Create in us clean hearts, O Lord (Ps 51:1-12); write your law on our hearts and forget our sins forever (Jer 31:31-34). Christ, who was divine, took on human flesh in order to give us eternal salvation (Heb 5:5-10). Follow him. Walk in the light (Jn 12:20-33).

OPENING PRAYER: *Fifth Sunday in Lent*

Almighty and merciful God, unto whose everlasting blessedness we ascend, not by the frailty of the flesh but by the activity of the soul; make us ever, by your inspiration, to seek after the courts of the heavenly city, and, by your mercy, confidently to enter them; through Jesus Christ our Lord. *The Leonine Sacramentary*

OLD TESTAMENT READING: *Jeremiah 31:31-34*

REFLECTIONS FROM THE CHURCH FATHERS

An Explicit Promise. AUGUSTINE: Nowhere, or hardly anywhere, except in this passage of the prophet, do we find in the Old Testament Scriptures any mention so made of the New Testament as to indicate it by its name. It is no doubt often referred to and foretold as about to be given, but not so plainly as to have its name mentioned. Consider, then, carefully what difference God has testified as existing between the two Testaments—the old covenant and the new. *On the Spirit and the Letter* 33.

Jesus Writes Grace. PROSPER OF AQUITAINE: The adulterous woman whom the law prescribed to be stoned was set free by him with truth and grace when the avengers of the law, frightened with the state of their own conscience, had left the trembling guilty woman to the judgment of him who had come "to seek and save what was lost." For that reason he, bowing down—that is, stooping down to our human level and intent on the work of our reformation—"wrote with his finger on the ground," in order to repeal the law of the commandments with the decrees of his grace and to reveal himself as the One who had said, "I will give my laws in their understanding, and I will write them in their hearts." This indeed he does every day when he infuses his will into the hearts of those who are called and when with the pen of the Holy Spirit the Truth mercifully rewrites on the pages of their souls all that the devil enviously falsified. *The Call of All Nations* 1.8.

Sacred Scripture Remains. BEDE: The teachers of the Word come and go, and others follow in the succession of those who pass away. But the sacred Scripture remains for all time without ever being abolished, until the time when the Lord shall appear at the end of the world. Then we shall have no further need for the Scriptures or for those who interpret them, since there will be a long-awaited fulfillment of that promise of the Lord that says, "And they shall not teach their neighbor and brother saying, 'Know the Lord,' for they shall all know me, from the least of them to the greatest." *On the Tabernacle* 1.7.

PSALM OF RESPONSE: *Psalm 51:1-12*

NEW TESTAMENT READING: *Hebrews 5:5-10*

REFLECTIONS FROM THE CHURCH FATHERS

His Petition Not to Enter Death. PHOTIUS: Now as regards the first matter we say that he did not make one petition but a twofold one. For the one petition asked to avoid death, the other petition asked for death. For he also says in the same prayer and petition, "However, not my will but yours be done." And John, showing this more clearly, says that the Son prayed by saying, "Father, glorify your Son, in order that your Son may glorify you," calling the cross and death glory, as is clear. So the excellent Paul says quite well, "He was heard." *Fragments on the Epistle to the Hebrews* 5.7-9.

A Fine and Useful Example. CYRIL OF ALEXANDRIA: It was not while bare and not participating in the limits of his emptying that God the Word became our model, but "in the days of his flesh." Then, quite legitimately, he could employ human limits and pray insistently and shed tears and even appear somehow to need a savior and learn obedience, though a Son. The inspired author is, so to speak, stupefied by the mystery that the Son, existing by nature truly and endowed with the glories of divinity, should so abase himself that he endured the low estate of our impoverished humanity. But this was for us, as I have said, a fine and useful example. *On the Unity of Christ* 755.

Salvation Accomplished. LEO THE GREAT: Our origin, corrupted right after its start, needed to be reborn with new beginnings. A victim had to be offered for reconciliation, a victim that was at one and the same time both related to our race and foreign to our defilement. In this way alone could the plan of God—wherein it pleased him that the sin of the world should be wiped away through the birth and passion of Jesus Christ—be of any avail for the times of every generation. Nor would the mysteries—as they pass through various developments in time—disturb us. Instead, they would reassure us, since the faith by which we live would not have differed at any stage. *Sermon* 23.3-4.

GOSPEL READING: *John 12:20-33*

REFLECTIONS FROM THE CHURCH FATHERS

The Glory Is the Cross. PROCLUS OF CONSTANTINOPLE:

"*The hour has come*
For the Son of man to be glorified."
Glorified—referring to the cross.
For from it the power of the Lord was made known,
Because it changed the shame into glory—
　the insult into honor,
　the curse into blessing,
　the gall into sweetness,
　the vinegar into milk,
　the slap in his face into freedom,
　death into life.
The hour has come,
For the Son of man to be glorified.
Homily 9.3, On the Palm Branches.

The Seed Must Die Before Being Resurrected. AMBROSE: How many more wonders appear, if you examine each plant, noticing how the seed when laid in the earth decays and, if it did not die, would bear no fruit. But when it decays, by that very act of death, it rises up to bear fruit in greater abundance. The pliable sod receives, then, a grain of wheat. The scattered seed is controlled by the use of the hoe, and mother earth cherishes it in firm embraces to her breast. When that grain decays, there comes the pleasing aspect of the green burgeoning shoot, which immediately reveals its kind from its similarity to its own seed, so that you may discover the nature of the plant even in the very beginning of its growth, and its fruit, too, is made evident to you. *Six Days of Creation* 3.8.34.

Imitation of Christ Is Service to Christ. AUGUSTINE: Christ's servants are those who look out for his things rather than their own. "Let him follow me" means "Let him walk in my ways and not in his own," as it is written elsewhere. . . . For if he supplies food for the hungry, he should do so in the way of mercy, not to brag about it. He should be looking for nothing else there but to do good and not letting his left hand know what his right hand does. In other words, any work of charity should be utterly devoid of any thought of "what's in it for me." The one who serves in this way serves Christ and will have it rightly said to him, "Inasmuch as you did it unto one of the least of those who are mine, you did it unto me." . . . And the one who serves Christ in this way will be honored by his Father with the peculiar honor of being with his Son and having nothing lacking in his happiness ever again. And so, when you hear the Lord saying, "Where I am, there shall also my servant be," do not think merely of good bishops and clergy. But you yourselves should also serve Christ in your own way by good lives, by giving to the poor, by preaching his name and doctrine as best as you can too. Every father [or mother] . . . too will be filling an ecclesiastical and episcopal kind of office by serving Christ in their own homes when they serve their families so that they too may be with him forever. *Tractates on the Gospel of John* 51.12-13.

Christ Sums Up All Things in Himself. IRENAEUS: He took up humanity into himself, the invisible becoming visible, the incomprehensible being made comprehensible, the impassible becoming capable of suffering and the Word being made human, thus summing up all things in himself: so that as in supercelestial, spiritual and invisible things, the Word of God is supreme, so also in things visible and corporeal he might possess the supremacy, and, taking to himself the preeminence, as well as constituting himself head of the church, he might draw all things to himself at the proper time. *Against Heresies* 3.16.6.

CLOSING PRAYER

We beseech you, Lord Jesus, that to whom you do vouchsafe sweet

draughts of the words of your knowledge, you will also, of your goodness, grant that we may in due time come to you, the Fountain of all
wisdom, and ever stand before your face; for your sake. *Bede*

Hosanna!

THEME

This is the day the Lord has made—let us rejoice and be glad in it (Ps 118:1-2, 19-29)! Jesus humbled himself on the cross for us (Phil 2:5-11). God's help for us is all-sufficient (Is 50:4-9a). Hosanna! Blessed is he who comes in the name of the Lord (Mk 11:1-11).

OPENING PRAYER: *Palm Sunday*

Almighty God, we beseech you graciously to behold this your family, for which our Lord Jesus Christ was contented to be betrayed and given up into the hands of wicked men, and to suffer death on the cross; who now lives and reigns with you and the Holy Spirit, ever one God, world without end. *The Gregorian Sacramentary*

OLD TESTAMENT READING: *Isaiah 50:4-9a*

REFLECTIONS FROM THE CHURCH FATHERS

Evils Will Quickly Pass. CHRYSOSTOM: For the railings and insults and reproaches and gibes inflicted by enemies and their plots are compared with a worn-out garment and moth-eaten wool when God says, "Do not fear the reproach of people, neither be afraid of their revilings, for they shall grow old as does a garment, and like moth-eaten wool so shall they be consumed." Therefore, let none of these things that are happening trouble you, but stop asking for the aid of this or that person and running after shadows (for such are human alliances); persistently call on Jesus, whom you serve . . . and in a moment of time all these evils will be dissolved. *Letters to Olympias* 7.2.

Human and Divine. CYRIL OF ALEXANDRIA: And the Father was Christ's helper. For he did not allow or concede that his own Son should be completely shamed or overwhelmed. For they were punished, those who sought to take their punishment out on me as those who dare to fight with God. . . . For though being with us, he was the only-begotten Word of God. He put on as an identical human likeness, by which reason alone he was believed to be of a nature with us. For every human being is subject to faults and sins, and no one alive is completely blameless. He alone in becoming man retained the divine dignity. . . . And being Word and God, his flesh was able to shoo away destruction. Thus, the Son became a man who was fit to be accepted by the Father. For all that human beings have is God-given. For the one God and Father, through him, undid the power of death through his resurrection from the dead. . . . He was the servant of God, who while being human was yet truly the Son of God and the Father. And to hear his voice means no transgression of the law but a confirming of the law through types and shadows discerning the truth that is Christ and the prophecies of him, as Paul notes. . . . His voice is the evangelical and divine preaching that calls us to the redemption that is through faith in Christ. He also calls us to a proper behavior that lives in a way that is, by far, more consistent than the way of the law. The law was given in the shadows. Faith was given in the bright and shining light. *Commentary on Isaiah* 4.5.50.6-9.

Sin Eats Away at Those Who Give It Origin. THEODORET OF CYR: "Behold, you will all like a garment grow old, and something like a worm will devour you." The parable is accurate, for the worm that comes from the clothes destroys them, and sin, which is born from us, ruins those who allow it to grow. *Commentary on Isaiah* 16.50.7-9.

⧉ PSALM OF RESPONSE: *Psalm 118:1-2, 19-29*

⧉ NEW TESTAMENT READING: *Philippians 2:5-11*

REFLECTIONS FROM THE CHURCH FATHERS

The Form of God. AMBROSIASTER: When he dwelled among humans he appeared as God by his acts and works. *For the form of God* differs in nothing from God. Indeed, the reason for his being called the form and image of God is to make it apparent that he himself, though distinguishable from God the Father, is everything that God is. . . . His works revealed his form. Since his works were not those of a human, he whose work or form was that of God was perceived to be God. For what is *the form of God?* Is it not shown by the evidences given of his divinity—by his raising of the dead, his restoration of hearing to the deaf, his cleansing of lepers? *Epistle to the Philippians* 2.6–2.8.5.

The Emptying Hides but Does Not Curtail the Divinity in Him. GREGORY OF ELVIRA: We do not believe that he was so emptied that he himself as Spirit became something else. Rather he, having put aside for this time the honor of his majesty, put on a human body. Only by assuming human form could he become the Savior of humanity. Note that when the sun is covered by a cloud its brilliance is suppressed but not darkened. The sun's light, which is suffused throughout the whole earth, penetrating all with its brilliant splendor, is presently obscured by a small obstruction of cloud but not taken away. So too that man, whom our Lord Jesus Christ put on, being our Savior, which means God and the Son of God, does not lessen but momentarily hides the divinity in him. *On the Faith* 88-89.

The Phrase Conveys Ineffability. GREGORY OF NYSSA: God is "above every name." The only proper way to name God is as above every name. God exceeds every operation of the intellect. God cannot be contained in any nominal definition. This is a sign to us of God's incommunicable greatness. *Against Eunomius* 2.587.

GOSPEL READING: *Mark 11:1-11*

REFLECTIONS FROM THE CHURCH FATHERS

Beasts of Burden in the Messianic Drama. EPHREM THE SYRIAN: "Untie the donkey and bring it to me." He began with a manger and finished with a donkey, in Bethlehem with a manger, in Jerusalem with a donkey. *Commentary on Tatian's Diatessaron.*

Embodying Humility. AUGUSTINE: The master of humility is Christ who humbled himself and became obedient even to death, even the death of the cross. Thus he does not lose his divinity when he teaches us humility. . . . What great thing was it to the king of the ages to become the king of humanity? For Christ was not the king of Israel so that he might exact a tax or equip an army with weaponry and visibly vanquish an enemy. He was the king of Israel in that he rules minds, in that he gives counsel for eternity, in that he leads into the kingdom of heaven for those who believe, hope and love. It is a condescension, not an advancement for one who is the Son of God, equal to the Father, the Word through whom all things were made, to become king of Israel. It is an indication of pity, not an increase in power. *Tractates on John* 51.3-4.

Spreading the Heart Before Him. METHODIUS: Instead of spreading our garments, let us spread our hearts before him. *Oration on the Psalms* 1.

The Tribute of Their Voices. JEROME: And others cut boughs . . . and strewed them in the way. They cut branches from the fruit-bearing trees with which the Mount of Olives was planted and spread them in the way so as to make the crooked ways straight and the rough ways smooth, that Christ the conqueror of sin might walk straightly and safely into the hearts of the faithful. . . . And when they had done all that was to be done by their hands, they offered also the tribute of their voices; and going before and following after they cry, not in a brief and wordless confession but with all their might: "Hosanna to the son of David. Blessed is he that comes in the name of the Lord." *Homilies* 94.

CLOSING PRAYER

Look down from heaven, O Lord, with the eye of pity and compassion on us, your humble servants, who now implore the pardon of our sins and trust alone in your mercies; through Jesus Christ our Lord. Amen.

The Gelasian Sacramentary

He Lives!

THEME

Give thanks to the Lord, for his steadfast love endures forever (Ps 118:1-2, 14-24). The Lord wipes away our tears and gives us the hope of the resurrection (Is 25:6-9). Christ died. His life was given as an exchange for all (1 Cor 15:1-11). Christ is risen! He lives! Hallelujah (Jn 20:1-18)!

OPENING PRAYER: *Easter*

O God of hope, the true light of faithful souls and perfect brightness of the blessed, who is truly the Light of the world, grant that our hearts may both render you a worthy prayer and always glorify you with the offering of praises; through Jesus Christ our Lord. Amen. *The Gelasian Sacramentary*

OLD TESTAMENT READING: *Isaiah 25:6-9*

REFLECTIONS FROM THE CHURCH FATHERS

A Shelter from the Heat. PRIMASIUS: They will not hunger because they will feed on living bread, for he said, "I am the living bread which came down from heaven." Neither will they thirst, because they will drink from a cup so splendid as to enact in them the truth he spoke: "Whoever believes in me will never thirst"; and again: "Whoever drinks from the water I give him will receive in himself a fountain of water

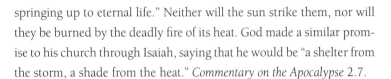

springing up to eternal life." Neither will the sun strike them, nor will they be burned by the deadly fire of its heat. God made a similar promise to his church through Isaiah, saying that he would be "a shelter from the storm, a shade from the heat." *Commentary on the Apocalypse* 2.7.

Love Overcomes Death. EUSEBIUS OF CAESAREA: Now the laws of love summoned him even as far as death and the dead themselves, so that he might summon the souls of those who were long time dead. And so because he cared for the salvation of all for ages past and that "he might bring to nothing him that has the power of death," as Scripture teaches, here again he underwent the dispensation in his mingled natures: as a man, he left his body to the usual burial, while as God he departed from it. For he cried with a loud cry and said to the Father, "I commend my spirit," and departed from the body free, in no way waiting for death, who was lagging as it were in fear to come to him. No, rather, he pursued him from behind and drove him on, trodden under his feet and fleeing, and he burst the eternal gates of his dark realms and made a road of return back again to life for the dead there bound with the bonds of death. *Proof of the Gospel* 4.12.

Christ Conquers Death. CYRIL OF ALEXANDRIA: It is appropriate and necessary that at the time the "mystery" is handed over, the "resurrection of the dead" is included. For at the time we make the confession of faith at holy baptism, we say that we expect the resurrection of the flesh. And so we believe. Death overcame our forefather Adam on account of his transgression and like a fierce wild animal it pounced on him and carried him off amid lamentation and loud wailing. Men wept and grieved because death ruled over all the earth. But all this came to an end with Christ. Striking down death, he rose up on the third day and became the way by which human nature would rid itself of corruption. He became the firstborn of the dead and the first fruits of those who have fallen asleep. We who come afterward will certainly follow the first fruits. He turned suffering into joy, and we cast off our sackcloth. We put on the joy given by God so that we can rejoice and say, "Where is your victory, O death?" Therefore every tear is taken away. For believing that Christ will surely raise the dead, we do not weep over them, nor are we overwhelmed by inconsolable grief like those who have no hope. Death itself is a "reproach of the people" for it had its beginning among us through sin. Corruption entered in on account of sin, and death's power ruled on earth. *Commentary on Isaiah* 3.1.25.

PSALM OF RESPONSE: *Psalm 118:1-2, 14-24*

NEW TESTAMENT READING: *1 Corinthians 15:1-11*

REFLECTIONS FROM THE CHURCH FATHERS

The Message of the Gospel. CHRYSOSTOM: When Paul calls the Corinthian Christians his brothers, he establishes the basis for most of his subsequent assertions. For we became brothers through the work of Christ in his earthly life and death. After all, what is the gospel but the message that God became man, was crucified and rose again? This is what the angel Gabriel announced to the Virgin Mary, what the prophets preached to the world and what all the apostles truthfully proclaimed. Homilies on the *Epistles of Paul to the Corinthians* 38.2.

The Justice Wrought in His Death. CYRIL OF JERUSALEM: The iniquity of sinners was not as great as the justice of the one who died for them. The sins we committed were not as great as the justice he embodied, when he laid down his life for us. *Catechesis* 13.

One Died for All. CYRIL OF ALEXANDRIA: He made his life be an exchange for the life of all. One died for all, in order that we all might live to God sanctified and brought to life through his blood, justified as a gift by his grace. *Letter* 41.11.

Who Was the Twelfth? ORIGEN: Evidently Matthias was chosen to replace Judas before Jesus ceased appearing to the disciples after his resurrection. *Commentary on 1 Corinthians* 4.77.

To Five Hundred. AMBROSIASTER: This is not recorded in the Gospels, but Paul knew it independently of them. *Commentary on Paul's Epistles.*

Some Have Fallen Asleep. CHRYSOSTOM: Paul does not say that some have died but that they have fallen asleep, thereby confirming the truth of the resurrection. *Homilies on the Epistles of Paul to the Corinthians* 38.5.

The Labors Imposed by Virtue. BASIL THE GREAT: He who spends his time in softness and all laxity because of his luxurious living, who is clothed in purple and fine linen and feasting every day in splendid fashion and who flees the labors imposed by virtue has neither labored in this life nor will live in the future, but he will see life afar off, while being racked in the fire of the furnace. *Unto the End* 19.5.

Grace and Labor. AUGUSTINE: Paul did not labor in order to receive grace, but he received grace so that he might labor. *Proceedings of Pelagius* 14.36.

GOSPEL READING: *John 20:1-18*

REFLECTIONS FROM THE CHURCH FATHERS

Proof No Theft Occurred. EUSEBIUS OF CAESAREA: The cloths lying within seem to me at once to furnish also a proof that the body had not been taken away by people, as Mary supposed. For no one taking away the body would leave the linens, nor would the thief ever have stayed until he had undone the linens and so be caught. And at the same time they establish the resurrection of the body from the dead. For God, who transforms the bodies of our humiliation so as to be conformed to the body of Christ's glory, changed the body as an organ of the power that dwelled in it, changing it into something more divine. But he left the linen cloths as superfluous and foreign to the nature of the body. *To Marinus*, Supplement 2.

Jesus the Spiritual Gardener. GREGORY THE GREAT: Perhaps this woman was not as mistaken as she appeared to be when she believed that Jesus was a gardener. Was he not spiritually a gardener for her when he planted the fruitful seeds of virtue in her heart by the force of his love? But why did she say to the one she saw and believed to be the gardener, when she had not yet told him whom she was seeking, "Sir, if you have taken him away"? She had not yet said who it was who made her weep from desire or mentioned him of whom she spoke. But the force of love customarily brings it about that a heart believes everyone else is aware of the one of whom it is always thinking. . . . After he had called her by the common name of "woman," he called her by her own name, as if to say, "Recognize him who recognizes you." . . . And so because Mary was called by name, she acknowledged her creator and called him at once "Rabboni," that is, "teacher." He was both the one she was outwardly seeking and the one who was teaching her inwardly to seek him. *Forty Gospel Homilies* 25.

Mary Recognizes the Voice of Her Shepherd. ROMANUS MELODUS:
He who searches the hearts
And grabs them by the reins,
Knowing that Mary would recognize his voice;
Like a shepherd, called his crying lamb,
Saying, "Mary."
She at once recognized him and spoke:
"Surely my good shepherd calls me;
In order that from this time forward he may
    number me among the ninety-nine lambs;
For I see behind the one who is calling me
The bodies of the saints, the ranks of the just,

Therefore, then, I do not say,
'Who are you who calls me?'
For I clearly know who he is who is calling me;
It is he, as he said ahead of time, My Lord, he
who offers resurrection to the fallen."
Kontakion on the Resurrection 29.10.

CLOSING PRAYER

O Lord, we beseech you, absolve your people from their offenses, that through your bountiful goodness we may all be delivered from the hands of those sins that by our frailty we have committed; grant this, O heavenly Father, for Jesus Christ's sake, our blessed Lord and Savior. Amen. *The Gregorian Sacramentary*

Walk in the Light

⸙ THEME

How wonderful it is to live in unity with each other (Ps 133)! What belongs to God belongs to all (Acts 4:32-35). Put aside doubts; Christ is faithful (Jn 20:19-31). Flee sin, and walk in the light (1 Jn 1:1–2:2).

⸙ OPENING PRAYER: *Second Sunday of Easter*

Give perfection to beginners, O Father; give intelligence to the little ones; give aid to those who are running their course. Give sorrow to the negligent; give fervor of spirit to the lukewarm. Give to the perfect a good consummation; for the sake of Christ Jesus our Lord. Amen. *Irenaeus*

⸙ READING FROM ACTS: *Acts 4:32-35*

REFLECTIONS FROM THE CHURCH FATHERS

God Is Love. AUGUSTINE: For . . . the love that God puts in people makes one heart of many hearts and makes the many souls of people into one soul, as it is written of them that believed and mutually loved one another, in the Acts of the Apostles, "They had one soul and one heart toward God." If, therefore, my soul and your soul become one soul, when we think the same thing and love one another, how much more must God the Father and God the Son be one God in the fountain of love! *Tractates on the Gospel of John* 18.4.

A Christian Is Not His Own. BASIL THE GREAT: The Christian ought to regard all the things that are given him for his use, not as his to hold as his own or to lay up. Moreover, giving careful heed to all things as the Lord's, he should not overlook any of the things that are being thrown aside and disregarded, should this be the case. No Christian should think of himself as his own master, but each should rather so think and act as though given by God to be slave to his fellow brothers and sisters. But "every person in his own order." *Letter* 22.1.

That Wealth of Greater Interest. ARATOR: Generous one, you do not do these things as a seller of property, but, ambitious one, as one who wishes to keep his privileges, and you abandon for a short time what you desire to be yours forever. Thus, to scatter the fields was the desire not to be in need; for of what advantage is property that perishes even though it is guarded? Whoever loses it has it to greater advantage laid up in the citadel of heaven. Seek there, creditor, the wealth of greater interest and lay up treasures where they can suffer no loss; there no misfortune wears away perpetual wealth; you will possess everlastingly what you cause the Lord to owe. *On the Acts of the Apostles* 1.

PSALM OF RESPONSE: *Psalm 133*

NEW TESTAMENT READING: *1 John 1:1–2:2*

REFLECTIONS FROM THE CHURCH FATHERS

The Central Theme—Love. AUGUSTINE: This book is very sweet to every healthy Christian heart that savors the bread of God, and it should constantly be in the mind of God's holy church. But I choose it more particularly because what it specially commends to us is love. The person who possesses the thing that he hears about in this epistle must rejoice when he hears it. His reading will be like oil to a flame. For others, the epistle should be like flame set to firewood; if it was not already burning, the touch of the word may kindle it. *Ten Homilies on 1 John, Prologue.*

Imparting Brightness to You. SYMEON THE NEW THEOLOGIAN: Let no one deceive you. God is light, and to those who have entered into union with him, he imparts of his own brightness to the extent that they have been purified. *Discourses 15.3.*

Those Surrounded by Darkness. BEDE: John calls sin heresies, and hatred darkness. Therefore the mere confession of one's faith is not enough for salvation if there is no sign of good works confirming that faith. But at the same time, the goodness of the works is of no value either, if they are not done in the simplicity of faith and love. Anyone who is in any way surrounded by darkness is totally unable to have fellowship with the one in whom there is no sign of wickedness at all. *On 1 John.*

God Is Faithful and Just. OECUMENIUS: To say that God is faithful means that he is reliable, for faithful is a word that is not just applied to those who believe but also to those who can be relied on. It is in this second sense that it is applied to God. He is also just in that he does not refuse anyone who comes to him, however seriously they may have sinned. *Commentary on 1 John.*

GOSPEL READING: *John 20:19-31*

REFLECTIONS FROM THE CHURCH FATHERS

The Holy Spirit Is the Breath of God. CYRIL OF ALEXANDRIA: The Son, sharing the same nature as God the Father, has the Spirit in the same manner that the Father would be understood to have the Spirit. In other words, the Spirit is not something added or that comes from without, for it would be naïve—even insane—to hold such an opinion. But God the Father has the Spirit, just as each one of us has our own breath within us that pours forth from the innermost parts of the body.

This is why Christ physically breathed on his disciples, showing that as the breath proceeds physically from the human mouth, so too does Christ, in a manner befitting God, pour forth the Spirit from the divine essence. *Commentary on the Gospel of John* 9.1.

The Father Sends the Son, the Son Sends You. GREGORY THE GREAT: The Father sent his Son, appointing him to become a human person for the redemption of the human race. He willed him to come into the world to suffer—and yet he loved his Son whom he sent to suffer. The Lord is sending his chosen apostles into the world, not to the world's joys but to suffer as he himself was sent. Therefore as the Son is loved by the Father and yet is sent to suffer, so also the disciples are loved by the Lord, who nevertheless sends them into the world to suffer. *Forty Gospel Homilies* 26.

Salvation Rests on More Than Eyes Can See. LEO THE GREAT: It is the strength of great minds and the light of firmly faithful souls unhesitatingly to believe what is not seen with the bodily sight and to focus your affections where you cannot direct your gaze. And from where should this godliness spring up in our hearts or how should someone be justified by faith, if our salvation rested on those things only that lie beneath our eyes? And so, our Lord said to Thomas, who seemed to doubt Christ's resurrection until he had tested by sight and touched the traces of his passion in his very flesh, "because you have seen me, you have believed; blessed are those who have not seen and yet have believed." *Sermon* 74.1.

Courageous Endurance. JOHN OF CARPATHUS: Blessed are those who, when grace is withdrawn, find no consolation in themselves but only continuing tribulation and thick darkness, and yet they do not despair. Rather, strengthened by faith, they endure courageously, convinced that they do indeed see him who is invisible. *Texts for the Monks in India* 71.

⸙ CLOSING PRAYER

O God, who by the power of your majesty dispenses the number of our days and the measure of our time, favorably regard the service that we humbly render, and grant that our times may be filled with the abundance of your peace and the grace of your bounty; through Jesus Christ our Lord. Amen. *The Gelasian Sacramentary*

Open Our Minds

THEME

Why are we troubled? Christ suffered, Christ died, Christ is alive. Open our minds so we might understand (Lk 24:36b-48) and do right (1 Jn 3:1-7). Lord, please hear us when we cry out to you (Ps 4); let us be your witnesses (Acts 3:12-19).

OPENING PRAYER: *Third Sunday of Easter*

You, almighty Ruler, did create all things for your name's sake; and did give food and drink to men for their enjoyment, that they may give thanks unto you: but us you have blessed with spiritual food and drink, and life eternal through your Child. *Didache*

READING FROM ACTS: *Acts 3:12-19*

REFLECTIONS FROM THE CHURCH FATHERS

True Excellence. JOHN CASSIAN: Nor did they think that anyone should be renowned for the gifts and marvels of God but rather for the fruits of his own good deeds, which are brought about by the efforts of his mind and the power of his works. For often, as was said above, people of corrupt minds, reprobate concerning the truth, both cast out devils and perform the greatest miracles in the name of the Lord. *Conference* 15.6.

The Power of the Kingdom. CASSIODORUS: It is through the saints' preaching that God's might and the glory of the kingdom are made known, in case they might be perhaps less sought if people did not know of them. His might was also made known when Peter and John made the man lame from birth walk, and they said, "Men of Israel, why marvel at this, as if by our strength or devotion we had made this man to walk?" And a little later they say that he was made whole in the name of Christ Jesus. The might of the Lord was also made known when the apostles invoked his name and made manifest diverse powers. *Exposition of the Psalms 144.12.*

Faith for Healing. AMMONIUS: "And the faith which is through him." This is said because someone is healed through the faith that is directed to Christ. For it is necessary that the faith of both concur, that is, the faith of the one healed and the faith of the one praying over the sick person. This we see in the case of the paralytic and the woman with the flow of blood. *Catena on the Acts of the Apostles 3.16.*

God Uses the Wickedness of People. CHRYSOSTOM: If indeed it was all the prophets and not only one of them who said this, it follows that, although the event took place through ignorance, it did not take place contrary to God's ordinance. See how great is the wisdom of God, when it uses the wickedness of others to bring about what must be. *Homilies on the Acts of the Apostles 9.*

PSALM OF RESPONSE: *Psalm 4*

NEW TESTAMENT READING: *1 John 3:1-7*

REFLECTIONS FROM THE CHURCH FATHERS

The World. CLEMENT OF ALEXANDRIA: The "world" means those who live in pleasure. *Adumbrations.*

The Inheritance Given Us. **ANDREAS:** God shows us the necessary patience because of the inheritance that he has given us. Here the "world" refers to wicked people. *Catena.*

We Shall See Him As He Is. **SEVERUS OF ANTIOCH:** Therefore we live as children of God even in this present life, sanctifying ourselves by virtue and striving toward the likeness of something even better. Encouraged by this, we shall be fashioned according to the brightness of the resurrection, when we shall see him, insofar as that is possible, as he is. *Catena.*

Faith Past and Present. **HILARY OF ARLES:** We shall see him as he is because we shall be like him. This is our hope for the future, our love in the present and our faith in both the past and the present. *Introductory Commentary on 1 John.*

Imitating God's Purity. **BEDE:** There are many who say they have faith in Christ but somehow seem to forget about this pure aspect of it. It is clear that anyone who has real faith will demonstrate that fact by living a life of good works . . . by rejecting ungodliness and worldly desires and by imitating Christ's sober, righteous and godly life. We are commanded to imitate the purity of God's holiness to the extent that we are capable of doing so, just as we are taught to hope for the glory of the divine likeness according to our capacity for receiving it. *Introductory Commentary on 1 John.*

No Excuse to Sin. **OECUMENIUS:** Since Christ, in whom there was no sin, came to take away your sins, now you have no excuse to go on sinning. *Commentary on 1 John.*

GOSPEL READING: *Luke 24:36b-48*

REFLECTIONS FROM THE CHURCH FATHERS

The Disciples Despised Death. **IGNATIUS OF ANTIOCH:** I myself am convinced and believe that he was in the flesh even after the resurrection. When he came to Peter and his friends, he said to them, "Take hold of me. Touch me, and see that I am not a bodiless ghost." They immediately touched him. They were convinced, clutching his body and his very breath. For this reason, they despised death itself and proved its victors. After the resurrection, he also ate and drank with them as a real human being, although in spirit he was united with the Father. *Letter to the Smyrnaeans* 3.1-2.

The Grilled Fish Represents the Faith of the Martyrs. AUGUSTINE: While they were still flustered for joy, they were rejoicing and doubting at the same time. They were seeing and touching, and scarcely believing. What a tremendous favor grace has done us! We have neither seen nor touched, and we have believed. While they were still flustered for joy, he said, "Have you got here anything to eat? Certainly you can believe that I am alive and well if I join you in a meal." They offered him what they had: a portion of grilled fish. Grilled fish means martyrdom, faith proved by fire. Why is it only a portion? Paul says, "If I deliver my body to be burned, but have not love, I gain nothing." Imagine a complete body of martyrs. Some suffer because of love, while others suffer out of pride. Remove the pride portion, offer the love portion. That is the food for Christ. Give Christ his portion. Christ loves the martyrs who suffered out of love. *Sermon* 229.3.

Jesus Recalls His Predictions and the Old Testament Prophecies. CYRIL OF ALEXANDRIA: When he restrained their thoughts by what he said, by the touch of their hands and by sharing food, he then opened their minds to understand that he had to suffer, even on the wood of the cross. The Lord reminds the disciples of what he said. He had forewarned them of his sufferings on the cross, according to what the prophets had long before spoken. He also opens the eyes of their hearts for them to understand the ancient prophecies. *Commentary on Luke,* Chapter 24.

The Necessary Sequence. **BEDE:** The disciples learned that their Maker subjected himself to countless kinds of abuses at the hands of the wicked and even to the sentence of death for their salvation. This effectively stirred them up to tolerate adversities of every kind for their salvation. They remembered that through his sacraments they had been cleansed, sanctified and united to the body of him who, when he had tasted death for them, presented an example of a speedy rising from death. For what other reason might they more fittingly receive the hope of their own resurrection? *Homilies on the Gospels* 11.9.

CLOSING PRAYER

Finished and perfected, as far as is in our power, O Christ, our God, is the mystery of your dispensation. For we have remembered your death . . . we have been filled with your unending life, we have enjoyed your inexhaustible bounty. Do you be pleased to count us worthy of them in the world to come. Through the grace of your eternal Father, and your holy, good and life-giving Spirit, now and ever, world without end. *The Liturgy of St. Basil*

The Good Shepherd

THEME

Lord, we are the sheep (Jn 10:11-18) and you are our good shepherd (Ps 23). The stone that has been rejected has become the chief cornerstone (Acts 4:5-12). Love one another; keep his commandments (1 Jn 3:16-24).

OPENING PRAYER: *Fourth Sunday of Easter*

Into your hands, O Lord, we commit ourselves this day. Give to each one of us a watchful, a humble and a diligent spirit that we may seek in all things to know your will, and when we know it may perform it perfectly and gladly, to the honor and glory of your name; through Jesus Christ our Lord. Amen. *The Gelasian Sacramentary*

READING FROM ACTS: *Acts 4:5-12*

REFLECTIONS FROM THE CHURCH FATHERS

The Promise Fulfilled. CHRYSOSTOM: And now recall what Christ said: "When they bring you before the synagogues, the rulers and the authorities, do not worry about how you are to defend yourselves or what you are to say; for the Holy Spirit will teach you at that very hour what you ought to say." *Homilies on the Acts of the Apostles* 10.

He Extends Throughout History. AUGUSTINE: For "there is one God, and one Mediator between God and men, the man Christ Jesus," since "there is no other name under heaven given to men, whereby we must be saved," and "in him God has defined to all men their faith, in that he has raised him from the dead." Now without this faith, that is to say, without a belief in the one Mediator between God and humankind, the man Christ Jesus; without faith, I say, in his resurrection by which God has given assurance to all people and which no one could of course truly believe were it not for his incarnation and death; without faith, therefore, in the incarnation and death and resurrection of Christ, the Christian truth unhesitatingly declares that the ancient saints could not possibly have been cleansed from sin so as to have become holy and justified by the grace of God. And this is true both of the saints who are mentioned in holy Scripture and of those also who are not indeed mentioned therein but must yet be supposed to have existed—either before the deluge or in the interval between that event and the giving of the law or in the period of the law itself—not merely among the children of Israel, as the prophets, but even outside that nation, as for instance Job. For cleansing from sin was by the self-same faith. The one Mediator cleansed the hearts of these too, and there also was "shed abroad in them the love of God by the Holy Spirit," "who blows where he wills," not following people's merits but even producing these very merits himself. For the grace of God will in no wise exist unless it be wholly free. *On Original Sin* 2.24.28.

Salvation Is Not in Any Other. BEDE: If the salvation of the world is in no other but in Christ alone, then the fathers of the Old Testament were saved by the incarnation and passion of the same Redeemer, by which we also believe and hope to be saved. For although the sacramental signs differed by reason of the times, nevertheless there was agreement in one and the same faith, because through the prophets they learned as something to come the same dispensation of Christ that we learned through the apostles as something that has been done. For there is no redemption of human captivity [to sinfulness] except in the blood of him who gave himself as a redemption for all. *Commentary on the Acts of the Apostles* 4.12.

PSALM OF RESPONSE: *Psalm 23*

NEW TESTAMENT READING: *1 John 3:16-24*

REFLECTIONS FROM THE CHURCH FATHERS

To the Least of These. CYPRIAN: If alms given to the least are given to Christ, there is no reason for anyone to prefer earthly things to heavenly ones or to place human things before divine ones. *Works and Almsgiving* 16.

Closing One's Heart. CHRYSOSTOM: When you see someone in need, do not run away, but think to yourself, if that were you, would you want to be treated like that? *Catena.*

Be Ready at Least to Give Goods. AUGUSTINE: If you are not yet able to die for your brother, at least show him your ability to give him of your goods. Let love be stirring your inmost heart to do it, not for display but out of the very marrow of compassion, thinking only of the brother and his need. *Ten Homilies on 1 John* 5.12.

Love Is Active. HILARY OF ARLES: Actions speak louder than words. *Introductory Commentary on 1 John.*

Offering Basic Necessities. BEDE: If a brother or sister has nothing and cannot even find enough to eat, we ought to give them the basic necessities of life. Likewise if we notice that they are deficient in spiritual things we ought to guide them in whatever way we can. Of course we must be sincere in doing this, not looking for praise from other people, not boasting and not pointing out that others who are richer than we are have not done nearly as much. For someone who thinks like that is full of wickedness, and the gift of truth does not dwell in him, even if it appears on the surface that he is showing love to others. *On 1 John.*

Do Unto Others. OECUMENIUS: What does John mean by this? It is exactly what Jesus said: "Whatever you want others to do to you, do the same to them." Therefore if we want our neighbors to be well-disposed toward us, we must be equally well-disposed toward them. If this is God's command, how much more ought we to obey it if we dwell in him and are sealed by him? He cannot deny himself, and it must surely be the case that whatever he has asked us to do he has already done or become in himself. Therefore if we do what he says, we know that he will give us whatever we ask and that his gift will be sealed in us. *Commentary on 1 John.*

GOSPEL READING: *John 10:11-18*

REFLECTIONS FROM THE CHURCH FATHERS

The Good Shepherd Wins the Sheep's Love. BASIL OF SELEUCIA: For the sake of his flock the shepherd was sacrificed as though he were a sheep. He did not refuse death. He did not destroy his executioners as he had the power to do, for his passion was not forced on him. He laid down his life for his sheep of his own free will. "I have the power to lay it down," he said, "and I have the power to take it up again." By his passion he made atonement for our evil passions, by his death he cured our death, by his tomb he robbed the tomb, by the nails that pierced his flesh he destroyed the foundations of hell. *Homily 26.2.*

The Hireling Rejoices in Pride of Position. GREGORY THE GREAT: There are some who love earthly possessions more than the sheep and do not deserve the name of a shepherd. . . . He is called a hireling and not a shepherd because he does not pasture the Lord's sheep out of his deep love for them but for a temporal reward. That person is a hireling who holds the place of shepherd but does not seek to profit souls. He is eager for earthly advantages, rejoices in the honor of preferment, feeds on temporal gain and enjoys the deference offered him by other people. *Forty Gospel Homilies* 15.

The Strength of Love in a Shepherd. PETER CHRYSOLOGUS: The force of love makes a person brave because genuine love counts nothing as hard or bitter or serious or deadly. What sword, what wounds, what penalty, what deaths can avail to overcome perfect love? Love is an impenetrable breastplate. It wards off missiles, sheds the blows of swords, taunts dangers, laughs at death. If love is present, it conquers everything. *Sermon* 40.

Christ's Death Not a Consequence of Sin. AUGUSTINE: Here he shows that his natural death was not the consequence of sin in him but of his own simple will, which was the why, the when and the how [of his death]. For because the Word of God is so commingled [with the flesh] as to be one with it, he says, "I have power to lay it down." *On the Trinity* 4.13.16.

CLOSING PRAYER

We beseech you, O Lord, to look on your servants, whom you have enabled to put their trust in you, and grant us both to ask such things as shall please you, and also to obtain what we ask; through Jesus Christ our Lord. Amen. *The Leonine Sacramentary*

Love One Another

☙ THEME

If we love each other, God lives in us (1 Jn 4:7-21). We are called to
share the good news (Acts 8:26-40) and be fruitful (Jn 15:1-8). Seek
the Lord. Praise his name (Ps 22:25-31).

☙ OPENING PRAYER: *Fifth Sunday of Easter*

Open our hearts, O Lord, and enlighten our minds by the grace of your
Holy Spirit, that we may seek what is well-pleasing to your will; and so
order our doings after your commandments that we may be found fit
to enter into your everlasting joy, through Jesus Christ our Lord. *Bede*

☙ READING FROM ACTS: *Acts 8:26-40*

REFLECTIONS FROM THE CHURCH FATHERS

The Ethiopian's Fervor. CHRYSOSTOM: Consider, I ask you, what a
great effort it was not to neglect reading even while on a journey, and
especially while seated in a chariot. Let this be heeded by those people
who do not even deign to do it at home but rather think reading the
Scriptures is a waste of time, claiming as an excuse their living with a
wife, conscription in military service, caring for children, attending to
domestics and looking after other concerns, they do not think it necessary for them to show any interest in reading the holy Scriptures. *Homilies on Genesis 35.3.*

The Spirit Spoke to Philip. **BEDE:** The Spirit spoke to Philip in his heart. God's Spirit utters certain words to us by a hidden power and tells us what must be done. *Commentary on the Acts of the Apostles* 8.29.

A Humble Learner. **ATHANASIUS:** He was not ashamed to confess his ignorance and implored to be taught. Therefore, to him who became a learner, the grace of the Spirit was given. But as for those Jews who persisted in their ignorance, as the proverb says, "Death came on them. For the fool dies in his sins." *Festal Letters* 19.5.

With or Without Human Mediation. **AUGUSTINE:** This same Philip, who had baptized people, and the Holy Spirit had not come on them until the apostles had come along and laid their hands on them, baptized the eunuch of queen Candace who had been worshiping in Jerusalem, and on his way back from there he was reading the prophet Isaiah in his chariot and not understanding it. Philip was prompted to approach the chariot, and he explained the reading, insinuated the faith, preached Christ. The eunuch believed in Christ and said, when they came to some water: "Look, here is water; who is to prevent me being baptized?" Philip said to him, "Do you believe in Jesus Christ?" He answered, "I believe that Jesus Christ is the Son of God." And immediately he went down with him into the water. Once the mystery and sacrament of baptism had been carried out, since there was no expectation of the apostles coming as on the previous occasion, so that no one should think the gift of the Holy Spirit was at the disposal of mortals, the Holy Spirit came immediately. *Sermon* 99.11.

PSALM OF RESPONSE: *Psalm 22:25-31*

NEW TESTAMENT READING: *1 John 4:7-21*

REFLECTIONS FROM THE CHURCH FATHERS

Let Us Love One Another. **DIDYMUS THE BLIND:** Just as the person who does not choose what he ought to choose has done wrong and does not love what he ought to love, so those who love only those who are worthy of love receive only that level of praise due to them. *Commentary on 1 John.*

What Kind of Love? CHRYSOSTOM: What kind of love are we talking about here? It is the true love and not simply what people use this word to mean. It comes from our attitude and knowledge and must proceed from a pure heart. For there is also a love of evil things. Robbers love other robbers, and murderers love each other too, not out of love that comes from a good conscience but from a bad one. *Catena.*

We Ought to Love One Another. OECUMENIUS: The love we show to one another ought to be like the love that God has shown to us. I mean by that it should be sincere and pure, without ulterior motives or other hidden thoughts of the kind we normally associate with robbers and other evildoers. *Commentary on 1 John.*

If We Love One Another. AUGUSTINE: Why does John say so much about loving our brothers but nothing at all about loving our enemies? Reaching out to our enemies does not exclude loving our brothers. Our love, like a fire, must first take hold of what is nearest and then spread to what is further off. *Ten Homilies on 1 John 8.1.*

Our Savior, Our Judge. BEDE: Let no one despair of being saved. For if the diseases of wickedness that oppress us are great, there is an almighty doctor coming who can deliver us. But all of us should remember that the same Son of God who comes in meekness to save us will come again in severity to judge us. *On 1 John.*

One Who Has Love. BASIL THE GREAT: If God is love, as John says, then it must be that the devil is hatred. As he who has love has God, so he who has hatred has the devil dwelling in him. *Ascetical Discourses 2.*

Love Perfected in Us. HILARY OF ARLES: In this world we must do our best to be generous, godly, merciful and patient, imitating God as closely as we can. *Introductory Commentary on 1 John.*

GOSPEL READING: *John 15:1-8*

REFLECTIONS FROM THE CHURCH FATHERS

The Winepress of the Cross. GAUDENTIUS OF BRESCIA: The wine of his blood, gathered from the many grapes of the vine planted by him, is pressed out in the winepress of the cross, and of its own power it begins to ferment in the capacious vessels of those who receive it with faithful heart. *Two Tractates on Exodus.*

The Vine as a Living Parable. AMBROSE: It seems clear, therefore, that the example of the vine is designed, as this passage indicates, for the instruction of our lives. It is observed to bud in the mild warmth of early spring, and next to produce fruit from the joints of the shoots from which a grape is formed. This gradually increases in size, but it still retains its bitter taste. When, however, it is ripened and mellowed by the sun, it acquires its sweetness. Meanwhile, the vine is decked in green leaves by which it is protected in no slight manner from frosts and other injuries and is defended from the sun's heat. Is there any spectacle that is more pleasing or any fruit that is sweeter? What a joy to behold the rows of hanging grapes like so many jewels of a beautiful countryside, to pluck those grapes gleaming in colors of gold and purple! . . . Let them praise you who behold you, and let them admire the marshaled bands of the church like the serried rows of vine branches. Let everyone among the faithful gaze on the gems of the soul. *Six Days of Creation* 3.12.52.

The Spirit Nourishes the Fruit. CYRIL OF ALEXANDRIA: Unless the branch is provided with the life-producing sap from its mother the vine, how will it bear grapes or what fruit will it bring forth—and from what source? . . . For no fruit of virtue will spring up anew in those of us who have fallen away from intimate union with Christ. To those, however, who are joined to the one who is able to strengthen them and who nourishes them in righteousness, the capacity to bear fruit will readily be added by the provision and grace of the Spirit, which is like a life-producing water. *Commentary on the Gospel of John* 10.2.

Branches Do Nothing Apart from the Vine. PROSPER OF AQUITAINE: It is the grace of Christ that allows freedom
To run, rejoice, endure, beware, choose, press on,
To have faith, hope, love, to be purified and justified.
For if anything we do is right, O Lord, we do it
With your help.
On the Ungrateful People 954-97.

CLOSING PRAYER

Grant us, Lord, we beseech you, not to mind earthly things but to seek things heavenly; so that though we are set among scenes that pass away, our heart and affection may steadfastly cleave to the things that endure forever; through Jesus Christ our Lord. *The Leonine Sacramentary*

Overcomers

THEME

Let us sing for joy! God is faithful (Ps 98) and sends us the gift of the
Holy Spirit (Acts 10:44-48). Keep God's commandments; overcome the
world (1 Jn 5:1-6); love one another (Jn 15:9-17).

OPENING PRAYER: *Sixth Sunday of Easter*

God of creation, wondrous might, eternal power that all adore,
You rule the changing day and night, yourself unchanging evermore.
Pour light on our fading day, so in our lives no dusk shall be,
So death shall bring us to the ray, of heavenly glory, Lord, with you.
Father of mercy, unto you, we lift our voice in prayer and praise,
And to the Son and Spirit be, like glory to the end of days.
Rerum Deus Tenax Vigor, *Ambrose*

READING FROM ACTS: *Acts 10:44-48*

REFLECTIONS FROM THE CHURCH FATHERS

Destroying the Dividing Wall. CHRYSOSTOM: Gentiles? What Gentiles now? They were no longer Gentiles, the Truth having come. It is
nothing wonderful, he says, if before the act of baptism they received
the Spirit: in our own case this same happened. Peter shows that not as
the rest were they baptized, but in a much better way. This is the reason
why the event takes place in this manner, that his opponents may have

nothing to say but even in this way may account the Gentiles equal with themselves. *Homilies on the Acts of the Apostles* 24.

The Outpouring of the Holy Spirit. ORIGEN: Hence, if you speak God's word and do so faithfully with a pure conscience, it can come about that while you are speaking the fire of the Holy Spirit will inflame the hearts of your hearers and immediately make them warm and eager to carry out all you are teaching in order to implement what they have learned. *Commentary on Romans* 6.13.

God Surprises Us to the Degree Necessary. SEVERUS OF ANTIOCH: At the beginning of the preaching, when the apostles announced the gospel, those who received holy baptism both spoke with tongues and prophesied in order to prove that they had received the Holy Spirit. When unbelief was at its climax, then, as was necessary, the miracles flourished. Yet, with the faith spread far and wide, there is no need of signs, for what comes from God is not for show but for the salvation, healing and benefit of those who receive. *Catena on the Acts of the Apostles* 10.44.

A Twofold Purification. CYRIL OF JERUSALEM: For since a person is of twofold nature, soul and body, the purification also is twofold, the one incorporeal for the incorporeal part, and the other bodily for the body. The water cleanses the body, and the spirit seals the soul, that we may draw near to God, "having our heart sprinkled" by the Spirit "and our body washed with pure water." . . . Neither does he who is baptized with water, but not found worthy of the Spirit, receive the grace in perfection; nor if a person is virtuous in his deeds, but receives not the seal by water, shall he enter into the kingdom of heaven. A bold saying, but not mine, for it is Jesus who has declared it, and here is the proof of the statement from holy Scripture. *Catechetical Lectures* 3.4.

PSALM OF RESPONSE: *Psalm 98*

⳨ NEW TESTAMENT READING: *1 John 5:1-6*

REFLECTIONS FROM THE CHURCH FATHERS

When We Love God. AUGUSTINE: To love the children of God is to love the Son of God; to love the Son of God is to love the Father. Nobody can love the Father without loving the Son, and anyone who loves the Son will love the other children as well. *Ten Homilies on 1 John* 10.3.

On Fire with Love. BEDE: Only someone who is on fire with the love of his Maker can be said to love his fellow humans in the right way. For if a person's love for his Creator starts to flag, his words of love for his fellows lose all their power. *On 1 John.*

We Love the Children of God. THEOPHYLACT: If we love God, then we must also love those whom God has brought to birth and who have become our brothers and sisters. Loving one another is a sign of how much we love God. *Commentary on 1 John.*

Who Overcomes? BEDE: The person who believes that Jesus is the Son of God overcomes the world by adding works worthy of that faith to it. If you think that faith in his divinity and a profession of that faith are enough by themselves, read on! *On 1 John.*

By Water and Blood. OECUMENIUS: Why did Jesus come? To give us new birth and to make us children of God. How are we born? Through water and blood. The Jesus who came gives us new birth by water and by blood. The water stands for his baptism, when Jesus was revealed as the Son of God. The blood, of course, stands for his crucifixion, when he prayed that the Father would glorify him and a voice answered from heaven: "I have glorified and I will glorify." *Commentary on 1 John.*

By Baptism, Passion and the Spirit. ISHO'DAD OF MERV: John calls Christ's baptism "water" and his passion "blood." He fulfilled all the dispensations for our sake, by means of his baptism, his passion and by the Holy Spirit. *Commentaries.*

GOSPEL READING: *John 15:9-17*

REFLECTIONS FROM THE CHURCH FATHERS

Hold to the Commandment of Love. BASIL THE GREAT: Do we fail to love according to the commandment of the Lord? Then we lose the distinctive mark imprinted on us. Are we puffed up till almost bursting with empty pride and arrogance? Then we fall into the inevitable condemnation of the devil. *Letter 56.*

God's Love Intertwined with Our Own. CHRYSOSTOM: "Love one another as I have loved you." Do you see that the love of God is intertwined with our own and connected like a sort of chain? Thus, it sometimes says that there are two commandments, sometimes only one. For it is not possible that the one who has taken hold of the first should not possess the second also. *Homilies on the Gospel of John 77.1.*

Love Your Enemy and Make a Friend. GREGORY THE GREAT: The unique, the highest proof of love is this, to love the person who is against us. This is why Truth himself bore the suffering of the cross and yet bestowed his love on his persecutors, saying, "Father, forgive them for they know not what they do." Why should we wonder that his living disciples loved their enemies, when their dying master loved his? He expressed the depth of his love when he said, "No one has greater love than this, than that he lay down his life for his friends." The Lord had come to die even for his enemies, and yet he said he would lay down his life for his friends to show us that when we are able to win over our enemies by loving them, even our persecutors are our friends. *Forty Gospel Homilies 27.*

Love Is the Fruit We Are to Bear. AUGUSTINE: For who can truly rejoice who does not love the good as the source of his joy? Who can have true peace, if he does not have it with one whom he truly loves? Who can be long-enduring through persevering continually in good, except through fervent love? Who can be kind, if he does not love the person he is helping? Who can be good, if he is not made so by loving? Who can be sound in the faith without that faith that works by love? Whose meekness can be beneficial in character, if not regulated by love? And who will abstain from that which is debasing, if he does not love that which dignifies? Appropriately, therefore, the good Master frequently commends love as the only thing needing to be commended. Without love, everything else that is good is no help, and you cannot have love without bringing with it all those other good things that make a person truly good. *Tractates on the Gospel of John 87.1.*

CLOSING PRAYER

Lord of all power and might, who art the author and giver of all good things; graft in our hearts the love of your name, increase in us true religion, nourish us with all goodness, and of your great mercy keep us in the same; through Jesus Christ our Lord. Amen. *The Gelasian Sacramentary*

Believe!

◊ THEME

We meditate on God's words and delight in them (Ps 1), taking comfort in God's mercy in the midst of change and disappointment (Acts 1:15-17, 21-26). Imitate Christ (Jn 17:6-19)! We believe, and are granted eternal life (1 Jn 5:9-13).

◊ OPENING PRAYER: *Seventh Sunday of Easter*

Let the prayers of your suppliants, O Lord, come up to the ears of your mercy; and that we may obtain what we ask, make us ever to ask what pleases you; through Jesus Christ our Lord. *The Leonine Sacramentary*

◊ READING FROM ACTS: *Acts 1:15-17, 21-26*

REFLECTIONS FROM THE CHURCH FATHERS

The Fisherman's Vocation Changed. ARATOR: Foremost among the band of apostles, Peter had been called from his small boat; the scaly throng were wont to be caught by this fisher; suddenly, seen from the shore as he drew his nets, he himself deserved to be drawn; Christ's fishing deigned to seize a disciple who must stretch the nets that are to catch the human race. To the hand that had borne the fishhook was transferred the key. He who had been eager to shift the dripping booty from the depths of the sea to the shore and to fill the craft with spoils, now in another area draws from the better waves [of baptism]; no longer pursuing his profits through the waters, he forsakes his profession. To him the Lamb entrusted the sheep which he saved by his passion; and he enlarges his flock throughout the whole world under this shepherd. *On the Acts of the Apostles* 1.

God Knows the Hearts of All People. AMBROSE: The imperial power is great, but consider . . . how great God is. He sees the hearts of all; he probes their inmost conscience; he knows all things before they come to pass; he knows the innermost secrets of your heart. You do not allow yourself to be deceived; do you expect to hide anything from God? *Letter* 11 (57).

Through the Twelve the Trinity Is Proclaimed Everywhere. AUGUSTINE: This saying, "I have chosen you twelve," may be understood in this way, that twelve is a sacred number. For the honor of that number was not taken away because one was lost, for another was chosen into the place of the one who perished. The number remained a sacred number, a number containing twelve. The twelve were to make known the Three [the Trinity] throughout the whole world, that is, throughout the four quarters of the world. That is the reason of the three times four. Judas, then, only cut himself off; he did not profane the number twelve. He abandoned his Teacher, but God appointed a successor to take his place. *Tractates on the Gospel of John* 27.10.

PSALM OF RESPONSE: *Psalm 1*

NEW TESTAMENT READING: *1 John 5:9-13*

REFLECTIONS FROM THE CHURCH FATHERS

The Testimony of People. HILARY OF ARLES: The testimony of men refers to the testimony of people like Moses and the prophets, who were all men of God. *Introductory Commentary on 1 John*.

The Testimony God Has Borne. **ANDREAS:** After giving us one testimony about his Son, God gave us another, which is eternal life. *Catena.*

Eternal Life. **BEDE:** John says that God has given us eternal life, and remember that he was saying this at a time when he was still in the flesh and subject to physical death. But God gave us eternal life in exactly the same way as he has given us the power to become his children. Right now we live on earth in the hope of his promise, which we shall receive in its fullness after we die and go to be with him. *On 1 John.*

This Life Is in His Son. **OECUMENIUS:** God has promised to give us eternal life because we have been adopted into him through his Son, of whom Scripture says, "In him was life." Therefore whoever has the Son by holy baptism also has life. *Commentary on 1 John.*

Life Only in Christ. **AUGUSTINE:** Here John testifies that no one has life unless he has Christ. *Against Julian 6.9.27.*

Reassured of Future Blessedness. **BEDE:** John writes these things so that those who believe in Christ will be reassured about their future blessedness. They will not be led astray by the deception of those who say that Jesus was not the Son of God and therefore has nothing to offer to those who have believed in him. *On 1 John.*

GOSPEL READING: *John 17:6-19*

REFLECTIONS FROM THE CHURCH FATHERS

Christ Carries Out His Father's Plan. **BASIL THE GREAT:** The Lord says "all mine are yours," as if he were submitting his lordship over creation to the Father, but he also adds "yours are mine," to show that the creating command came from the Father to him. The Son did not need help to accomplish his work, nor are we to believe that he received a separate commandment for each portion of his work. Such extreme inferiority would be entirely inadequate to his divine glory. Rather, the

Word was full of his Father's grace. He shines forth from the Father and accomplishes everything according to his parent's plan. He is not different in essence, nor is he different in power from his Father, and if their power is equal, then their works are the same. Christ is the power of God and the wisdom of God. All things were made through him and all things were created through him and for him, not as if he were discharging the service of a slave, but instead he creatively fulfills the will of his Father. *On the Holy Spirit* 8.19.

A Prayer of Thanks for the Holy Name. DIDACHE:
We give you thanks, holy Father,
For your holy name that you
Have caused to dwell in our hearts,
And for the knowledge and faith and immortality
Which you have made known to us
Through Jesus your servant;
To you be the glory forever. . . .
Remember your church, Lord,
To deliver it from all evil
And to make it perfect in your love;
And gather it, the one that has been sanctified,
From the four winds into your kingdom,
Which you have prepared for it;
For yours is the power and the glory forever.
Didache 10.2-5.

Christians Look to Another City. CAESARIUS OF ARLES: There are two cities, dearest brothers. . . . The first is the city of this world, the second, the city of paradise. The first city is full of labor, the second is restful. The first is full of misery, the second is blessed. If a person lives sinfully in the first, he cannot arrive in the second. We must be pilgrims in this world in order to be citizens of heaven. If one wants to love this world and remain a citizen on it, he has no place in heaven, for we prove our pilgrim status by our longing for our true country. Let no one deceive himself, beloved brothers. The true country of Christians is in heaven, not here. The angels are our fellow citizens. Our parents are the patriarchs, prophets, apostles and martyrs. Our King is Christ. May we live, therefore, in this earthly sojourn in a manner that will enable us to long for such a country during our stay here. *Sermon* 151.2.

CLOSING PRAYER

May the Spirit, O Lord, who proceeds from you illuminate our minds, and as your Son has promised, lead us into all truth, through the same our Lord Jesus Christ. Amen. *The Gelasian Sacramentary*

Counselor, Comforter

⊰ THEME

God raises the dead and offers us the promise of resurrection (Ezek 37:1-14). The Holy Spirit helps us in our weakness, interceding for us (Rom 8:22-27). He is our counselor, our comforter (Jn 15:26-27; 16:4b-15). May the glory of the Lord, who made all things, endure forever (Ps 104:24-34, 35b)!

⊰ OPENING PRAYER: *Day of Pentecost*

O God, who has taught us to keep all your heavenly commandments by loving you and our neighbor; grant us the spirit of peace and grace, that we may be both devoted to you with our whole heart and united to each other with a pure will; through Jesus Christ our Lord. Amen. *The Leonine Sacramentary*

⊰ OLD TESTAMENT READING: *Ezekiel 37:1-14*

REFLECTIONS FROM THE CHURCH FATHERS

The Mystery of the Resurrection. ORIGEN: The mystery of the resurrection is great and difficult for many of us to understand. It is mentioned also in many other passages of the Scripture and is proclaimed no less through these words in Ezekiel. *Commentary on the Gospel of John* 10.233.

Faith in the Resurrection Is Fundamental. CYRIL OF JERUSALEM: The hope of resurrection is the root of every kind of good work, for expectation of reward braces the soul to productive toil. And whereas every worker is ready to sustain his toil if he can look forward to being repaid for his labors, where toil has no recompense the soul is soon discouraged and the body flags with it. A soldier who expects his share of the spoils is ready for war. But no one is prepared to die serving a king so undiscerning that he does not provide rewards for labors. In the same way, any soul that believes in resurrection takes care for itself, as is right, but any soul that disbelieves the resurrection abandons itself to destruction. A person who believes that the body survives to rise again is careful of this garment and does not soil it. *Catechetical Lectures* 18.1.

The Weak Are Supported by the Strong. BASIL THE GREAT: There should . . . be certain bones of the inner person in which the bond of union and harmony of spiritual powers is collected. Just as the bones by their own firmness protect the tenderness of the flesh, so also in the church there are some who through their own constancy are able to carry the infirmities of the weak. And as the bones are joined to each other through articulations by sinews and fastenings that have grown on them, so also would be the bond of charity and peace, which achieves a certain natural junction and union of the spiritual bones in the church of God. *Homilies on the Psalms* 16.13.

The Wonder of Resurrection. AMBROSE: We notice here how the operations of the Spirit of life are again resumed; we know in what way the dead are raised from the opening tombs. And is it in truth a matter of wonder that the sepulchers of the dead are opened at the bidding of the Lord, when the whole earth from its utmost limits is shaken by one thunderclap, the sea overflows its bounds and again checks the course of its waves? *On His Brother Satyrus* 2.76.

PSALM OF RESPONSE: *Psalm 104:24-34, 35b*

NEW TESTAMENT READING: *Romans 8:22-27*

REFLECTIONS FROM THE CHURCH FATHERS

First Fruits. ORIGEN: Even though because of the fact that we believe in Christ our salvation is assured, nevertheless it still remains something to be hoped for; it has not been realized. *Commentary on the Epistle to the Romans.*

World as Stormy Ocean. AMBROSIASTER: For Christians, this world is like the ocean. For just as the sea is whipped up by adverse winds and produces storms for sailors, so also this world, moved by the scheming of wicked people, disturbs the minds of believers. And the enemy does this in so many different ways that it is hard to know what to avoid first, for sources of tribulation are by no means wanting. *Commentary on Paul's Epistles.*

Patient Waiting. CYPRIAN: Patient waiting is necessary that we may fulfill what we have begun to be and, through God's help, that we may obtain what we hope for and believe. *The Good of Patience 13.*

The Spirit Intercedes. AUGUSTINE: We must not deduce from this that either the apostle or those to whom he spoke were unacquainted with the Lord's Prayer. We think that the reason Paul says that we do not know how to pray . . . was because temporal trials and troubles are often useful for curing the swelling of pride or for proving and testing our patience, and by this proving and testing winning for it a more glorious and precious reward; or for chastising and wiping out certain sins, while we, ignorant of these benefits, wish to be delivered from all trouble. *Letter 130.*

The Spirit Intercedes. THEODORET OF CYR: Do not think that you will be set free by things which are harmful. You do not know what is good for you in the way that God does. Therefore, give yourselves to him who holds the key to the universe. For even if you ask nothing but merely groan under the impulse of the grace that dwells in you, he handles your affairs wisely and will ensure that you get what you need. *Interpretation of the Letter to the Romans.*

GOSPEL READING: *John 15:26-27; 16:4b-15*

REFLECTIONS FROM THE CHURCH FATHERS

The Comforter Is with Us in Our Troubles. CYRIL OF JERUSALEM: He is called the Comforter because he comforts and encourages us and helps our infirmities. We do not know what we should pray for as we should, but the Spirit himself makes intercession for us, with groanings that cannot be uttered, that is, he makes intercession to God. Very often, someone has been outraged and dishonored unjustly for the sake of Christ. Martyrdom is at hand; tortures on every side, and fire, and sword, and savage beasts and the pit. But the Holy Spirit softly whispers to him, "Wait on the Lord." What is now happening to you is a small matter; the reward will be great. Suffer a little while, and you will be with angels forever. "The sufferings of this present time are not worth comparing with the glory that shall be revealed in us." He portrays to the person the kingdom of heaven. He gives him a glimpse of the paradise of delight. *Catechetical Lectures* 16.20.

Procession Belongs to the Spirit. GREGORY OF NAZIANZUS: The Holy Spirit always existed, and exists and always will exist, Who neither had a beginning nor will have an end . . . Ever being partaken but no partaking; Perfecting, not being perfected; Sanctifying, not being sanctified; deifying, not being deified . . . Life and Lifegiver; Light and Lightgiver; Absolute Good and Spring of Goodness . . . By whom the Father is known and the Son is glorified . . .

Why make a long discourse of it? All that the Father has the Son has also; except the being unbegotten. And all that the Son has the Spirit has also, except the generation.
On Pentecost, Oration 41.9.

Come, Holy Spirit. AMBROSE:
Come, Holy Spirit, who ever One
Are with the Father and the Son,
It is the hour, our souls possess
With your full flood of holiness.

Let flesh, and heart, and lips and mind,
Sound forth our witness to humankind;
And love light up our mortal frame,
Till others catch the living flame.

Grant this, O Father, ever One
With Christ, your sole begotten Son
And Holy Spirit we adore,
Reigning and blest forever more. Amen.
Liturgy of Hours, Terce.

The Lord's Voice. TERTULLIAN: The Lord sent the Paraclete because, since human weakness could not receive everything at once, it might gradually be directed and regulated and brought to perfection of discipline by the Lord's vicar, the Holy Spirit. . . . And so, he declared the world of the Spirit. This, then, is the Paraclete's guiding office: the direction of discipline, the revelation of the Scriptures, the reforming of the intellect and the progress in us toward "better things." *On the Veiling of Virgins* 1.

The Holy Spirit Not Inferior. AUGUSTINE: For the Holy Spirit is not inferior to the Son, as certain heretics have imagined, as if the Son received from the Father and the Holy Spirit received from the Son in reference to some kind of gradation of natures. . . . He himself immediately solves this difficulty and explains his own words: "All things that the Father has are mine; therefore said I, that he shall take of mine and shall show it to you." *Tractates on the Gospel of John* 100.4.

CLOSING PRAYER

O God, who by the grace of the Holy Spirit has poured the gifts of love into the hearts of your faithful people, grant unto all your servants in your mercy health of body and soul, that they may love you with all their strength, and with perfect affection fulfill your pleasure; through Jesus Christ our Lord. Amen. *The Gregorian Sacramentary*

Send Me!

⁙ THEME

Jesus tells us to be born again—the baptism of water by which we receive the Holy Spirit (Jn 3:1-17)—and to then let the Holy Spirit lead
us into new life (Rom 8:12-17). The Lord offers us peace and gives us
strength (Ps 29). Here am I, Lord! Send me (Is 6:1-8)!

⁙ OPENING PRAYER: *Trinity Sunday*

O God, who was pleased to send on your disciples the Holy Spirit in
the burning fire of your love, grant to your people to be fervent in the
unity of faith, that, abiding in you evermore, they may be found both
steadfast in faith and active in work; through Jesus Christ our Lord.
Amen. *The Gelasian Sacramentary*

⁙ OLD TESTAMENT READING: *Isaiah 6:1-8*

REFLECTIONS FROM THE CHURCH FATHERS

Awe and Wonder. CHRYSOSTOM: Do you desire to learn how the
powers above pronounce that name; with what awe, with what terror,
with what wonder? "I saw the Lord," says the prophet, "sitting on a
throne, high, and lifted up; around him stood the seraphim; and one
cried to another and said, 'Holy, holy, holy, Lord God of hosts; the
whole earth is full of his glory!'" Do you perceive with what dread, with
what awe, they pronounce that name while glorifying and praising

him? But you, in your prayers and supplications, call on him with much listlessness; when it would become you to be full of awe and to be watchful and sober! *Homily Concerning the Statues* 7.9.

Sinners Before God. SAHDONA: Let us therefore tremble at the magnitude of the sight of the ineffable one and at the sound that ceaselessly utters the praise of the hidden Being. And let us be filled with awe and trembling, falling on our faces in fear before him. *Book of Perfection* 5-9.

Worldly Conversation. GREGORY THE GREAT: Purity of heart and simplicity are most precious in the sight of Almighty God, who is fully pure and simple in nature. Set apart from the ways of the world, the servants of God are strangers to its vain talk and thus avoid disturbing and soiling their minds in idle conversation. *Dialogues* 3.15.

Obedient Service to God. JEROME: "Whom shall I send? Who will go for us?" O divine secrets of Scripture! As long as Isaiah's tongue was treacherous and his lips unclean, the Lord does not say to him, "Whom shall I send, and who shall go?" His lips are cleansed, and immediately he is appointed the Lord's spokesman; hence it is true that the person with unclean lips cannot prophesy, nor can he be sent in obedient service to God. "With fiery coals of the desert." Would to heaven this solitude were granted us, that it would clear away all wickedness from our tongue, so that where there are thorns, where there are brambles, where there are nettles, the fire of the Lord may come and burn all of it and make it a desert place, the solitude of Christ. *Homilies on the Psalms* 41 (Psalm 119).

PSALM OF RESPONSE: *Psalm 29*

NEW TESTAMENT READING: *Romans 8:12-17*

REFLECTIONS FROM THE CHURCH FATHERS

We Are Debtors. AMBROSIASTER: It is right and clear that we are not obliged to follow Adam, who lived according to the flesh, and who by being the first to sin left us an inheritance of sin. On the contrary, we ought rather to obey the law of Christ who, as was demonstrated above, has redeemed us spiritually from death. We are debtors to him who has washed our spirits, which had been sullied by carnal sins, in baptism, who has justified us and who has made us children of God. *Commentary on Paul's Epistles.*

Debtors Not to the Flesh. CHRYSOSTOM: Once again, Paul is not speaking here about the nature of the flesh. . . . For in many ways we are indebted to that. We have to give it food, warmth, rest, medicine, clothing and a thousand other things. In order to show us that this is not what he is talking about, Paul adds the words "to live according to the flesh." . . . It is not to take charge of our life. The flesh must follow, not lead, and it must receive the laws of the Spirit, not seek to control us. *Homilies on Romans* 14.

Putting to Death the Deeds of the Body. ORIGEN: Putting to death the deeds of the body works like this: Love is a fruit of the Spirit, but hate is an act of the flesh. Therefore hate is put to death and extinguished by love. Likewise, joy is a fruit of the Spirit, but sadness is of this world, and because it brings death it is a work of the flesh. Therefore it is extinguished if the joy of the Spirit dwells in us. Peace is a fruit of the Spirit, but dissension or discord is an act of the flesh; however, it is certain that discord can be eliminated by peace. Likewise the patience of the Spirit overcomes the impatience of the flesh, goodness wipes out evil, meekness does away with ferocity, continence with intemperance, chastity with license, and so on. *Commentary on the Epistle to the Romans.*

You Will Live. AUGUSTINE: That we *should* mortify the deeds of the flesh by the Spirit is *required* of us, but that we *may* live is *offered* to us. *Predestination of the Saints* 11.22.

GOSPEL READING: *John 3:1-17*

REFLECTIONS FROM THE CHURCH FATHERS

Jesus Explains the Meaning of the New Birth. THEODORE OF MOP-
SUESTIA: Since Nicodemus had asked, "Can one enter again into the
mother's womb and be born?" our Lord explained that this occurs
through both water and Spirit. He said water because the action takes
place in water, Spirit because the Spirit exercises his power through the
water. This is called the Spirit of adoption, not water, because we receive new birth through his power. For this reason in baptism we name
the Spirit together with the Father and the Son, but we do not mention
the water, so that it may be clear that water is employed as a symbol
and for a [visible] use. But we invoke the Spirit as the effective agent
together with the Father and the Son. *Commentary on John* 2.3.4-5.

New Birth Manifests a Radical Break with the Past. BASIL THE
GREAT: First of all, it is necessary that the continuity of the old life be
cut. And this is impossible unless one is born again, according to the
Lord's word. For the regeneration, as indeed the name shows, is a beginning of a second life. So before beginning the second, it is necessary
to put an end to the first. For just as in the case of runners who turn
and take the second course, a kind of break and pause intervenes between the movements in the opposite direction, so also in making a
change in lives it seems necessary for death to come as a mediator between the two, ending all that goes before, and beginning all that comes
after. *On the Spirit* 15.35.

He Gave What Was Most Precious to Show His Abundant Love.
ISAAC OF NINEVEH: The sum of all is God, the Lord of all, who
from love of his creatures has delivered his Son to death on the cross.
For God so loved the world that he gave his only-begotten Son for it.
Not that he was unable to save us in another way, but in this way it was
possible to show us his abundant love abundantly, namely, by bringing

us near to him by the death of his Son. If he had anything more dear to him, he would have given it to us, in order that by it our race might be his. And out of his great love he did not even choose to urge our freedom by compulsion, though he was able to do so. But his aim was that we should come near to him by the love of our mind. And our Lord obeyed his Father out of love for us. *Ascetical Homilies* 74.

CLOSING PRAYER

O holy Lord God, carry onward in us the gifts of your grace, and mercifully bestow by your Spirit what human frailty cannot attain— through Jesus Christ our Lord. Amen. *The Leonine Sacramentary*

Live by Faith

⊰ THEME

Trust in God, who supports and helps us when we call on his name (Ps 20). Leaders may fail (1 Sam 15:34–16:13), but God never fails (Mk 4:26-34). Live by faith, making it your goal to please the Lord (2 Cor 5:6-17).

⊰ OPENING PRAYER: *Proper 6*

Grant us your Holy Spirit, that those things may please you, which we do at present, and that the rest of our life hereafter may be pure and holy; through the grace of Jesus Christ our Lord. *Gelasian Sacramentary*

⊰ OLD TESTAMENT READING: *1 Samuel 15:34–16:13*

REFLECTIONS FROM THE CHURCH FATHERS

God's Human Ascriptions. GREGORY OF NYSSA: Holy Scripture is often accustomed to attributing expressions to God such that seem quite like our own, for example, "The Lord was angry, and he was grieved because of their sins"; and again, "He repented that he had anointed Saul king" . . . and besides this, it makes mention of his sitting, and standing, and moving, and the like, which are not as fact connected with God but are not without their use as an accommodation to those who are under teaching. For in the case of the too unbridled, a show of anger restrains them by fear. And to those who need the medicine of repentance, it says that the Lord repents along with them of the evil, and those who grow insolent through prosperity it warns, by God's repentance in respect to Saul, that their good fortune is no certain possession, though it seems to come from God. *Answer to Eunomius's Second Book.*

Zeal for Souls. **JEROME:** Good people have always sorrowed for the sins of others. Samuel of old lamented for Saul because he neglected to treat the ulcers of pride with the balm of penitence. And Paul wept for the Corinthians who refused to wash out with their tears the stains of fornication. *Letter* 122.

Refrain from Judging. **GREGORY OF NAZIANZUS:** Do not say, "I do not mind a mere priest, if he is a celibate, and a religious person and of angelic life; for it would be a sad thing for me to be defiled even in the moment of my cleansing." Do not ask for credentials of the preacher or the baptizer. For another is his judge and the examiner of what you can't see. For humans look on the outward appearance, but the Lord looks on the heart. *On Holy Baptism,* Oration 40.26.

PSALM OF RESPONSE: *Psalm 20*

NEW TESTAMENT READING: *2 Corinthians 5:6-17*

REFLECTIONS FROM THE CHURCH FATHERS

Absent from the Lord. **AMBROSIASTER:** God is still present, but because we cannot see him we are said to be absent from him as long as we are in the body. *Commentary on Paul's Epistles.*

Hastening Home. **JEROME:** We who in this world "are exiled from the Lord" walk about on earth, it is true, but we are hastening on our way to heaven. For here we do not have a lasting place, but we are wayfarers and pilgrims, like all our fathers. *Homily 63 on Psalms.*

The Hope of the Future. **AUGUSTINE:** Man indeed brought death to himself and to the Son of man, but the Son of man, by dying and rising again, brought life to man. . . . . He wished to suffer this in the sight of his enemies, that they might think him, as it were, forsaken, and that the grace of the New Testament might be entrusted to us, to make us learn to seek another happiness, which we now possess by faith, but then we shall behold it. "For while we are in the body," says the apostle, "we are absent from the Lord, for we walk by faith and not by sight." Therefore, we now live in hope, but then we shall enjoy reality. *Letter 140, to Honoratus 9.*

The Judgment Seat. **CHRYSOSTOM:** Having alarmed and shaken his hearers by mentioning the judgment seat, Paul softens what he says by mentioning the possibility of receiving good rewards, as well as bad. *Homilies on the Epistles of Paul to the Corinthians 10.5.*

The Mark of a Lazy Soul. **ORIGEN:** Why do we ourselves not believe that we all will stand "before the judgment seat of Christ so that each one may obtain the things proper to the body according to what he has done, whether good or evil"? If we would believe these things entirely, there would be applied to us what was written: "Redemption of a man's soul is his wealth." But how can we either know or believe or understand these things when we indeed do not come together to hear them? For who of you, when the Scriptures are read, really pays attention? God through the prophet threatens indeed in great anger, "I will send famine on the earth; not a famine of bread or the thirst of water but a famine of hearing the word of God." But now God has not sent "a famine" on his church or "a thirst to hear the word of God." For we have "living bread that came down from heaven." We have "living water springing up into eternal life." Why in this time of fruitfulness do we destroy ourselves by famine and thirst? It is the mark of a lazy and lingering soul to suffer want in all this abundance. *Homilies on Leviticus 9.5.*

GOSPEL READING: *Mark 4:26-34*

REFLECTIONS FROM THE CHURCH FATHERS

Patterns of Increase. TERTULLIAN: Observe how the created order has advanced little by little toward fruitfulness. First comes the grain, and from the grain arises the shoot, and from the shoot emerges the shrub. From there the boughs and leaves gather strength, and the whole that we call a tree expands. Then follows the swelling of the germen, and from the germen bursts the flower, and from the flower the fruit opens. The fruit itself, primitive for a while, and unshapely, keeping the straight course of its development, is matured, little by little, to the full mellowness of its flavor. In just this way has righteousness grown in history. *On the Veiling of Virgins* 1.

Sharp and Pungent. CLEMENT OF ALEXANDRIA: The word that proclaims the kingdom of heaven is sharp and pungent as mustard. It represses bile (anger) and checks inflammation (pride). From this word flows the soul's true vitality and fitness for eternity. To such increased size did the growth of the word come that the tree that sprang from it (that is, the church of Christ now being established over the whole earth) filled the world, so that the birds of the air (that is, holy angels and lofty souls) dwelled in its branches. *Fragments from the Catena of Nicetas, Bishop of Heraclea* 4.

The Bruised Seed. AMBROSE: Its seed is indeed very plain and of little value; but if bruised or crushed it shows forth its power. So faith first seems a simple thing; but if it is bruised by its enemies it gives forth proof of its power, so as to fill others who hear or read of it with the odor of its sweetness. . . . The Lord himself is the grain of mustard seed. He was without injury; but the people were unaware of him as a grain of mustard seed of which they took no notice. He chose to be bruised, that we might say, "For we are the good odor of Christ unto God." *Exposition on the Gospel of Luke* 7.178-79.

The Spreading Tree. **PETER CHRYSOLOGUS:** It is up to us to sow this mustard seed in our minds and let it grow within us into a great tree of understanding reaching up to heaven and elevating all our faculties; then it will spread out branches of knowledge, the pungent savor of its fruit will make our mouths burn, its fiery kernel will kindle a blaze within us inflaming our hearts, and the taste of it will dispel our unenlightened repugnance. Yes, it is true: a mustard seed is indeed an image of the kingdom of God. Christ is the kingdom of heaven. Sown like a mustard seed in the garden of the virgin's womb, he grew up into the tree of the cross whose branches stretch across the world. Crushed in the mortar of the passion, its fruit has produced seasoning enough for the flavoring and preservation of every living creature with which it comes in contact. As long as a mustard seed remains intact, its properties lie dormant; but when it is crushed they are exceedingly evident. So it was with Christ; he chose to have his body crushed, because he would not have his power concealed. . . . Christ became all things in order to restore all of us in himself. *Sermon* 98.

CLOSING PRAYER

O Lamb of God, who takes away the sin of the world, look on us and have mercy on us; you who are yourself both victim and priest, yourself both reward and redeemer, keep safe from evil all those whom you have redeemed, O Savior of the world. *Irenaeus*

Open Your Heart

THEME

The Lord is our refuge and help in times of trouble (Ps 9:9-20). With God, the impossible becomes possible (1 Sam 17:1a, 4-11, 19-23, 32-49). What have we to fear, knowing God has power even over the wind and waves (Mk 4:35-41)? Let us open our hearts to the Lord, trusting him for all things (2 Cor 6:1-13).

OPENING PRAYER: *Proper 7*

God the Father of our Lord Jesus Christ, increase in us faith and truth and gentleness and grant us part and lot among the saints. *Polycarp*

OLD TESTAMENT READING: *1 Samuel 17:1a, 4-11, 19-23, 32-49*

REFLECTIONS FROM THE CHURCH FATHERS

Fortified by Faith. CHRYSOSTOM: In my discourse I showed that Goliath was protected by the power of his weapons and the strength of a full set of armor, whereas David had none of that panoply. But he was fortified by his faith. Goliath had the external protection of his glittering breastplate and shield; David shone from within with the grace of the Spirit. This is why a boy prevailed over a man, this is why the one wearing no armor conquered the one fully armed, this is why the shepherd's hand crushed and destroyed the bronze weapons of war. *Against the Anomoeans* 11.4-5.

The Devil Prefigured. CAESARIUS OF ARLES: When David had been anointed by blessed Samuel before he came here, he had killed a lion and a bear without any weapons, as he himself told King Saul. Both the lion and the bear typified the devil, for they had been strangled by the strength of David for having dared to attack some of his sheep. All that we read prefigured in David at that time, dearly beloved, we know was accomplished in our Lord Jesus Christ; for he strangled the lion and the bear when he descended into hell to free all the saints from their jaws. Moreover, listen to the prophet entreating the person of our Lord: "Rescue my soul from the sword, my loneliness from the grip of the dog. Save me from the lion's mouth." Since a bear possesses his strength in his paw and a lion has his in his mouth, the same devil is prefigured in those two beasts. Thus, this was said concerning the person of Christ, in order that his sole church might be removed from the hand, that is, the power or mouth of the devil. *Sermon* 121.4.

Faith Prevails over Weapons. PAULINUS OF NOLA: Having trust in Christ, consigning everything to the God of powers, regarding God alone as all that is highest—this has always been efficacious in achieving every good. This is the faith that has prevailed over all weapons. This was the strength that made that slight boy great, for he grew stronger by spurning weapons and brought low the armed giant by the power of a stone. *Poems* 26.150.

PSALM OF RESPONSE: *Psalm 9:9-20*

NEW TESTAMENT READING: *2 Corinthians 6:1-13*

REFLECTIONS FROM THE CHURCH FATHERS

Do Not Accept God's Grace in Vain. CAESARIUS OF ARLES: What does it mean to receive the grace of God in vain except to be unwilling to perform good works with the help of his grace? *Sermon* 126.5.

Varied Dangers. BASIL THE GREAT: That man, indeed, is in danger who does not throughout his whole life place before himself the will of God as his goal, so that in health he shows forth the labor of love by his zeal for the works of the Lord and in sickness displays endurance and cheerful patience. The first and greatest peril is that by not doing the will of God, he separates himself from the Lord and cuts himself off from fellowship with his own brothers; second, that he ventures, although undeserving, to claim a share in the blessings prepared for those who are worthy. *The Long Rules* 34.

Persistence in Prayer. SAHDONA: If we go on crying out and do not receive any answer, this is for our advantage: instead of losing heart and growing weary, we should go on brazenly asking God, for it is certain that "at an acceptable time" and at the appropriate hour he will answer us and deliver us. *Book of Perfection.*

A Warning Against Indifference. GREGORY OF NYSSA: For this is the grace of the Holy Spirit, possessing the entire soul and filling the dwelling place with gladness and power, making sweet for the soul the sufferings of the Lord and taking away the perception of the present pain because of the hope of the things to come. So, govern yourselves thus as you are about to ascend to the highest power and glory through your co-operation with the Spirit; endure every suffering and trial with joy with a view toward appearing to be worthy of the dwelling of the Spirit within you and worthy of the inheritance of Christ. Never be puffed up or enfeebled by indifference to the point of falling yourselves or being the cause of another's sin. *On the Christian Mode of Life.*

Only One Person's Opinion Matters. JEROME: Do not angle for compliments, lest while you win the popular applause, you dishonor God. "If I yet pleased men," says the apostle, "I should not be the servant of Christ." He ceased to please men when he became Christ's servant. Christ's soldier marches on through good report and evil report, the one on the right hand and the other on the left. No praise elates him, no reproaches crush him. He is not puffed up by riches nor depressed by poverty. Joy and sorrow he alike despises. The sun will not burn him by day or the moon by night. *Letter* 52.

Lacking Love, Restrictions Appear. CHRYSOSTOM: The heart of one who loves is wide open. He walks with great freedom. It is when love is lacking that restrictions appear. Paul did not want to accuse them openly of lack of love. He merely points to the behavioral result and encourages them to perceive the cause for themselves. *Homilies on the Epistles of Paul to the Corinthians* 13.1.

GOSPEL READING: *Mark 4:35-41*

REFLECTIONS FROM THE CHURCH FATHERS

The Bark of the Church. ORIGEN: For as many as are in the little ship of faith are sailing with the Lord; as many as are in the bark of holy church will voyage with the Lord across this wave-tossed life; though the Lord himself may sleep in holy quiet, he is but watching your patience and endurance: looking forward to the repentance, and to the conversion of those who have sinned. Come then to him eagerly, instant in prayer. *Fragments on Matthew* 3.3.

Who Was Asleep? GREGORY OF NAZIANZUS: He was tired—yet he is the "rest" of the weary and the burdened. He was overcome by heavy sleep—yet he goes lightly over the sea, rebukes the winds, and relieves the drowning Peter. *Oration* 29, On the Son 20.

Awakening the Christ Asleep in You. AUGUSTINE: When you have to listen to abuse, that means you are being buffeted by the wind. When your anger is roused, you are being tossed by the waves. So when the winds blow and the waves mount high, the boat is in danger, your heart is imperiled, your heart is taking a battering. On hearing yourself insulted, you long to retaliate; but the joy of revenge brings with it another kind of misfortune—shipwreck. Why is this? Because Christ is asleep in you. What do I mean? I mean you have forgotten his presence. Rouse him, then; remember him, let him keep watch within you, pay heed to him. . . . A temptation arises: it is the wind. It disturbs you: it is the surging of the sea. This is the moment to awaken Christ and let him remind you of those words: "Who can this be? Even the winds and the sea obey him." *Sermon* 63.1-3.

The Author of the Deep. PRUDENTIUS:

His power and miracles proclaim him God.
I see the wild winds suddenly grow calm
When Christ commands; I see the storm-tossed sea
Grow smooth, with tranquil surface bright,
At Christ's behest; I see the waves grow firm
As the raging flood sustains his treading feet.
He walks dry-shod upon the flowing tide
And bears upon the flood with footsteps sure.
He chides the winds and bids the tempest cease.
Who would command the stormy gales: "Be still,
Your strongholds keep and leave the boundless sea,"
Except the Lord and maker of the winds?
A Hymn on the Trinity.

CLOSING PRAYER

O God, who delights in the devotion of the faithful, make your people, we pray you, to be devoted to your holy things; that they who depart from their duties by ungodly depravity of mind may be converted by your grace and return from the snares of the devil wherein they are held captive; through Jesus Christ our Lord. *The Gelasian Sacramentary*

Caring for Others

⊰ THEME

Let us wait on the Lord and put our hope in his Word (Ps 130). Lord, give us true friends who help us grow stronger in our relationship with you (2 Sam 1:1, 17-27). With faith, all things are possible (Mk 5:21-43); with this in mind, let us give to others as they have need (2 Cor 8:7-15).

⊰ OPENING PRAYER: *Proper 8*

Grant, we beseech you, Almighty God, that pressing onwards in your way with devout minds, we may escape the snares of the sins that beset us; through Jesus Christ our Lord. *The Leonine Sacramentary*

⊰ OLD TESTAMENT READING: *2 Samuel 1:1, 17-27*

REFLECTIONS FROM THE CHURCH FATHERS

On Spreading Rumors. CHRYSOSTOM: You have heard David's lament for Saul. . . . Do not say to me, "I told so-and-so." Keep the story to yourself. If you did not manage to keep quiet, neither will he manage to keep his tongue from wagging. *Discourses Against Judaizing Christians* 8.4.10.

The Condemnation of the Elements. AMBROSE: Nature, therefore, by withholding its gifts from those places which were to be witnesses of a parricidal act and by its condemnation of innocent soil, makes clear to us the severity of the future punishments of the guilty. The very elements are, therefore, condemned because of the crime of people. Hence David condemned the mountains, in which Jonathan and his father were slain, to be punished with perpetual sterility, saying "You mountains of Gilboa, let neither dew nor rain come on you, mountains of death." *Cain and Abel* 2.8.26.

A Wonderful Friendship. CHRYSOSTOM: I will now cite from the Scriptures a wonderful instance of friendship. Jonathan, the son of Saul, loved David, and his soul was so knit to him that David in mourning over him says, "Your love to me was wonderful, passing the love of women. You were wounded fatally." What then? Did Jonathan envy David? Not at all, though he had great reason. Why? Because, by the events he perceived that the kingdom would pass from himself to him, yet he felt nothing of the kind. He did not say, "This one is depriving me of my paternal kingdom," but he favored David obtaining the sovereignty; and he didn't spare his father for the sake of his friend. Yet let not any one think him a parricide, for he did not injure his father but restrained Saul's unjust attempts. . . . He did not permit Saul to proceed to an unjust murder. He was many times willing even to die for his friend, and far from accusing David, he strained even his father's accusation. Instead of envying, Jonathan joined in obtaining the kingdom for him. Why do I speak of wealth? He even sacrificed his own life for David. For the sake of his friend, he did not even stand in awe of his father, since his father entertained unjust designs, but his conscience was free from all such things. Thus justice was conjoined with friendship. *Homilies on 2 Timothy 7.*

PSALM OF RESPONSE: *Psalm 130*

NEW TESTAMENT READING: *2 Corinthians 8:7-15*

REFLECTIONS FROM THE CHURCH FATHERS

You Become Rich. CHRYSOSTOM: If you do not believe that poverty is productive of great wealth, think of the case of Jesus and you will be persuaded otherwise. For if he had not become poor, you would not have become rich. By riches, Paul means the knowledge of godliness, the cleansing away of sins, justification, sanctification, the countless good things that God bestowed on us and that he intends to bestow. *Homilies on the Epistles of Paul to the Corinthians* 17.1.

Hidden Riches. AUGUSTINE: What human being could know all the treasures of wisdom and knowledge hidden in Christ and concealed under the poverty of his humanity? For, "being rich, he became poor for our sake that by his poverty we might become rich." When he assumed our mortality and overcame death, he manifested himself in poverty, but he promised riches though they might be deferred; he did not lose them as if they were taken from him. How great is the multitude of his sweetness that he hides from those who fear him but that he reveals to those that hope in him! For we understand only in part until that which is perfect comes to us. To make us worthy of this perfect gift, he, equal to the Father in the form of God, became like to us in the form of a servant and refashions us into the likeness of God. *Feast of the Nativity* 194.3.

The Likeness of Christ's Poverty. BASIL THE GREAT: If, then, we keep in reserve any earthly possessions or perishable wealth, the mind sinks down as into mire and the soul inevitably becomes blind to God and insensible to the desire for the beauties of heaven and the good things laid up for us by promise. These we cannot gain possession of unless a strong and single-minded desire leads us to ask for them and lightens the labor of their attainment. This, then, is renunciation, as our discourse defines it: the severance of the bonds of this material and transient life and freedom from human concerns whereby we render ourselves more fit to set out on the road leading to God. It is the unhindered impulse toward the possession and enjoyment of inestimable goods. . . . In short, it is the transference of the human heart to a heavenly mode of life. *The Long Rules* 8.

Translate Willingness into Action. THEODORET OF CYR: Paul knows and respects their willingness to help, but the time has now come for that willingness to be translated into action. *Commentary on the Second Epistle to the Corinthians* 329.

Giving as They Are Able. AMBROSIASTER: Paul is saying that the Corinthians should give as much as they are willing and able to give. That way their conscience would become clear and not be clouded by pretense, pleasing man but not God. *Commentary on Paul's Epistles.*

GOSPEL READING: *Mark 5:21-43*

REFLECTIONS FROM THE CHURCH FATHERS

The Cry of Anguish. JEROME: The woman with the hemorrhage had spent all that she had on doctors. Hungering and thirsting, her spirit had died within her. Having lost everything she possessed, because her life was wasting away within her, she cried out to the Lord in anguish. Her touch on the hem of his garment was the cry of a believing heart. In this she is the figure of the assembly of God gathered from all nations. *Homily 33.*

Drawing Near to the Physician. PETER CHRYSOLOGUS: No seas were ever so troubled by the ebb and flow of the tide, as the mind of this woman, pulled to and fro by the sway of her thoughts. After all the hopeless strivings of physicians, after all her outlay on useless remedies, after all the usual but useless treatment, when skill and experience had so long failed, all her substance was gone. This was not by chance, but divinely ordered, that she might be healed solely through faith and humility, whom human knowledge had failed through so many years. . . . She who feels unworthy in body, draws near in heart to the physician. In faith she touches God. . . . In an instant, faith cures where human skill had failed through twelve years. *Sermon* 33.4.

The Way of Healing. APOSTOLIC CONSTITUTIONS: Provide remedies suitable to every patient's case. Cure them, heal them by all means possible. Restore them soundly to the church. Feed the flock, "not with insolence and contempt, as lording it over them," but as a gentle shepherd, "gathering the lambs into your bosom, and gently leading those which are with young." *Constitutions of the Holy Apostles* 2.3.20.

The Sole Requisite to Receiving New Life. APHRAHAT: When the chief of the synagogue asked him about his daughter, Jesus said to him: "Only firmly believe and your daughter shall live." He believed and so his daughter lived and arose. . . . Faith causes the barren to sprout forth. It delivers from the sword. It raises up from the pit. It enriches the poor. It releases the captives. It delivers the persecuted. It brings down the fire. It divides the sea. It cleaves the rock, and gives to the thirsty water to drink. It satisfies the hungry. It raises the dead, and brings them up from Sheol. It stills the billows. It heals the sick. It conquers hosts. It overthrows walls. It stops the mouths of lions and quenches the flame of fire. It humiliates the proud and brings the humble to honor. All these mighty works are wrought by faith. *Demonstration* 4.17-19.

CLOSING PRAYER

O God, who dwells in the holy and forsakes not pious hearts, deliver us from earthly desires and carnal appetites; that no sin may reign in us, but that we may with free spirits serve you, our only Lord; through Jesus Christ. *The Gelasian Sacramentary*

God's Help

THEME

The Lord is great and worthy of our praise (Ps 48). We can accomplish things we could never do on our own through God's power (2 Sam 5:1-5, 9-10) and through Jesus Christ (Mk 6:1-13). We also accept our weaknesses, acknowledging that everything we accomplish is done with the help of the Lord (2 Cor 12:2-10).

OPENING PRAYER: *Proper 9*

O Lord, give ear unto our prayers and dispose the way of your servants in safety under your protection, that amid all the changes of this our pilgrimage, we may ever be guarded by your almighty aid; through Jesus Christ our Lord. Amen. *The Gelasian Sacramentary*

OLD TESTAMENT READING: *2 Samuel 5:1-5, 9-10*

REFLECTIONS FROM THE CHURCH FATHERS

The Word Flesh Is Used with Different Meanings. JOHN CASSIAN:
We find that the word *flesh* is used in holy Scripture with many different meanings: for sometimes it stands for the whole person, that is, for that which consists of body and soul, as here: "And the Word was made flesh," and "All flesh shall see the salvation of our God." Sometimes it stands for sinful and carnal people, as here: "My spirit shall not remain in those men, because they are flesh." Sometimes it is used for sins

themselves, as here: "But you are not in the flesh but in the spirit," and again, "Flesh and blood shall not inherit the kingdom of God." Lastly there follows, "Neither shall corruption inherit incorruption." Sometimes [as with David] it stands for unity and relationship, as here: "Behold, we are your bone and your flesh," and the apostle says, "If by any means I may provoke to emulation them who are my flesh, and save some of them." We must therefore inquire in which of these four meanings we ought to take the word flesh in this place. *Conference* 4.10.

David's Integrity. **AMBROSE:** What more should I say? He did not open his mouth to those planning deceit, and, as though he did not hear, he thought no word should be returned, nor did he answer their reproaches. When he was cursed, he blessed. He walked in simplicity of heart and fled from the proud. He was a follower of those unspotted from the world, one who mixed ashes with his food when bewailing his sins, and mingled his drink with weeping. Worthily, then, was he called for by all the people. All the tribes of Israel came to him, saying, "Behold, we are your bone and your flesh. Also yesterday and the day before when Saul lived, and reigned, you were he that led out and brought in Israel. And the Lord said to you, you shall feed my people!" And why should I say more about him of whom the word of the Lord has gone forth to say: "I have found David according to my heart." Who else always walked in holiness of heart and in justice as he did, so as to fulfill the will of God; for whose sake pardon was granted to his children when they sinned, and their rights were preserved to his heirs? *Duties of the Clergy* 2.7.35.

PSALM OF RESPONSE: *Psalm 48*

NEW TESTAMENT READING: *2 Corinthians 12:2-10*

REFLECTIONS FROM THE CHURCH FATHERS

Prayer in Our Suffering. **AUGUSTINE:** Therefore, in these trials that can be both our blessing and our bane, "we don't know how we should pray," yet, because they are hard, because they are painful, because they go against the feeling of our human weakness, by a universal human will we pray that our troubles may depart from us. But this need of devotion we owe to the Lord our God, that, if he does not remove them, we are not to think that he has deserted us but rather, by lovingly bearing evil, we are to hope for greater good. This is how power is made perfect in infirmity. To some, indeed, who lack patience, the Lord God, in his wrath, grants them what they ask, just as, on the other hand, he in his mercy refused the apostle's requests. *To Proba* 130.

A Plea Not Granted. AMBROSIASTER: Although he asked three times, his request was not granted. It is not that he was disregarded but that he was making a plea that was against his own best interests. *Commentary on Paul's Epistles.*

Answers to Our Advantage. CHRYSOSTOM: Accordingly, whether we have our requests granted or not, let us persist in asking and render thanks not only when we gain what we ask but also when we fail to. Failure to gain, you see, when that is what God wants, is not worse than succeeding; we do not know what is to our advantage in this regard in the way he does understand. The result is, then, that succeeding or failing we ought to give thanks. Why are you surprised that we don't know what is to our advantage? . . . So we ought to yield to the Creator of our nature, and with joy and great relish accept those things that he has decided on and have an eye not to the appearance of events but to the decisions of the Lord. After all, he who knows better than we what is for our benefit also knows what steps must be taken for our salvation. *Homilies on Genesis* 30.16.

Paul Coped. THEODORET OF CYR: Paul does not say that he enjoyed these things but that he had learned to cope with them. *Commentary on the Second Epistle to the Corinthians* 350.

GOSPEL READING: *Mark 6:1-13*

REFLECTIONS FROM THE CHURCH FATHERS

On Your Behalf. PETER CHRYSOLOGUS: How can he be said to go out and to come in, whom no space can enclose? What country can be his, who made, and who possesses, the whole universe? In truth, Christ goes out and comes in not of himself, nor for himself, but in you, and on behalf of you, until he recovers you from your exile and calls you home from your captivity. *Sermon* 49.

Impeding God's Gifts. JOHN CASSIAN: In some cases he so richly poured forth the mighty work of healing that the Evangelist was led to exclaim: "He healed all their sick." But among others the unfathomable depth of Christ's goodness was so thwarted that it was said: "And Jesus could do there no mighty works because of their unbelief." So the bounty of God is actually curtailed temporarily according to the receptivity of our faith. So it is said to one, "according to your faith may it be to you," and to another, "Go your way, and as you have believed so let it be to you," and to another, "Let it be to you according as you will," and again to another, "Your faith has made you whole." *Third Conference of Abbot Chaermeon* 15.

Resources for Apostolic Mission. PRUDENTIUS:
To wish for nothing more than need demands
Is rest supreme, with simple food and dress
To feed and clothe our bodies and to seek
No more than is prescribed by nature's wants.
When going on a journey, take no purse,
Nor of a second tunic think, and be
Not anxious for the morrow, lest for food
The belly lack. Our daily bread returns
With every sun. Does any bird take thought
Of tomorrow, certain to be fed by God?
The Spiritual Combat.

On Not Wearing Two Coats. AUGUSTINE: What is forbidden is neither the carrying nor the possessing of two coats but more distinctly the
wearing of two coats at the same time. The words say: "And not put on
two coats." What counsel is conveyed to them by this? They ought to
walk not in duplicity but in simplicity. *Harmony of the Gospels* 2.32.75.

CLOSING PRAYER

Have mercy, O Lord, on those whom you have associated with us in the
bonds of friendship and kindredship and grant that they, with us, may
be so perfectly conformed to your holy will, that being cleansed from
all sin, we may be found worthy, by the inspiration of your love, to be
partakers together of the blessedness of your heavenly kingdom;
through Jesus Christ our Lord. Amen. *The Gallican Sacramentary*

Give God Glory

THEME

Give me a clean heart, Lord (Ps 24); let me sing praises to you for your goodness (2 Sam 6:1-5, 12b-19). Even in the face of suffering and injustice (Mk 6:14-29) we give God glory and honor, for we know in him all things will be reconciled, and we have our inheritance (Eph 1:3-14).

OPENING PRAYER: *Proper 10*

O Lord our God, whose compassion is the cause of our fearing and loving your name, mercifully pour your grace into our hearts, that we, casting away what displeases you, may be united to you with an honest will; through Jesus Christ our Lord. Amen. *The Leonine Sacramentary*

OLD TESTAMENT READING: *2 Samuel 6:1-5, 12b-19*

REFLECTIONS FROM THE CHURCH FATHERS

Noble Through Humility. GREGORY THE GREAT: But because secret pride of heart is reproved by this which Elihu says, "All who seem to themselves to be wise will not dare to contemplate him," it seems good to observe what great gifts of virtues David had obtained, and in all these with how firm a humility he maintained himself. For whom would it not puff up to break the mouths of lions, to rend asunder the arms of bears, to be chosen, when his elder brothers had been despised, to be anointed to the government of the kingdom when the kings had been rejected, to slay with a single stone Goliath who was dreaded by all, to bring back, after the destruction of the aliens, the numerous foreskins proposed by the king, to receive at last the promised kingdom, and to possess the whole people of Israel without any contradiction? . . . Before God he acted with the most extreme lowliness, in order to strengthen by his humility the bold deeds he had performed in the sight of people. *Morals on the Book of Job* 27.46.

Extravagant Living Condemned. CLEMENT OF ALEXANDRIA: So it is that he who of all philosophers so praised truth, Plato, gave new life to the dying ember of Hebrew philosophy by condemning a life spent in revelry. "When I arrived," he said, "what is here called a life of pleasure, filled with Italian and Syracusan meals, was very repulsive to me. It is a life in which one gorges oneself twice a day, sleeps not only during the night, and engages in all the pastimes that go with this sort of life. No one on earth could ever become wise in this way, if from his youth he had followed such pursuits as these, nor would he ever attain in that way any reputation for an excellent physique." *Christ the Educator* 2.1.18.

Dancing in God's Honor. AMBROSE: But we also find praiseworthy bodily dancing in honor of God, for David danced before the ark of the Lord. Michal, however, the daughter of Saul, saw him dancing and beating a drum in the presence of the Lord and asked him, after receiving him into her home, "How is it honorable for the king of Israel to dance naked today in the presence of his maidservants?" And David answered Michal in the presence of the Lord: "Blessed be the Lord who chose me above your father and above his entire house to be established as prince over his people Israel. I will make merry in the presence of the Lord and run naked, and I will be lighthearted in your presence, and I will be honored by the maids with whom you called me naked." *Exposition on Psalm 118.*

PSALM OF RESPONSE: *Psalm 24*

NEW TESTAMENT READING: *Ephesians 1:3-14*

REFLECTIONS FROM THE CHURCH FATHERS

Called to Persevere. AMBROSIASTER: God, foreknowing all, knew who were going to believe in Christ. . . . Therefore those whom God is said to call will persevere in faith. These are the ones whom he elected before the world in Christ, so that they might be blameless before God through love—that is, so that the love of God might give them holy lives. For no one can show greater respect toward another than when he obeys in love. *Epistle to the Ephesians* 1.4.

He Chose Us in Him. CHRYSOSTOM: What he means is this: The one through whom he has blessed us is the one through whom he has elected us. . . . Christ chose us to have faith in him before we came into being, indeed even before the world was founded. The word *foundation* was well chosen, to indicate that it was laid down from some great height. For great and ineffable is the height of God, not in a particular place but rather in his remoteness from nature. So great is the distance between creature and Creator. *Homily on Ephesians* 1.1.4.

Our Sonship by Adoption. MARIUS VICTORINUS: God in his love has predestined us to adoption through Christ. How could God possibly have Christ for his Son by adoption? . . . We speak of ourselves as heirs of God the Father and heirs through Christ, being sons through adoption. Christ is his Son, through whom it is brought about that we become sons and fellow heirs in Christ. *Against the Arians* 1.2.

How Our Forgiveness Relates to Christ's Redemptive Grace. ORIGEN: Forgiveness of sins follows redemption, for there would be no forgiveness of sin for anyone before redemption occurs. First then we need to be redeemed, to be no longer subject to our captor and oppressor, so that having been freed and taken out of his hands we may be able to receive the benefit of remission of sins. Once our wounds have been healed we are called to live in accord with piety and the other virtues. *Epistle to the Ephesians.*

He Sacrificed His Beloved Son for Those Who Hated Him. CHRYSOSTOM: The wonder is not only that he gave his Son but that he did so in this way, by sacrificing the one he loved. It is astonishing that he gave the Beloved for those who hated him. See how highly he honors us. If even when we hated him and were enemies he gave the Beloved, what will he not do for us now? *Homily on Ephesians* 1.1.8.

GOSPEL READING: *Mark 6:14-29*

REFLECTIONS FROM THE CHURCH FATHERS

Calamities Accumulate. AUGUSTINE: A girl dances, a mother rages, there is rash swearing in the midst of the luxurious feast and an impious fulfillment of what was sworn. *Harmony of the Gospels* 2.33.

When a Lesser Sin Elicits a Greater. BEDE: His love for the woman prevailed. She forced him to lay his hands on a man whom he knew to be holy and just. Since he was unwilling to restrain his lechery, he incurred the guilt of homicide. What was a lesser sin for him became the occasion of a greater sin. By God's strict judgment it happened to him that, as a result of his craving for the adulteress whom he knew he ought to refuse, he caused the shedding of the blood of the prophet he knew was pleasing to God. . . . Already holy, John became more holy still when, through his office of spreading the good news, he reached the palm of martyrdom. *Homilies on the Gospels* 2.23.

His Tongue Did Not Remain Silent. AMBROSE: Look, most savage king, at the spectacle of your feast. Stretch out your right hand and see the streams of holy blood pouring down between your fingers. Nothing is lacking in your cruelty. The hunger for such unheard-of cruelty could not be satisfied by banquets, or the thirst by goblets. So as you drink the blood pouring from the still flowing veins of the cut-off head, behold those eyes. Even in death those eyes are the witnesses of your crime, turning away from the sight of the delicacies. The eyes are closing, not so much owing to death as to horror of excess. That bloodless golden mouth, whose sentence you could not endure, is silent, and yet it is still dreaded. Meanwhile, the tongue, which even after death is apt to observe its duty as when living, continues to condemn the incest with trembling motion. *Concerning Virgins* 3.5.30.

Death as a Crown. CHRYSOSTOM: In what way, then, was this just man harmed by this demise, this violent death, these chains, this imprisonment? Who are those he did not set back on their feet—provided they had a penitent disposition—because of what he spoke, because of what he suffered, because of what he still proclaims in our own day—the same message he preached while he was living. Therefore, do not say: "Why was John allowed to die?" For what occurred was not a death but a crown, not an end but the beginning of a greater life. Learn to think and live like a Christian. You not only will remain unharmed by these events but also will reap the greatest benefits. *On the Providence of God.*

CLOSING PRAYER

Into your hands, O God, we commend ourselves and all who are dear to us this day. Let the gift of your special presence be with us even to its close. Grant us never to lose sight of you all the day long, but to worship and pray to you, that at eventide we may again give thanks unto you; through Jesus Christ our Lord. Amen. *The Gelasian Sacramentary*

The Chief Cornerstone

THEME

God is our rock (Ps 89:20-37). He keeps his promises (2 Sam 7:1-14a)
and cares for us, as a shepherd cares for his sheep (Mk 6:30-34, 53-56).
Christ is our peace and our chief cornerstone (Eph 2:11-22).

OPENING PRAYER: *Proper 11*

Abba, Father, fulfill the office of your name toward your servants: do
you govern, protect, preserve, sanctify, guide and console us. Let us be
so enkindled with love for you, that we may not be despised by you, O
most merciful Lord, most tender Father, for Jesus Christ's sake. Amen.
The Gallican Sacramentary

OLD TESTAMENT READING: *2 Samuel 7:1-14a*

REFLECTIONS FROM THE CHURCH FATHERS

Christ's Kingdom Is Promised. **TERTULLIAN**: That new dispensation,
then, that is found in Christ now, will prove to be what the Creator then
promised under the appellation of "the sure mercies of David," which
were Christ's, inasmuch as Christ sprang from David, or rather his very
flesh itself was David's "sure mercies," consecrated by religion, and
"sure" after its resurrection. Accordingly the prophet Nathan . . . makes
a promise to David for his seed, "which shall proceed," he says, "from
your own body." Now, if you explain this simply of Solomon, you will

send me into a fit of laughter. For David will evidently have brought forth Solomon! But is not Christ here designated the seed of David, as of that womb that was derived from David, that is, Mary's? Now, because Christ rather than any other was to build the temple of God, that is to say, a holy manhood, wherein God's Spirit might dwell as in a better temple, Christ rather than David's son Solomon was to be looked for as the Son of God. Then, again, the throne forever with the kingdom forever is more suited to Christ than to Solomon, a mere temporal king. *Against Marcion* 3.20.

An Indestructible Kingdom. **BASIL THE GREAT** However, the tribe of Judah did not fail until he came for whom it was reserved, who did not himself sit on a material throne, for the kingdom of Judea had now been transferred to Herod, the son of Antipater, the Ascalonite, and to his sons, who divided Judea into four provinces when Pilate was governor and Tiberius held the power over the whole Roman province. But his indestructible kingdom he calls the throne of David on which the Lord sat. He himself is "the expectation of nations," not of the least part of the world. "For there will be the root of Jesse," it is said, "and he who rises up to rule the Gentiles, in him the Gentiles will hope." "For I have placed you for a covenant of the people, for a light of the Gentiles." "And I shall establish," it is said, "his seed forever, and his throne as the days of the heavens." *Letter* 236.

Messianic Prophecies. **JUSTIN MARTYR:** Now, I have explained the meaning of the words "The Lord swore, you are a priest forever according to the order of Melchizedek." I have also shown that the prophecy of Isaiah, "His burial has been taken away from the midst," referred to Christ, who was to be buried and to rise again. I have stated at length that this same Christ will be the judge of both the living and the dead. Further, Nathan spoke thus of him to David: "I will be his Father, and he shall be my Son, and I will not take my mercy away from him, as I did from those who were before him; and I will establish him in my house, and in his kingdom forever." And Ezekiel states that he shall be the only prince in this house, for he is the Son of God. And do not suppose that Isaiah or the other prophets speak of sacrifices of blood or libations being offered on the altar at his second coming, but only of true and spiritual praises and thanksgiving. *Dialogue with Trypho* 118.

PSALM OF RESPONSE: *Psalm 89:20-37*

NEW TESTAMENT READING: *Ephesians 2:11-22*

REFLECTIONS FROM THE CHURCH FATHERS

Remembering the Circuitous Path of Salvation. CHRYSOSTOM: Many are the evidences of God's love of humanity. God has saved us through himself, and through himself in such a special way, remembering what we were when he saved us and to what point he has now brought us. For each of these stages in itself is a great proof of his benevolence. Paul now reviews at each stage what he writes. He has already said that God has saved us when we were dead in sins and children of wrath. Now Paul shows to what extent God has raised us. *Homily on Ephesians* 5.2.11-12.

Brought Near by the Blood of Christ. AMBROSIASTER: He reminds us that we were brought close to God by the blood of Christ in order to show how great is God's affection toward us, since he allowed his own Son to die. We too, enduring in faith, should not yield to despair in any of the agonies inflicted on us for his sake, knowing that what he deserves from us exceeds all that our enemies can bring on us. *Epistle to the Ephesians* 2.13.

The Peacemaker Destroys the Wall of Partition. MARIUS VICTORINUS: Christ, he says, "is our peace." Elsewhere Paul calls him mediator. He interposed himself of his own accord between divided realms. Souls born of God's fountain of goodness were being detained in the world. There was a wall in their midst, a sort of fence, a partition made by the deceits of the flesh and worldly lusts. Christ by his own mystery, his cross, his passion and his way of life destroyed this wall. He overcame sin and taught that it could be overcome. He destroyed the lusts of the world and taught that they ought to be destroyed. He took away the wall in the midst. It was in his own flesh that he overcame the enmity. The work is not ours. We are not called to set ourselves free. Faith in Christ is our only salvation. *Epistle to the Ephesians* 1.2.14-15.

Christ Uniquely Fitted to Create a New Humanity. TERTULLIAN: He was born in a singular way from a virgin by the Spirit of God. He was born to reconcile both Gentile and Jew to God, both of whom had offended God. He reconciled them into one body through the cross. The enmity was in this way slain. This reconciliation took place in his flesh through his body as he suffered on the cross. *Against Marcion* 5.17.15.

Full Consummation Yet Awaiting. JEROME: However, it should not be thought possible to achieve perfect and complete reconciliation in this world. . . . The making of the new person in Christ will be fully consummated when earthly and heavenly things have been reconciled, when we come to the Father in one Spirit and with one affection and understanding. *Epistle to the Ephesians* 1.2.15.

GOSPEL READING: *Mark 6:30-34, 53-56*

REFLECTIONS FROM THE CHURCH FATHERS

Hard Work. BEDE: The great happiness of those days can be seen from the hard work of those who taught and the enthusiasm of those who learned. If only in our time such a concourse of faithful hearers would again press round the ministers of the word. *Homilies on the Gospels* 2.20.

Breaking Open the Word. BEDE: As he broke up the five loaves and two fishes and distributed them to his disciples, he opened their minds to understand everything that had been written about him in the law of Moses and in the Prophets and the Psalms. *Homilies on the Gospels* 2.2.

Life to All. AMBROSE: The Lord of hosts was not signaling weakness as he gave sight to the blind, made the crooked to stand upright, raised the dead to life, anticipated the effects of medicine at our prayers and cured those who sought after him. Those who merely touched the fringe of his robe were healed. Surely you did not think it was some divine weakness, you speculators, when you saw him wounded. Indeed there were wounds that pierced his body, but they did not demonstrate weakness but strength. For from these wounds flowed life to all, from the One who was the life of all. *Of the Christian Faith* 4.5.54-55.

CLOSING PRAYER

We beseech you, O Lord our God, that the relief from anxiety that your mercy has bestowed on us may not make us negligent but rather cause us to become more acceptable worshipers of your name; through Jesus Christ our Lord. *The Leonine Sacramentary*

Strengthen Our Faith

THEME

Only fools say there is no God (Ps 14), but even those nearest to God's heart are capable of great sin (2 Sam 11:1-15). Let us not doubt the One who works great miracles (Jn 6:1-21). Strengthen us, Lord, with power through the Holy Spirit (Eph 3:14-21).

OPENING PRAYER: *Proper 12*

Almighty and everlasting God, at evening and morning and noonday, we humbly beseech you that you would drive from our hearts the darkness of sin and make us to come to the true Light, which is Christ; through the same Jesus Christ your Son. Amen. *The Gelasian Sacramentary*

OLD TESTAMENT READING: *2 Samuel 11:1-15*

REFLECTIONS FROM THE CHURCH FATHERS

The Use of the Eyes. JEROME: David was a man after God's own heart, and his lips had often sung of the Holy One, the future Christ. Yet as he walked on his housetop he was fascinated by Bathsheba's nudity, and he added murder to adultery. Notice here how, even in his own house, a man cannot use his eyes without danger. Then repenting, he says to the Lord, "Against you, you only, have I sinned and done this evil in your sight." Being a king he feared no one else. *Letter* 22.12.

The Affairs of Prudence. CHRYSOSTOM: And the prophet was found in adultery, the pearl in mud. However, he did not yet understand that he had sinned, the passion raged him to such a great extent. Because, when the charioteer gets drunk, the chariot moves in an irregular, disorderly manner. What the charioteer is to the chariot, the soul is to the body. If the soul becomes darkened, the body rolls in mud. As long as the charioteer stands firm, the chariot drives smoothly. However, when he becomes exhausted and is unable to hold the reins firmly, you see this very chariot in terrible danger. This exact same thing happens to human beings. As long as the soul is sober and vigilant, this very body remains in purity. However, when the soul is darkened, this very body rolls in mud and in lusts. . . . So you may learn that the affairs of prudence rely on the will and do not depend on age, just remember that David was found in his venerable years falling into adultery and committing murder; and he reached such a pathetic state that he was unaware that he had sinned, because his mind, which was the charioteer, was drunk from debauchery. *Homilies on Repentance and Almsgiving* 2.2.4-7.

The Failure of David. GREGORY THE GREAT: Well-pleasing in almost all of his actions in the judgment of him who had chosen him, so soon as the burden of his obligations was not on him, he broke out into festering conceit and showed himself as harsh and cruel in the murder of a man as he had been weakly dissolute in his desire for a woman. And he who had known how in pity to spare the wicked learned afterwards without let or hesitation to pant for the death of even the good. At first he had, indeed, been unwilling to strike down his captive persecutor, but afterwards, with loss to his wearied army, he killed even his loyal soldier. His guilt would, in fact, have removed him a long way from the number of the elect, had not scourgings restored him to pardon. *Pastoral Care* 1.3.

PSALM OF RESPONSE: *Psalm 14*

NEW TESTAMENT READING: *Ephesians 3:14-21*

REFLECTIONS FROM THE CHURCH FATHERS

Strengthened in the Inner Man. MARIUS VICTORINUS: What are these "riches of the glory of God"? They are "being strengthened with might through his Spirit," so that they may be strong against the sinful nature, the desires of the flesh and the dreadful powers of this world. This strengthening happens through the Spirit of God. But how are persons strengthened and made firm through the Spirit of God? By "Christ's dwelling in the inner man," he says. For when Christ begins to dwell in the inner citadel of the soul, persons are made strong by might through the Spirit. In this way everything of a hostile nature is evicted. *Epistle to the Ephesians* 1.3.16-17.

Prayer for Christ's Indwelling. AMBROSIASTER: Paul prays that believers be made more steadfast, not doubting but believing increasingly that Christ dwells in them even when they do not see him with their physical eyes. He prays that the Spirit which has been given them might infuse into them a certainty that Christ lives and is the Son of God, so that he lives by faith in their hearts. Thus when we have faith in him we behold him in our hearts. The benefit of this is that we grow more sure of his blessing. He does not desert us. He is always present through that faith in him that he guards in us. The gift of the Spirit, which is also the gift of God the Father, is given to us that he may keep us safe, to his glory. *Epistle to the Ephesians* 3.17.1-2.

The Fourfold Figure of the Cross. GREGORY OF NYSSA: The divine mind of the apostle did not imagine this fourfold figure of the cross to no purpose. He knew that this figure, which is divided into four segments from the common center, represents the power and providence of the one displayed on it. This dimensionality runs through all things.

For this reason he calls each of four projections by its own name. By the height he means what is above, by the depth the underworld, by the length and breadth the intermediate domain that is under the control of his all-governing power. Hence the worship of the cross is viewed in relation to the fourfold figure of the cross. The heavenly order is symbolically paying its devotion to the Lord in the upper part, the cosmic order in the middle part and even the infernal order in the lower part. *On the Three Days.*

Glory Forever. JEROME: This glory does not extend over the present time only, as if terminating in the age to come. Rather it extends throughout all generations and all ages. It is eternally ineffable. It abides, develops and increases. *Epistle to the Ephesians* 2.3.20-21.

Glory in All Generations. THEODORET: God is to be worshiped both in the present life and in the next. Having thus revealed God's goodness to them, he proceeds to urge them on to the particular virtues. *Epistle to the Ephesians* 3.20-21.

⸙ **GOSPEL READING:** *John 6:1-21*

REFLECTIONS FROM THE CHURCH FATHERS

A Mountain Vantage Point. CHRYSOSTOM: He went up onto the mountain because of the miracle he was going to do. The disciples alone ascended with him, which implies that the people who stayed behind were at fault for not following. He went up to the mountain too as a lesson to us to retire from the tumult and confusion of the world. For solitude is appropriate for the study of wisdom. Jesus often went up alone onto a mountain in order to pray, even spending the night there. He did this in order to teach us that the one who will come most near to God must be free from all disturbance and must seek times and places away from all the confusion. *Homilies on the Gospel of John* 42.1.

Miracle Not Evident While Happening. HILARY OF POITIERS: Five loaves are then set before the multitude, and broken. While the apostles are dividing them, a succession of newly created portions passes—they cannot tell how—through their hands. The loaf that they are dividing does not grow smaller, and yet their hands are continually full of the pieces. The speed of the process baffles the sight. You follow with the eye a hand full of portions, and in the meantime you see that the contents of the other hand are not diminished. And all the while the heap of pieces grows. The carvers are busy at their task, the eaters hard at work at theirs. The hungry are satisfied, and the fragments fill twelve baskets. Neither sight nor any of the other senses can discover how such an amazing miracle happened. What did not exist was created; what we see passes our understanding. It only remains for us to believe that God can do all things. *On the Trinity* 3.6.

Flee from Worldly Glory. CYRIL OF ALEXANDRIA: When Christ flees from those who want to give him honor and refuses that highest earthly prize of a kingdom . . . he teaches us that it is unseemly for those who pursue divine grace and thirst for everlasting glory to seek after worldly greatness. We must then forego the love of glory, the sister and neighbor of arrogance, residing not far from its borders. Let us have nothing to do with illustrious honor in this present life which is hurtful. Let us rather seek after a holy humility giving preference to one another. *Commentary on the Gospel of John* 3.4.

CLOSING PRAYER

Mercifully regard, O Lord, the prayers of your family, and while we submit ourselves to you with our whole heart, do you prosper, support and encompass us; that, relying on you as our guide, we may be entangled in no evil and replenished with all good; through Jesus Christ our Lord. Amen. *The Leonine Sacramentary*

Forgive Us

✥ THEME

Wash away our sins (Ps 51:1-12) and forgive us for our transgressions (2 Sam 11:26–12:13a). Give us the bread of life (Jn 6:24-35) and help us to build up the body of Christ in love (Eph 4:1-16).

✥ OPENING PRAYER: *Proper 13*

Accept, we beseech you, our . . . thanksgiving, O you fountain of all good, who has led us in safety through the length of the day; who daily blesses us with so many temporal mercies and has given us the hope of resurrection to eternal life; through Jesus Christ our Lord. Amen. *From an Ancient Collect*

✥ OLD TESTAMENT READING: *2 Samuel 11:26–12:13a*

REFLECTIONS FROM THE CHURCH FATHERS

***Challenging the Powerful.* GREGORY THE GREAT:** But at times, in taking to task the powerful of this world, they are first to be dealt with by drawing diverse comparisons in a case ostensibly concerning someone else. Then, when they give a right judgment on what apparently is another's case, they are to be taken to task regarding their own guilt by a suitable procedure. Thus a mind puffed up with temporal power cannot possibly lift itself up against the reprover, for by its own judgment it has trodden on the neck of pride; and it cannot argue to defend itself, as it stand convicted by the sentence out of its own mouth. *Pastoral Care* 3.2.

The Character of David's Sin. AUGUSTINE: When this same king, carried away by the heat of passion and by temporal prosperity, had taken unlawful possession of one woman, whose husband also he ordered to be put to death, he was accused of his crime by a prophet, who, when he had come to show him his sin, set before him the parable of the poor man who had but one ewe lamb and whose neighbor, though he had many, yet when a guest came to him, refused to take one of his own flock but set his poor neighbor's one lamb before his guest to eat. And David's anger being kindled against the man, he commended that he should be put to death and the lamb restored fourfold to the poor man; thus unwittingly condemning the sin he had wittingly committed. *Christian Instruction* 3.21.

God Sees and Judges Secret Actions. SALVIAN THE PRESBYTER: What do you say to this, you who believe that God does not judge our actions and who believe that he has no concern whatsoever for us? Do you not see that the eyes of God were never absent even from that secret sin through which David fell once? Learn from this that you are always seen by Christ, understand and know that you will be punished, and perhaps very soon, you, who, perhaps in consolation for your sins, think that our acts are not seen by God. You see that the holy David was unable to hide his sin in the secrecy of his inmost rooms; neither was he able to claim exemption from immediate punishment through the privilege of great deeds. *The Governance of God* 2.4.

PSALM OF RESPONSE: *Psalm 51:1-12*

NEW TESTAMENT READING: *Ephesians 4:1-16*

REFLECTIONS FROM THE CHURCH FATHERS

A Physical Analogy to a Spiritual Truth. ORIGEN: Here is a physical analogy to a spiritual truth: We can agree that the sun is "above all" things on earth. But by its rays it might be said at the same time to be "through all." And insofar as the power of its light penetrates everywhere, it could also be said to be "in all." It is in this way, I think, that God's majesty is denoted by the phrase "above all." God's all-sufficiency is denoted in the words "through all." It also belongs to the power of God to penetrate into all, so that because of his being in all no one is entirely void of him. *Epistle to the Ephesians* 18.

From the Father, Through the Son, in the Spirit. AUGUSTINE: Those who read very closely recognize the Trinity in this passage. Paul writes of God the Father "who is above all and through all and in all." All things are "from God," who owes his existence to no one. All things are "through him," as though to say through the Mediator. All things are "in him," as though to say in the One who contains them, that is, reconciles them into one. *On Faith and the Creed* 19.

He Descended in Order to Ascend. AMBROSIASTER: The truth incarnate is that he is said to have descended in order to ascend, unlike humans, who have descended in order to remain there. For by decree they were held in the lower world. But this decree could not hold the Savior. He has conquered sin. Therefore, after his triumph over the devil, he descended to the heart of the world, so that he might preach to the dead, that all who desired him might be set free. It was necessary for him to ascend. He had descended to trample death underfoot by the force of his own power, then only to rise again with the former captives. *Epistle to the Ephesians* 4.9.

The Proportional Distribution of Gifts. CHRYSOSTOM: One might say that the whole body receives increase as each member partakes of the distribution of gifts proportionally. In this way . . . the members, receiving the distribution in accordance with their own capacities, are thus increased. The Spirit, flowing abundantly from above, comes into contact with all the limbs and distributes according to the ability of each one to receive, thus "enabling bodily growth." *Homily on Ephesians 11.4.15-16.*

GOSPEL READING: *John 6:24-35*

REFLECTIONS FROM THE CHURCH FATHERS

Do Not Be Nailed to the Things of This Life. CHRYSOSTOM: To "take no thought" does not mean "not to work" but "not to be nailed to the things of this life." In other words, do not worry about tomorrow's comfort; in fact, consider it superfluous. There are those who do no work and yet lay up treasures for tomorrow. There are also others who do work and yet are careful for nothing. Carefulness and work are not the same thing. People do not work because they trust in their work but so that they may give to the person who is in need. *Homilies on the Gospel of John 44.1.*

Through Christ We Can Receive the Divine Seal. CYRIL OF ALEXANDRIA: The countenance of God the Father is the Son who is the imprint of God. But the light of God is the grace that passes into creation through the Spirit by which we are refashioned to God through faith. We receive through God, as with a seal, the being conformed to his Son. *Commentary on the Gospel of John 3.5.*

Christ Is Our Daily Bread. TERTULLIAN: For Christ is our Bread because Christ is Life, and bread is life. "I am," says he, "the Bread of life." And, a little above he says, "The bread of God is that which comes down from heaven." Then we find, too, that his body is reckoned in bread: "This is my body." And so, in petitioning for "daily bread," we ask for perpetuity in Christ and indivisibility from his body. But, because "bread" is admissible in a carnal sense too, it cannot be so used without the religious remembrance of spiritual discipline. For the Lord commands that bread be prayed for which is the only food necessary for believers. *On Prayer 6.*

Desire the Bread of God. **IGNATIUS OF ANTIOCH:** Do not talk about Jesus Christ while you desire the world. Do not let envy dwell among you. . . . I take no pleasure in corruptible food or the pleasures of this life. I want the bread of God, which is the flesh of Christ who is of the seed of David; and for drink I want his blood, which is incorruptible love. *Epistle to the Romans 7.*

Jesus Gives Real Food, Real Life. **THEODORE OF HERACLEA:** Because we have all died to sin—or because after the eternal, incorruptible resurrection he will give life to those who believe, when there will be neither food nor drink perceived by the senses—therefore we "will certainly not hunger." To be sure, the manna of those who ate it "in the desert" nourished the body for a little while, but it did not contribute anything to the soul to help it live virtuously and nobly. All of them (except for a few) were discovered to have been godless. But the living Bread recovered the souls of the believers by his words of life and procured real life for the world. *Fragments on John 31.*

CLOSING PRAYER

Lighten our darkness, we beseech you, O Lord; and by your great mercy defend us from all perils and dangers of this night; for the love of your only Son, our Savior, Jesus Christ. Amen. *The Gelasian Sacramentary*

Draw Us Close

⊰ THEME

Lord, hear my voice; let my cries come to you (Ps 130) in life's deepest sorrows (2 Sam 18:5-9, 14-15, 31-33). You are the bread of life (Jn 6:35, 41-51). Help us to put away all that keeps us from drawing closer to you (Eph 4:25–5:2).

⊰ OPENING PRAYER: *Proper 14*

Yours is the day, O Lord, and yours is the night. Grant that the Sun of righteousness may abide in our hearts to drive away the darkness of evil thoughts. *The Gelasian Sacramentary*

⊰ OLD TESTAMENT READING: *2 Samuel 18:5-9, 14-15, 31-33*

REFLECTIONS FROM THE CHURCH FATHERS

The Name and Terms of Judgment. SALVIAN THE PRESBYTER: When his rebellious son chased him from his kingdom, the Lord soon delivered David. Not only did the Lord deliver him, but he delivered him more fully than the one delivered wished. This was that God might show that the injustice is more grievous to himself than to those who suffer it. . . . Thus, when for his attempted patricide, David's son being hanged on a cross not made by human hands, the Scripture says that the punishment, divinely brought on him, was thus announced: "I bring good tidings, my lord, the king: for the Lord has judged on your behalf this day from the hand of all that have risen up against you." You see how the Scriptures prove by divine witnesses that God judges not only by deeds and by examples, as I have already said, but does so today by the very name and terms of judgment. *The Governance of God* 2.3-4.

Grief over Punishment. AUGUSTINE: When King David had endured this affliction from his wicked and treacherous son, he had not only tolerated his uncontrolled passion but even lamented his death. He was not held ensnared by a carnal jealousy, since it was not the outrages inflicted on him, but rather the sins of his son that troubled him. For he had forbidden that his son be killed if he were conquered in order that opportunity for repentance might be reserved for him after he was vanquished. Since this was impossible, he did not grieve because of his bereavement in the death of his son but because he realized into what punishments such a wickedly adulterous and murderous soul was precipitated. *Christian Instruction* 3.21.30.

The Concern of a Good Pastor. CHRYSOSTOM: So great is the concern and sympathy of a good pastor. For David was deeply moved at their falling, as when one's own children are killed. And on this ground he begged that the wrath might come on himself. And in the beginning of the slaughter he would have done this, unless he had seen it advancing and expected that it would come to himself. When therefore he saw that this did not happen, but that the calamity was raging among them, he no longer forebore but was touched more than for Amnon his firstborn. For then he did not ask for death, but now he begs to fall in preference to the others. Such ought a ruler to be and to grieve rather at the calamities of others than his own. *Homilies on Romans* 29.

PSALM OF RESPONSE: *Psalm 130*

NEW TESTAMENT READING: *Ephesians 4:25–5:2*

REFLECTIONS FROM THE CHURCH FATHERS

Created for Truth, We Must Tell the Truth. AMBROSIASTER: Since we have been "created in truth and righteousness" and reborn in baptism, in order to remain in it we are instructed to put away lying altogether. Hold fast to the truth. Do not cheat your brother in any way. Being members of one body, support one another's causes in turn. *Epistle to the Ephesians* 4.25.

Treat the Neighbor As We Wish Him to Become. AUGUSTINE: Let no one mistake this. The apostle is not giving us room to tell a lie to those who are not yet members of Christ with us. The point of the saying is that each of us should consider everyone as we wish him to become, even if he has not become so. . . . We ought to deal with a person in such a way that he will cease to be an outsider. Regard him as your neighbor already, rather than as an outsider. It may be that, because of the fact that he is not yet a partaker of our faith and sacraments, certain truths must be concealed from him. But that is no reason for telling him falsehoods. *Against Lying* 15.

Do Not Let the Sun Leave You as Enemies. CHRYSOSTOM: Do you wish to have your fill of anger? One hour, or two or three is enough for you. But do not let the sun go down and leave you both as enemies. It was God's goodness that did not leave us in anger. He did not let us part in enmity. He shed his light on those of us who were sinners. So when evening is coming on, be reconciled. Quell the evil impulses while they are fresh. For if night overtakes you, the next day will not be enough time to extinguish the further evil that has been increasing overnight. *Homily on Ephesians* 14.4.25-27.

How the Devil Gains Entry. ORIGEN: He is showing us how an opportunity is being given to the devil by these acts and desires. Once he has entered our body, he takes full possession of us. Or if he cannot take full possession, he at least pollutes the soul, having stuck his flaming darts into us unawares. At times these pierce us with a wound that goes down very deep. At other times we are merely temporarily inflamed. But it is indeed seldom that these burning darts are easily extinguished. They find their place to wound. *On First Principles* 3.2.4.

After Cutting Weeds, Plant Good Seeds. CHRYSOSTOM: Tell me what good it is to weed a garden if we do not plant good seed. . . . Sow good habits and dispositions. To be free from a bad habit does not mean we have formed a good one. We need to take the further step of forming good habits and dispositions to replace what we have left behind. *Homily on Ephesians* 16.4.31-32.

Gentleness Overcomes Bitterness. JEROME: Paul wants us to be gentle, approachable people, people who have left anger, bitterness, wrath and slander behind. If we are merciful and serene, taking the initiative in reaching out to others, our very approachability will overcome the shyness and fear of those for whom we reach out. *Epistle to the Ephesians* 3.5.1.

GOSPEL READING: *John 6:35, 41-51*

REFLECTIONS FROM THE CHURCH FATHERS

Lacking Hunger of the Inner Person. AUGUSTINE: But they were far from being fit for that heavenly bread and did not know how to hunger for it. . . . For this bread requires the hunger of the inner person. *Tractates on the Gospel of John* 26.1.

Christ Leads to the Father and the Father to Christ. HILARY OF POITIERS: There is no approach to the Father except through Christ. But there is also no approach to Christ, unless the Father draws us. *On the Trinity* 11.33.

Faith Can Be Learned Only from God. CHRYSOSTOM: He then shows the way in which the Father draws. "It is written in the prophets,

'And they shall all be taught of God.' " You see the excellence of faith: that it cannot be learned from people or by the teaching of people but only from God. . . . If then all shall be taught by God, how is it that some shall not believe? Because *all* here only means in general. Besides, the prophecy does not mean absolutely everyone but all who have the desire. For the Teacher sits ready to impart what he has to everyone and dispenses his truth to all. *Homilies on the Gospel of John* 46.1.

The Advantage of Living Bread. **AMBROSE:** It has been proven that the sacraments of the church are more ancient; now realize that they are more powerful. In very fact it is a marvelous thing that God rained manna on the ancestors and they were fed by daily nourishment from heaven. Therefore, it is said, "Humankind has eaten the bread of angels." And yet all those who ate that bread died in the desert, but this food that you receive, this "living bread, which came down from heaven," furnishes the substance of eternal life, and whoever eats this bread "will not die forever," for it is the body of Christ. *On the Mysteries* 8.47.

⌐ CLOSING PRAYER

Grant, O Lord, we beseech you, to your people firmness of faith, that as we confess your only begotten Son, the everlasting partaker of your glory, to have been born in our very flesh of the Virgin Mother, we may be delivered from present adversities and admitted into joys that shall abide; through the same Jesus Christ your Son, our Lord and Savior. Amen. *The Leonine Sacramentary*

A Wise Heart

THEME

Great are the works of the Lord (Ps 111)! Give us wisdom (1 Kings 2:10-12; 3:3-14) and help us to make the most of every opportunity (Eph 5:15-20) because you are the bread of life (Jn 6:51-58).

OPENING PRAYER: *Proper 15*

Almighty and everlasting God, the brightness of faithful souls, who did bring the Gentiles to your light and made known unto them him who is the true Light, and the bright and morning Star, fill, we beseech you, the world with your glory, and show yourself by the radiance of your Light unto all nations; through Jesus Christ our Lord. Amen. *The Gregorian Sacramentary*

OLD TESTAMENT READING: *1 Kings 2:10-12; 3:3-14*

REFLECTIONS FROM THE CHURCH FATHERS

The Christian Who Cleaves to God. AMBROSE: By Abel we understand the Christian who cleaves to God, as David says: "It is good for me to adhere to my God," that is, to attach oneself to heavenly things and to shun the earthly. Elsewhere he says, "My soul has fainted in your word," thus indicating his rule of life was directed toward reflections on the Word and not on the pleasures of this world. Wherefore we realize that what we read concerning David in the book of Kings is not an idle statement but is said with due weight and reflection: "And he was laid with his fathers." We are given to understand that his faith was like that of his father's. It is clear, then, that there is reference here to participation in life and not to the burial of a body. *Cain and Abel* 1.5.

Ask for What Is Important. ISAAC OF NINEVEH: Do not be foolish in the request you make to God, otherwise you will insult God through your ignorance. Act wisely in prayer so that you may become worthy of glorious things. Ask for things that are honorable from him who will not hold back so that you may receive honor from him as a result of the wise choice your free will has made. Solomon asked for wisdom—and along with it he also received the earthly kingdom, for he knew how to ask wisely of the heavenly King, that is, for things that are important. *Discourse* 3.

The Author of Proverbs. HIPPOLYTUS: Proverbs are words of exhortation that serve the whole path of life. They serve as guides and signs for those who are seeking their way to God by reviving them when they become tired by the length of the road. These, moreover, are the proverbs of "Solomon," that is to say, the "peacemaker," who, in truth, is Christ the Savior. And since we understand the words of the Lord without offense as being the words of the Lord, that no one may mislead us by likeness of name, he tells us who wrote them and of what people he was king in order that the credit of the speaker may make the discourse acceptable and the hearers attentive. For these proverbs are the words of that Solomon to whom the Lord said, "I will give you a wise and understanding heart; so that there has been no one like you on the earth, and after you there shall not arise any one like you." . . . Now he was the wise son of a wise father. This is why David's name, by whom Solomon was begotten, was added. From a child he was instructed in the sacred Scriptures and obtained his dominion not by lot or by force but by the judgment of the Spirit and the decree of God. *Fragment on Proverbs.*

⌑ PSALM OF RESPONSE: *Psalm 111*

⌑ NEW TESTAMENT READING: *Ephesians 5:15-20*

REFLECTIONS FROM THE CHURCH FATHERS

Avoid Constant Change. JEROME: Christ, the Sun of righteousness, has risen. Rise up from the sleep of the age. Walk cautiously and prudently. Cast off folly. Take hold of wisdom. In this way you will be able to avoid changing yourself constantly as you walk through the vicissitudes of the times. Rather you will find a unity within yourself even amid the diversity of the times. *Epistle to the Ephesians* 3.5.16.

The Will of the Lord. AMBROSIASTER: Do what you have to do with moderation. This is the will of the Lord. Do not allow commotion and din or discord with bad feeling to give rise to estrangement. So Paul adds these words to what he has said about his wish that the servants of God should admonish wrongdoing. *Epistle to the Ephesians* 5.17.

The Spirit's Filling. CHRYSOSTOM: Be ready for the Spirit's filling. This happens only when we have cleansed our souls of falsehood, anger, bitterness, sexual impurity, uncleanness and covetousness. It happens only when we have become compassionate, meek and forgiving to one another, only when facetiousness is absent, only when we have made ourselves worthy. Only then does the Spirit come to settle within our hearts, only when nothing is there to prevent it. Then he will not only enter but also fill us. *Homily on Ephesians* 19.5.19-21.

Extol God Always and in Everything. JEROME: Paul now calls us to "give thanks always and in everything." This is to be understood in a double sense, both in adversity and in good times. . . . In this way the mind rejoices and bursts out in gratitude to God, not only for what we think good but for what troubles us and happens against our will. . . . It is obvious that generally we are called to give thanks to God for the

sun that rises, for the day that goes by and for the night that brings rest
. . . for the rains that come, for the earth that brings forth fruit and for
the elements in their course. . . . Finally, we are thankful that we are
born, that we have being, that our wants are sufficiently taken care of
in the world, as if we lived in the house of an extremely powerful family
patriarch, knowing that whatever is in the world has been created on
our account. In this way we give thanks when we are grateful for the
benefits that come to us from God. All these things, however, the heathen also does, and the Jew and the publican and the Gentile. But the
second sense of giving thanks is seen in the special gift of Christians to
give thanks to God even in seeming adversity. . . . Those who are saintly
in their own eyes are prone to give thanks to God because they have
been released from dangers and afflictions. But according to the apostle
the greater virtue is to give thanks to God precisely amid those very
dangers and afflictions. *Epistle to the Ephesians* 3.5.20.

GOSPEL READING: *John 6:51-58*

REFLECTIONS FROM THE CHURCH FATHERS

Let Faith Confirm You. CYRIL OF JERUSALEM: Failing to understand his words spiritually, [the Jews] were offended and drew back,
thinking that the Savior was urging them to cannibalism. Then again in
the old covenant there was the showbread. But that, since it belonged
to the old covenant, has come to an end. In the new covenant there are
the bread of heaven and the cup of salvation, which sanctify body and
soul. For as bread corresponds to the body, so the Word is appropriate
to the soul. So do not think of them as mere bread and wine. In accordance with the Lord's declaration, they are body and blood. And if our
senses suggest otherwise, let faith confirm you. Do not judge the issue
on the basis of taste, but on the basis of faith be assured beyond all
doubt that you have been allowed to receive the body and blood of
Christ. *Mystagogical Lectures* 4.4-6.

The Medicine of Immortality. IGNATIUS OF ANTIOCH: Come together in common one and all without exception in charity, in one faith and in one Jesus Christ, who is of the race of David according to the flesh, the Son of man and Son of God . . . and break one bread, which is the medicine of immortality and the antidote against death, enabling us to live forever in Jesus Christ. *Epistle to the Ephesians* 20.

Earthly and Heavenly Bread. IRENAEUS: For we offer to him his own, announcing consistently the fellowship and union of the flesh and Spirit. For as the bread that is produced from the earth, when it receives the invocation of God, is no longer common bread but the Eucharist, consisting of two realities, earthly and heavenly, so also our bodies when they receive the Eucharist are no longer corruptible, having the hope of the resurrection to eternity. *Against Heresies* 4.18.5.

The Shared Being of the Father and the Son. GREGORY OF NAZIANZUS: All things that the Father has are the Son's. On the other hand, all that belongs to the Son is the Father's. Nothing then is unique to either one, because all things are in common. For their being [essence] itself is common and equal, even though the Son receives it from the Father. It is in this respect . . . that it is said, "I live by the Father," not as though his life and being were kept together by the Father but because he has his being from him beyond all time and beyond all cause. *Theological Oration* 4(30).11, On the Son.

CLOSING PRAYER

Sunrise marks the hour for toil to begin, but in our souls, Lord, prepare a dwelling for the day that will never end. *Ephrem the Syrian*

Stand Firm

⌘ THEME

Better is one day in your courts, Lord, than a thousand elsewhere (Ps 84). Hear our prayers, Lord, for there is no one like you (1 Kings 8:1, 6, 10-11, 22-30, 41-43), the bread of life (Jn 6:56-69). Help us to stand firm and to be fearless (Eph 6:10-20).

⌘ OPENING PRAYER: *Proper 16*

Almighty and everlasting God, who governs all things in heaven and earth: Mercifully hear the supplications of your people, and grant us your peace all the days of our life; through Jesus Christ our Lord. *The Gregorian Sacramentary*

⌘ OLD TESTAMENT READING: *1 Kings 8:1, 6, 10-11, 22-30, 41-43*

REFLECTIONS FROM THE CHURCH FATHERS

Solomon's Prayer Was for All. EPHREM THE SYRIAN: Now notice that Solomon did not only pray for his people but also for the foreigners and the strangers who distrusted the nation of Israel and were often hostile to it, so that the son of David might show the God of David to everyone in general, by praying for his enemies and by speaking ahead of time for us those future words: "But I say to you, Love your enemies and pray for those who persecute you." *On the First Book of Kings 8.21.*

A Foreshadowing of the Lord's Incarnation. CLEMENT OF ALEX-
ANDRIA: Solomon the son of David, in the books styled The Reigns of
the Kings, comprehending not only that the structure of the true temple was celestial and spiritual but had also a reference to the flesh,
which he who was both the Son and the Lord of David was to build up,
both for his own presence, where, as a living image, he resolved to
make his shrine, and for the church that was to rise up through the
union of faith, says expressly, "Will God in very deed dwell with humans on the earth?" He dwells on the earth clothed in flesh, and his
abode with humans is effected by the conjunction and harmony that
obtain among the righteous and that build . . . a new temple. For the
righteous are the earth, being still encompassed with the earth; and
earth, too, in comparison with the greatness of the Lord. Thus also the
blessed Peter does not hesitate to say, "You also, as living stones, are
built up, a spiritual house, a holy temple, to offer up spiritual sacrifices,
acceptable to God by Jesus Christ." And with reference to the body,
which by circumscription he consecrated as a hallowed place for himself on earth, he said, "Destroy this temple, and in three days I will raise
it up again." The Jews therefore said, "In forty-six years was this temple
built, and will you raise it up in three days?" "But he spoke of the temple of his body." *Fragment* 12.3.

Solomon's Words Announce the Coming of Christ. CYRIL OF JERU-
SALEM: Afterwards Solomon, hearing his father David say these
things, and having built a wondrous house and foreseeing him who
would come to it, says in astonishment, "Is it then to be thought that
God should indeed dwell on earth?" Yes, says David in anticipation in
the psalm inscribed "For Solomon," wherein it is said, "He shall be like
rain coming down on the fleece"; "rain" because of his heavenly origin
but "on the fleece" because of his humanity. For rain, falling on fleece,
falls noiselessly; so that, the mystery of his birth being unknown, the
wise men said, "Where is he that is born king of the Jews?" And Herod,

being troubled, inquired concerning him who had been born, and said, "Where is the Christ born?" *Catechetical Lectures* 12.9.

God Cannot Be Contained by Any Material Space. **FULGENTIUS OF RUSPE:** Since the Father and the Son and the Holy Spirit by nature are one God, eternal and infinite, there is nothing in heaven, nothing on earth, nothing above the heavens, nothing in any nature that he made that has not been made, where the same one God, Father, Son and Holy Spirit, could be missing. In God, just as there is no mutability of times, so there is no spatial capacity. As Solomon truly said at the dedication of the temple in these words: "Even heaven and the highest cannot contain you, much less this house that I have built." *Letter* (Fulgentius to Scarila) 10.7.

PSALM OF RESPONSE: *Psalm 84*

NEW TESTAMENT READING: *Ephesians 6:10-20*

REFLECTIONS FROM THE CHURCH FATHERS

The Strength of His Might. **ORIGEN:** To be "strong in the Lord" is to be strengthened in word and wisdom and the contemplation of truth. All these qualities are encompassed in the titles applying to Christ. The greatest of these is the strength of his might, which is stronger than all human virtues combined. Moral corruption lacks power in his presence. This one virtue, being strong in the Lord, is inconceivably powerful. Those who are wise in these matters call it the strength of his might. It has some analogy with bodily might but far exceeds it. This strength is beautiful, as a strong body is beautiful. *Epistle to the Ephesians.*

Why Is It Called a Breastplate? **JEROME:** One who has put on a sturdy breastplate is difficult to wound. Especially well-protected are those essential parts of the body on which life depends. So put on the breastplate. Strap it together by iron rings and insert the hooks in their place. One protected by such a breastplate of righteousness will not be like a vulnerable stag that receives the arrow in his liver. He will not lapse into rage or lust. Rather he will be protected, having a clean heart, having God as the fashioner of his breastplate, since he fashions the whole armor for every one of the saints. *Epistle to the Ephesians* 3.6.14.

Quenching Fiery Darts. CHRYSOSTOM: By "his darts" Paul means both temptations and perverse desires. He calls them fiery because that is the nature of the appetite. Faith is capable of commanding hosts of demons. How much more is faith capable of ordering the passions of the soul? *Homily on Ephesians* 24.6.14-17.

With a Clean Conscience. AMBROSIASTER: Insofar as our conduct is right we are rightly prepared for the Holy Spirit to abide in us. Hence we are more ready to obtain what we request. This therefore is what it means to pray in the Spirit at all times. We are directing our prayer to God with a clean conscience and sincere faith. One who prays with a polluted mind prays only in the flesh, not in the spirit. *Epistle to the Ephesians* 6.20.1.

GOSPEL READING: *John 6:56-69*

REFLECTIONS FROM THE CHURCH FATHERS

Jesus Knows Our Thoughts. HILARY OF POITIERS: Jesus Christ knows the thoughts of the mind, as it is now, stirred by present motives, and as it will be tomorrow, aroused by the impulse of future desires. . . . By its virtue his nature could perceive the unborn future and foresee the awakening of passions yet dormant in the mind. Do you believe that it did not know what is through itself and within itself? He is Lord of all that belongs to others; is he not Lord of his own? *On the Trinity* 9.59.

No Room for Fickle Faith. TERTULLIAN: Let the chaff of a fickle faith fly off as much as it will at every blast of temptation, all the purer will be that heap of corn that shall be laid up in the garner of the Lord. Did not certain of the disciples turn back from the Lord himself when they were offended? Yet the rest did not therefore think that they must turn away from following him. But because they knew that he was the Word of Life and had come from God, they continued in his company to the very last, after he had gently inquired of them whether they also would go away. *Prescriptions Against Heretics* 3.

No Compulsion. ATHANASIUS: For it is the part of true godliness not to compel but to persuade. Our Lord himself does not employ force but offers the choice, saying to everyone, "If anyone will follow after me," and to his disciples in particular, "Will you also go away?" *History of the Arians* 8.67.

Son of God Always, Son of Man in Time. AUGUSTINE: Therefore Christ is one, the Word, soul and flesh, one Christ; the Son of God and the Son of man, one Christ. The Son of God always, the Son of man in time, nevertheless, one Christ according to the unity of the person. He was in heaven when he was speaking on earth. So the Son of man was in heaven as the Son of God was on earth. The Son of God was on earth in the flesh he had taken, the Son of man was in heaven in the unity of person. *Tractates on the Gospel of John* 27.4.1-2.

Peter Confesses the Resurrection. CHRYSOSTOM: Peter's was a speech of the greatest love, proving that Christ was more precious to them than father or mother. And that it might not seem to be said as a result of thinking that there was no one whose guidance they could look to, he adds, "You have the words of eternal life." . . . These men already confessed the resurrection and all the apportionment that shall happen there. *Homilies on the Gospel of John* 47.3.

CLOSING PRAYER

We beseech you, O Lord, to keep us in perpetual peace, as you have vouchsafed us confidence in you; through Jesus Christ our Lord. Amen. *The Gelasian Sacramentary*

Guide Our Steps

THEME

Lord, you love righteousness and hate wickedness (Ps 45:1-2, 6-9); you call to us amid the beauties of creation (Song 2:8-13). Help us to love you with our hearts, rather than holding on to legalism (Mk 7:1-8, 14-15, 21-23), and to be righteous in all we think and do (Jas 1:17-27).

OPENING PRAYER: *Proper 17*

We beseech you, Almighty God, mercifully to look on your people, that by your great goodness they may be governed and preserved evermore, both in body and soul; through Jesus Christ our Lord. *The Gregorian Sacramentary*

OLD TESTAMENT READING: *Song of Songs 2:8-13*

REFLECTIONS FROM THE CHURCH FATHERS

Down from Heaven and Back Again. GREGORY THE GREAT: The church speaks through Solomon: "See how he comes leaping on the mountains, bounding over the hills!" . . . If I can put it this way, by coming for our redemption the Lord leaped! My friends, do you want to become acquainted with these leaps of his? From heaven he came to the womb, from the womb to the manger, from the manger to the cross, from the cross to the sepulcher, and from the sepulcher he returned to heaven. You see how Truth, having made himself known in the flesh, leaped for us to make us run after him. *Forty Gospel Homilies* 29.

The Dove's Voice Can Be Heard. AMBROSE: "Arise, come, my dearest one," that is, arise from the pleasures of the world, arise from earthly things and come to me, you who still labor and are burdened, because you are anxious about worldly things. Come over the world, come to me, because I have overcome the world. Come near, for now you are fair with the beauty of everlasting life, now you are a dove, that is, you are gentle and mild, now you are filled entirely with spiritual grace. . . . "Winter is now past"; that is, the Pasch has come, pardon has come, the forgiveness of sins has arrived, temptation has ceased, the rain is gone, the storm is gone, and the affliction. Before the coming of Christ it is winter. After his coming there are flowers. On this account he says, "The flowers appear on the earth." Where before there were thorns, now flowers are there. "The time of pruning has come." Where before there was desert, the harvest is there. "The voice of the dove is heard in our land." *Isaac, or the Soul* 4.34-35.

Significance of Winter and Its Passing. GREGORY OF ELVIRA: There is thus no doubt that winter has a double meaning, either that harshness and severity belong to it, or that it is a time for sowing with the coming of the rain. When it says winter, therefore, it refers to the present world, where the Word of God is sowed in this age like a seed of righteousness by prophets and apostles, or priests, and is fertilized by assiduous preaching, as though by rains from heaven. . . . But with the passing of winter, that is, the tribulations of this world, and the cessation of the rains, that is, the preaching of the Word of God, and the subsequent arrival of the joy of spring (which designates the coming of Christ's vernal kingdom in great peace), then the bodies of the saints everywhere will emerge from the graves of the earth like flowers—lilies or roses—pure white with holiness and red with passion. *Explanation of the Song of Songs* 4.13, 15.

The Rock Is Christ. **CYRIL OF ALEXANDRIA:** The rock is Christ. He is a wall and a shelter to us who believe and a perfect guardian, which is denoted by the wall. When you arrive, he says, you will be protected with every defense. *Fragments in the Commentary on the Song of Songs* 2.14.

PSALM OF RESPONSE: *Psalm 45:1-2, 6-9*

NEW TESTAMENT READING: *James 1:17-27*

REFLECTIONS FROM THE CHURCH FATHERS

Undeserved Gift. **AUGUSTINE:** Man's merit is a free gift, and no one deserves to receive anything from the Father of lights, from whom every good gift comes down, except by receiving what he does not deserve. *Letter* 186.

Avoid Habituation to Wickedness. **OECUMENIUS:** What James wants to say is this. Although a person may often fall into uncleanness, the faster he gets out of it the better. Otherwise, if he remains in it and carries on, he will make the evil stronger by force of habit and have a harder time washing it away. *Commentary on James.*

The New Testament Mirrors Perfection. **HILARY OF ARLES:** There are two kinds of mirrors—large and small. In a small mirror you see small things—this is the Old Testament, which leads no one to perfection. But in a big mirror you see great things—this is the New Testament, because in it the fullness of perfection is seen. *Introductory Tractate on the Letter of James.*

Good Intentions. **BEDE:** Spiritual happiness is gained not by empty words but by putting our good intentions into practice. *Concerning the Epistle of St. James.*

The Unbridled Tongue. **BASIL THE GREAT:** Anger causes tongues to become unbridled and speech unguarded. Physical violence, acts of contempt, reviling, accusations, blows and other bad effects too numerous to recount are born of anger and indignation. *Sermon* 10.

Which Fields Are to Be Bought. HERMAS: Instead of fields, buy souls that are in trouble, according to your ability. Look after widows and orphans. Do not neglect them. Spend your riches on these kinds of fields and houses. *Parables* 1.8.

Become More Like God. CHRYSOSTOM: We can become more like God if we are merciful and compassionate. If we do not do these things, we have nothing at all to our credit. God does not say that if we fast we shall be like him. Rather he wants us to be merciful, as he himself is. "I desire mercy," he says, "and not sacrifice." *Catena.*

GOSPEL READING: *Mark 7:1-8, 14-15, 21-23*

REFLECTIONS FROM THE CHURCH FATHERS

Marks of Pharisaic Living. JOHN OF DAMASCUS: *Pharisee* is a name meaning "those who are set apart." They followed a way of life that they regarded as most perfect. They esteemed their way as superior to others. They affirmed the resurrection of the dead, the existence of angels and holiness of life. They followed a rigorous way of life, practicing asceticism and sexual abstinence for periods of time and fasting twice a week. They ceremonially cleansed their pots and plates and cups, as did the scribes. They observed the paying of tithes, the offering of first fruits and the recitation of many prayers. *On Heresies* 15.

Verbal Religion. CLEMENT OF ROME: So let us devote ourselves to those at peace in their devotion to God, and not to those who seek peace through hypocrisy. For he says in one place: "This people honors me with their lips, but their heart is far from me." And again: "They blessed with their mouth, but they cursed in their heart." And again he says: "They flattered him with their mouths; they lied to him with their tongues. Their heart was not steadfast toward him; they were not true to his covenant." *The Letter to the Corinthians* 14.

Mixing Water with Wine. IRENAEUS: The Pharisees claimed that the traditions of their elders safeguarded the law, but in fact it contravened the law Moses had given. By saying, "Your merchants mix water with the wine," Isaiah shows that the elders mixed their watery tradition with God's strict commandment. They enjoined an adulterated law at cross-purposes with the divine law. The Lord made this clear when he asked them, "Why do you transgress God's commandment for the sake of your tradition?" By their transgression they not only falsified God's law, mixing water with the wine, but they also set against it their own law, called to this day the Pharisaic law. In this their rabbis suppress some of the commandments, add new ones and give others their own interpretation, thus making the law serve their own purposes. *Against Heresies* 4.12.1-2.

The Cycle of Bitterness Broken by Forbearance. TERTULLIAN: Let us, then, his servants, follow our Lord and patiently submit to denunciations that we may be blessed! If, with slight forbearance, I hear some bitter or evil remark directed against me, I may return it, and then I shall inevitably become bitter myself. Either that, or I shall be tormented by unexpressed resentment. If I retaliate when cursed, how shall I be found to have followed the teaching of our Lord? For his saying has been handed down that one is defiled not by unclean dishes but by the words that proceed from his mouth. *On Patience* 8.

Evil Willed. BEDE: This is an answer to those who consider that evil thoughts are simply injected by the devil and that they do not spring from our own will. He can add strength to our bad thoughts and inflame them, but he cannot originate them. *Homilies on the Gospels* 2.

CLOSING PRAYER

I beg you, most loving Savior, to reveal yourself to us, that knowing you
we may desire you, that desiring you we may love you, that loving you
we may ever hold you in our thoughts. *Columbanus*

Loving Our Neighbor

◈ THEME

Those who trust God are like Mount Zion, strong and enduring (Ps 125). Help us to share what we have with others (Prov 22:1-2, 8-9, 22-23), to have faith in your power (Mk 7:24-37; Jas 2:1-10, 11-13, 14-17) and to love our neighbor as ourselves.

◈ OPENING PRAYER: *Proper 18*

Good Jesus, as you have graciously allowed me here to drink in the sweetness of your word, so at the last, I pray, you will bring me into your presence, that I may listen to your voice, which is the source of all wisdom, and watch your face forever. *Bede*

◈ OLD TESTAMENT READING: *Proverbs 22:1-2, 8-9, 22-23*

REFLECTIONS FROM THE CHURCH FATHERS

The Wise Possess Much More Than Riches. **AMBROSE:** A good name is more excellent than money, and good favor is better than heaps of silver. Faith itself redounds to itself, sufficiently rich and more than rich in its possession. There is nothing that is not the possession of the wise person except what is contrary to virtue, and wherever he goes he finds all things to be his. The whole world is his possession, since he uses it all as his own. *Letter* 15.

To Lighten the Load of the Rich. AUGUSTINE: Both of you are traveling the same road; you are companions on the journey. Lightly laden are the poor man's shoulders, but yours are burdened with heavy luggage. Give away some of the load that is weighing you down; give away some of your luggage to the needy man—and you will thus afford relief both to yourself and to your companion. The Scripture says, "The rich and the poor have met one another, but the Lord has made them both." Where have they met, except in this life? The one is now arrayed in costly garments, while the other is clad in rags. When did they meet? Both were born naked, and even the rich man was born poor. Let him disregard what he found when he had come; let him consider what he brought with him. *Sermon* 11.6.

Holy Sharing of Poor and Rich. CAESARIUS OF ARLES: I beseech you, beloved brethren, be eager to engage in divine reading whatever hours you can. Moreover, since what a person procures in this life by reading or good works will be the food of his soul forever, let no one try to excuse himself by saying he has not learned letters at all. If those who are illiterate love God in truth, they look for learned people who can read the sacred Scriptures to them. This even illiterate merchants have learned to do, for they hire literate mercenaries and through their reading or writing acquire great profits. Now, if people do this for earthly wealth, how much more should we do it for the sake of eternal life? It often happens that a learned person may be poor in food or clothing, while one who does not know letters has more abundant wealth. The illiterate person who abounds in earthly goods summons the poor learned one, and they mutually give each other what they need. The one by reading feeds the other with the sweet word of God, while the other by giving material substance does not allow his neighbor to suffer want. The learned man should satisfy the soul of the rich man, while the latter should warm the body of the poor man with clothing and refresh him with earthly food. If this is done with charity, there will be fulfilled what is written: "The rich and poor have met one another: the Lord is the maker of them both." Being pressed down with a heavy burden by possessing more than was necessary, the rich man was unable to walk, while the poor man perhaps was learned but was failing because of not having the necessities of life. For this reason, there was holy sharing on the part of both men. While the rich man gave the poor material wealth from his possessions, the poor man imparted the sacred lessons to the rich, and they both happily reach the eternal country on the road of this life. *Sermon* 8.1.

PSALM OF RESPONSE: *Psalm 125*

NEW TESTAMENT READING: *James 2:1-10, 11-13, 14-17*

REFLECTIONS FROM THE CHURCH FATHERS

The Art of Showing Mercy. CHRYSOSTOM: Mercy is the highest art and the shield of those who practice it. It is the friend of God, standing always next to him and freely blessing whatever he wishes. It must not be despised by us. For in its purity it grants great liberty to those who respond to it in kind. It must be shown to those who have quarreled with us, as well as to those who have sinned against us, so great is its power. It breaks chains, dispels darkness, extinguishes fire, kills the worm and takes away the gnashing of teeth. By it the gates of heaven open with the greatest of ease. In short, mercy is a queen that makes men like God. *Catena.*

Forgiving as We Are Forgiven. OECUMENIUS: If we forgive others the sins that they have committed against us and give alms to the poor and needy among us, then God's mercy will deliver us from judgment. But if, on the other hand, we are not well-disposed toward those around us, we shall receive the condemnation handed out to the wicked servant, along with the retribution that is mentioned in the

Lord's Prayer. For there we ask God to forgive us as we forgive those who have sinned against us, but if we do not forgive them, we shall not be forgiven either. *Commentary on James.*

Words Alone Do Not Help. BEDE: It is obvious that words alone are not going to help someone who is naked and hungry. Someone whose faith does not go beyond words is useless. Such faith is dead without works of Christian love that alone can bring it back to life. *Concerning the Epistle of St. James.*

Care for the Body. VALERIAN OF CIMIEZ: Who does not hate this kind of "mercy"? In it an idle piety flatters the sick with elegant language. Fruitless tears are offered to heaven. What does it profit to bewail another man's shipwreck if you take no care of his body, which is suffering from exposure? What good does it do to torture your soul with grief over another's wound if you refuse him a health-giving cup? *Sermon 7.5.*

The Strength of Faith. LEO THE GREAT: While faith provides the basis for works, the strength of faith comes out only in works. *Sermon 10.3.*

Works Give Life to Faith. HILARY OF ARLES: Works give life to faith, faith gives life to the soul, and the soul gives life to the body. *Introductory Tractate on the Letter of James.*

GOSPEL READING: *Mark 7:24-37*

REFLECTIONS FROM THE CHURCH FATHERS

Eliciting the Lord's Compassion. CHRYSOSTOM: Have you not heard of the Syrophoenician woman? By the constancy of her entreaty, she elicited the Lord's compassion. *Homily 24 on Ephesians.*

The Finger of God. GREGORY THE GREAT: The Spirit is called the finger of God. When the Lord put his fingers into the ears of the deaf

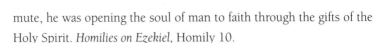

mute, he was opening the soul of man to faith through the gifts of the Holy Spirit. *Homilies on Ezekiel,* Homily 10.

Petition for an Open Way. AMBROSE: So open your ears and enjoy the good odor of eternal life that has been breathed on you by the grace of the sacraments. This we pointed out to you as we celebrated the mystery of the opening and said: "Ephphatha," that is "Be opened," so that everyone about to come to the table of grace might know what he was asked and remember the way he once responded. Christ celebrated this mystery in the Gospel, as we read, when he healed the one who was deaf and dumb. *Concerning the Mysteries* 1.3-4.

The Hearing of the Gentiles. LACTANTIUS: He thereby declared that it would shortly come to pass that those who were destitute of the revealed truth would both hear and understand the majestic words of God. Accordingly you may truly call those deaf who do not hear the heavenly things that are true and worthy of being performed. He loosed the tongues of the dumb. They spoke plainly—a power worthy of admiration even in its ordinary operation. But there was also contained in this display of power another meaning. It would shortly come to pass that those who were previously ignorant of heavenly things, having received the instruction of wisdom, might soon speak God's own truth. *Divine Institutes* 4.2.6.

Tongues Unloosed. PRUDENTIUS:
Deafened ears, of sound unconscious,
every passage blocked and closed,
At the word of Christ responding,
all the portals open wide,
Hear with joy friendly voices and
the softly whispered speech.
Every sickness now surrenders,
every listlessness departs,

Tongues long bound by chains of silence
are unloosed and speak aright,
While the joyful paralytic
bears his pallet through the streets.
Hymns 9.

CLOSING PRAYER

O God, at whose bidding man goes forth to his work and to his labor until the evening: grant us to cherish the lessons we have learned out of your holy Word. Support us when we are tested in duty, that in all our doings we may remember that you have chosen us that we should go and bear fruit and that our fruit should abide. *The Gelasian Sacramentary*

Pleasing Words

⋄ THEME

May the words of our mouths and meditations of our hearts be pleasing to God (Ps 19). Help us to learn wisdom (Prov 1:20-33), keeping watch over our tongues lest we stumble (Jas 3:1-12); as we proclaim Christ to all (Mk 8:27-38).

⋄ OPENING PRAYER: *Proper 19*

O God, the life of the faithful, the strong helper of them that call on you: hearken to our supplications; and as you do put within us a hearty desire to pray, so grant us, O most Loving, your aid and comfort in our prayers; and may the souls that thirst for your promises be filled from your abundance; through Jesus Christ or Lord. Amen. *The Gelasian Sacramentary*

⋄ OLD TESTAMENT READING: *Proverbs 1:20-33*

REFLECTIONS FROM THE CHURCH FATHERS

Beneficial Correction. CLEMENT OF ALEXANDRIA: The correction of the Lord is very beneficial. He calls the same people, through David, also, "a perverse and exasperating generation, a generation that set not their heart aright: and whose spirit was not faithful to God. They kept not the covenant of God: and in his law they would not walk." These are the reasons for his exasperation, and for these reasons he will come as judge to pass sentence on those who are unwilling to preserve goodness in their lives. Therefore, he treats them severely in the hope that perhaps he might curb their impulse toward death. . . . He knew that they repented out of fear, after neglecting his love; as a general rule, men always neglect the good that is kind but serve it with loving fear if it keeps recalling justice. *Christ the Educator* 85-86.

We Must Take Heed. ORIGEN: If there is someone who meditates on the law of the Lord day and night and someone who is like the mouth of the righteous that meditates on wisdom, he will be able to inquire more carefully and to find. This is so, provided he seeks rightly and in seeking knocks on the door of wisdom to ask God that it may be opened to him and that he be worthy to receive through the Holy Spirit the word of wisdom and the word of knowledge and to become a fellow of Solomon's wisdom. For it was the latter who said, "I stretched out my words and you did not hear." And he rightly says that he stretched out words in his heart, because, as we said a moment ago, God gave him largeness of heart. For that person's heart is enlarged who can explain what is briefly said in mysteries by a broader teaching with assertions taken from the divine books. *Commentary on the Song of Songs,* Prologue.

PSALM OF RESPONSE: *Psalm 19*

NEW TESTAMENT READING: *James 3:1-12*

REFLECTIONS FROM THE CHURCH FATHERS

Great Ships, Strong Winds, Small Rudder. BEDE: These great ships stand for the minds of people in this life, whether they are good or bad. The strong winds that threaten them are the desires of these minds, by which they are naturally forced to act and that bring them either to a good or to a bad end. The rudder that directs them is the intention of the heart by which the elect cross the waves of this life and finally reach the harbor of their heavenly home. *Concerning the Epistle of St. James.*

Guiding the Tongue. ANDREAS: James says that if we can contain the spirits of a horse by putting a bit into his mouth and control the direction of a ship with a small rudder, how much more ought we to be able to guide the tongue by right words toward doing good. *Catena.*

Great Good and Great Evil. JEROME: The sword kills the body, but the tongue kills the soul. The tongue knows no moderation—either it is a great good or it is a great evil. It is a great good when it acknowledges that Christ is God and a great evil when it denies that. Let no one deceive himself into thinking that he has never sinned, for if I have sinned, it is with my tongue. What more monstrous sin is there than blasphemy against God? The devil did not fall because he committed theft, murder or adultery; he fell because of his tongue. He said: "I will scale the heavens; above the stars I will set up my throne, I will be like the most high." *Sermon 41.*

Mixing Human and Divine Things. ANDREAS: For being power-hungry and filled with the wisdom of the world, they preached with the force and zeal of orthodox teachers, gathering a crowd with no trouble at all and deceiving them, mixing human things with the divine, so that the hearers might be dazzled by the newness of what was being said. That is how heresy arose. But James forbids that kind of teaching and whatever comes from a wisdom that is not divine but diabolical. He said all this in order to praise good teaching, the wisdom that comes from humility in words and in useful deeds. *Catena.*

GOSPEL READING: *Mark 8:27-38*

REFLECTIONS FROM THE CHURCH FATHERS

His Humanity and Divinity Foreshadowed. BEDE: We note that the

Lord called himself "Son of man," while Nathanael proclaimed him "Son of God." Similar is the account in the Gospels where Jesus himself asks the disciples who people say the Son of man is, and Peter answers, "You are the Christ, Son of the living God." This was done under the guidance of the economy of righteousness. It shows that the two natures of the one mediator are affirmed: his divinity and his humanity, and attested both by our Lord himself and by human mouths. By this means the God-man declared the weakness of the humanity assumed by him. Those purely human would themselves declare the power of eternal divinity in him. *Homilies on the Gospels* 1.17.

Why Believers Are Called Christians. BEDE: *Messiah* in the Hebrew language means *Christ* in Greek; in Latin it is interpreted as "the Anointed One." Hence *chrisma* in Greek means "anointing" in Latin. The Lord is named *Christ,* that is, the Anointed One, because, as Peter says, "God has anointed him with the Holy Spirit and with power." Hence the psalmist also speaks in his praise, "God, your God, has anointed you with the oil of gladness above your companions." He calls us his companions since we have also been fully anointed with visible chrism for the reception of the grace of the Holy Spirit in baptism, and we are called *Christians* from Christ's name. *Homilies on the Gospels* 1.16.

He Helps Effect What He Commands. CAESARIUS OF ARLES: What he commands is not difficult, since he helps to effect what he commands. . . . Just as we are lost through loving ourselves, so we are found by denying ourselves. Love of self was the ruin of the first man. If he had not loved himself in the wrong order, he would have been willing to be subject to God, preferring God to self. *Sermon 159.*

Deflecting Self-Hate. AUGUSTINE: This precept by which we are enjoined to lose our life does not mean that a person should kill himself, which would be an unforgivable crime, but it does mean that one should kill that in oneself which is unduly attached to the earthly, which makes one take inordinate pleasure in this present life to the neglect of the life to come. This is the meaning of "shall hate his life" and "shall lose it." Embedded in the same admonition he speaks most openly of the profit of gaining one's life when he says, "He that loses his life in this world shall find it unto life eternal." *Letter* 243, to Laetus.

The Enjoyment of Earthly Goods. CLEMENT OF ALEXANDRIA: Those who neglect good works may fail to grasp just how much the good work of God has benefited them. Hence they are less capable of praying fittingly so as to receive good things from God. And even if they receive them, they will likely be unaware of what has been given them. And even if they enjoy them, they will not enjoy worthily what they have not understood. For from their lack of knowledge they will not grasp how to use the good things given them. And from their impulsiveness they will remain ignorant of how to avail themselves of the divine gifts offered. *Stromateis* 6.14.

CLOSING PRAYER

O Love ever burning, never quenched! O Charity, my God, set me on fire with your love! . . . Give me the grace to do as you command, and command me to do what you will! *Augustine*

Pursue Wisdom

THEME

Lord, let us meditate on your law at all times (Ps 1), showing by our works that we follow you (Prov 31:10-31). Give us a childlike faith; help us not strive for power (Mk 9:30-37) or selfish ambition but to pursue wisdom (Jas 3:13–4:3, 7-8a).

OPENING PRAYER: *Proper 20*

We beseech you, O Lord, to purify our consciences by your daily visitation; that when your Son our Lord comes, he may find in us a mansion prepared for himself; through the same Jesus Christ our Lord. *The Gelasian Sacramentary*

OLD TESTAMENT READING: *Proverbs 31:10-31*

REFLECTIONS FROM THE CHURCH FATHERS

An Ideal Sister. GREGORY OF NAZIANZUS: The divinely inspired Solomon in his instructive wisdom, I mean in his Proverbs, praises the woman who keeps her house and loves her husband. And in contrast to the woman who wanders abroad, who is uncontrolled and dishonorable, who hunts precious souls with wanton ways and words, he praises her who is engaged honorably at home, who performs her womanly duties with fearless courage, her hands constantly holding the spindle as she prepares double cloaks for her husband, who buys a field in season, and carefully provides food for her servants, and receives her friends at a bountiful table, and who exhibits all other qualities for which he extols in song the modest and industrious woman. If I were to praise my sister on such counts, it would be like praising a statue for its shadow. *On His Sister St. Gorgonia,* Oration 8.9.

Wool and Linen. AUGUSTINE: The sacred text describes this housewife as a weaver of woolens and linen. But what we want to find out is what wool represents and what linen does. I think wool means something of the flesh, linen something of the spirit. I hazard this conjecture from the order we wear our clothes in; our underclothes or inner garments are linen, our outer garments woolen. Now everything we do in the flesh is public, whatever we do in the spirit is private. Now to act in the flesh and not to act in spirit may seem good but is in fact worthless, whereas to act in spirit and not act in the flesh is downright laziness. *Sermon* 37.6.

The Trees of Knowledge and Life. ORIGEN: The text speaks of the church as a virtuous soul possessing the tree of knowledge and the tree of life. The church possesses knowledge as the law, and life as the Word. For she herself [is the church] who came out of the rib of Christ and was found by her bridegroom to be a woman of sound mind and strength, guarding the faith of her bridegroom as she awaits his return again from heaven. *Exposition on Proverbs,* Fragment 31.1.

By Caring for the Poor, You Practice Holy Works. CAESARIUS OF ARLES: Brethren, let us not be ashamed to practice holy works of wool. If anyone has a full storeroom or granary, all those things are on the distaff; let them pass over to the spindle. They are on the left side as long as you do not give to the poor, but as soon as you begin to practice almsgiving, they are transferred to the right side and become a work from which a garment may result. *Sermon* 139.4.

Action and Spirit, Faith and Works. AMBROSE: The beauty of a good thing pleases the more if it is shown under various aspects. For those are good things, whereof the texture of the priestly robe was the token, that is to say, either the Law or the church, which latter has made two garments for her spouse, as it is written—the one of action, the other of spirit, weaving together the threads of faith and works. *On the Christian Faith* 2, Introduction 11.

❧ PSALM OF RESPONSE: *Psalm 1*

❧ NEW TESTAMENT READING: *James 3:13–4:3, 7-8a*

REFLECTIONS FROM THE CHURCH FATHERS

Jealousy Elicits Strife. CASSIODORUS: The mature faithful should not have any bitterness or jealousy in them, since such things are not given by God but are conceived by diabolical fraud. For where there is jealousy there is strife, disloyalty and every kind of evil that divine authority condemns. *Summary of James.*

Filth and Ambition Blind. CHRYSOSTOM: Let us cleanse the eyes of our souls of all filth. For just as filth and mud blind the eyes of the flesh, so too worldly concerns and discussions about moneymaking can dull the hearing of our minds more effectively than any filth, and not only corrupt them but do wicked things as well. *Catena.*

The Struggle Within. BEDE: Your passions are at war in your members whenever your hands or your tongue or some combination of your bodily parts obeys the promptings of your depraved mind. It is also possible that the passions mentioned here are in fact good desires, pointing toward the riches and benefits of God's kingdom. On account of these and many other such things there is often a struggle between good and evil going on in our minds. *Concerning the Epistle of St. James.*

❧ GOSPEL READING: *Mark 9:30-37*

REFLECTIONS FROM THE CHURCH FATHERS

The Reason for Grief. **CHRYSOSTOM:** If ignorant, how could they be sorrowful? Because they were not altogether ignorant. They knew that he was soon to die, for they had continually been told about it. But just what this death might mean they did not grasp clearly, nor that there would be a speedy recognition of it, from which innumerable blessings would flow. They did not see that there would be a resurrection. This is why they grieved. *The Gospel of St. Matthew,* Homily 58.

Rooting by Downward Movement. **AUGUSTINE:** Observe a tree, how it first tends downwards, that it may then shoot forth upwards. It fastens its root low in the ground, that it may send forth its top toward heaven. Is it not from humility that it endeavors to rise? But without humility it will not attain to higher things. You are wanting to grow up into the air without a root. Such is not growth but a collapse. *The Gospel of John,* Sermon 38.

Guileless Cohesion. **GREGORY OF NYSSA:** Let vanity be unknown among you. Let simplicity and harmony and a guileless attitude weld the community together. Let each remind himself that he is subordinate not only to the brother at his side, but to all. If he knows this, he will truly be a disciple of Christ. *On the Christian Mode of Life.*

The Pursuit of Meekness. **CHRYSOSTOM:** If you are in love with precedence and the highest honor, pursue the things in last place, pursue being the least valued of all, pursue being the lowliest of all, pursue being the smallest of all, pursue placing yourselves behind others. *The Gospel of St. Matthew,* Homily 58.

The Child as Pattern. **SHEPHERD OF HERMAS:** They are as veritable infants, whose hearts do not invent evil, who hardly know what corruption is and who have remained childlike forever. People such as these, therefore, undoubtedly dwell in the kingdom of God, because they in no way defile God's commandments but have continued in innocence all the days of their lives in the same state of mind. *Shepherd of Hermas* 3.9.39.

Receiving and Offering Refreshment. TERTULLIAN: Do not receive without prayer one who enters your house, especially if that one is a stranger, lest he turn out to be an angelic messenger. Do not offer your earthly refreshments prior to receiving heavenly refreshment. *On Prayer* 26.

CLOSING PRAYER

Almighty and everlasting God, mercifully grant unto your church that deadly pleasures may be cast aside, and that it may rather rejoice in the gladness of your eternal salvation; through Jesus Christ our Lord. *The Leonine Sacramentary*

Lead by Example

◈ THEME

Just as Esther trusted the Lord for her life (Esther 7:1-6, 9-10; 9:20-22), help us to remember that our help comes from God (Ps 124). Let us not lead others into sin; rather (Mk 9:38-50), let us confess our sins to each other and pray (Jas 5:13-20).

◈ OPENING PRAYER: *Proper 21*

Grant, we beseech you, O God, that for the lively reception of your truth, the minds of the faithful may be prepared and the hearts of the proud subdued; through Jesus Christ our Lord. Amen. *The Gelasian Sacramentary*

◈ OLD TESTAMENT READING: *Esther 7:1-6, 9-10; 9:20-22*

REFLECTIONS FROM THE CHURCH FATHERS

The Judgment of the Law. RABANUS MAURUS: It is written in the book of Proverbs: "Whoever digs a pit will fall into it, and a stone will come back on the one who starts it rolling." So also Haman was forced to support the cross that he had prepared for Mordecai. *Explanation on the Book of Esther* 10.

A Feast for the Lord. ATHANASIUS: In the face of all this, brothers and sisters, what should we do but give thanks to God, the king of all?

Let us start by crying out the words of the psalm, "Blessed is the Lord, who has not let them eat us up." Let us keep the feast in that way that he has established for our salvation—the holy day of Easter—so that we, along with the angels, may celebrate the heavenly feast. Remember that Israel, coming out of affliction to a state of rest, sang a song of praise for the victory as they kept the feast. And in the time of Esther the people kept a feast to the Lord because they had been delivered from a deadly decree. They called a feast, thanking and praising the Lord because he had changed the situation for them. Therefore, let us keep our promises to the Lord, confess our sins and keep the feast to him—in behavior, moral conduct and way of life. Let us keep it by praising the Lord, who has disciplined us so lightly but has never failed us nor forsaken us nor stopped speaking to us. *Festal Letters* 8.

Celebration of the Victory. ATHANASIUS: When the whole nation of Israel was about to perish, blessed Esther defeated the tyrant's anger simply by fasting and praying to God. By faith she changed the ruin of her people into safety. Those days are feast days for Israel; they used to call a feast when an enemy was slain or a conspiracy against the people was broken up and Israel was delivered. That is why Moses established the Feast of the Passover: because Pharaoh was killed and the people were delivered from bondage. So then, especially when tyrants were slain, temporal feasts and holidays were established in Judea. Now, however, the devil, that tyrant against the whole world, is slain. Therefore, our feast does not relate only to time but to eternity. It is a heavenly feast! We do not announce it as a shadow or a picture or a type but as the real thing. *Festal Letters* 4.

PSALM OF RESPONSE: *Psalm 124*

NEW TESTAMENT READING: *James 5:13-20*

REFLECTIONS FROM THE CHURCH FATHERS

In Good Times or Bad. **ANDREAS:** What should you do when you are in trouble? Call on God. And what should you do when you are happy? Praise him. *Catena.*

Boring and Detailed Confession Not Needed. **BRAULIO OF SARAGOSSA:** Since it would be a long and unpleasant task to reveal my sinful ways to you and to tell you everything in detail, it must suffice for me to reveal to your most holy mind that I am not what you believe, though I beg you to pray to God that he might make me what you believe. *Letter* 44.

The Lord's Example. **AUGUSTINE:** The Lord himself sets an example for us in this also. For if he who neither has, nor had, nor will have any sin prays for our sins, how much more ought we to pray for each other's sins! And if he for whom we have nothing to forgive forgives us, how much more should we forgive one another, knowing that we cannot live on earth without sinning! *Tractates* 58.2.

Rescuing a Soul from Death. **GREGORY THE GREAT:** If it is a great thing to rescue someone's body when it is on the point of death, how much greater is it to deliver someone's soul from death, so that it might live forever in the heavenly country? *Lessons in Job* 19.31.

The Motive of Love. **BEDE:** James does all he can here to ensure that imperfect people like ourselves do not gloat over winning others away from their wicked ways and converting them to the truth by reminding us that we should be engaged in such work out of love for our brothers and sisters. *Concerning the Epistle of St. James.*

GOSPEL READING: *Mark 9:38-50*

REFLECTIONS FROM THE CHURCH FATHERS

Judgmental Excess. **AUGUSTINE:** Some who are intent on severe disciplinary principles that admonish us to rebuke the restless, not to give what is holy to dogs, to consider a despiser of the church as a heathen, to cut off from the unified structure of the body the member that causes scandal, so disturb the peace of the church that they try to separate the wheat from the chaff before the proper time. Blinded by this error, they are themselves separated instead from the unity of Christ. *Faith and Works* 4.6.

Simplicity in Service. GREGORY OF NYSSA: God never asks his servants to do what is impossible. The love and goodness of his Godhead is revealed as richly available. It is poured out like water on all. God furnishes to each person according to his will the ability to do something good. None of those seeking to be saved will be lacking in this ability, given by the one who said, "Whoever gives you a cup of water to drink because you bear the name of Christ will by no means lose his reward." *On the Christian Mode of Life.*

Literally Cut Off? CLEMENTINA: Let none of you think that the Lord is here commending the cutting off of members. His meaning is that the incentive should be cut off, not the members. The causes that allure to sin are to be cut off, in order that our thought, borne up on the chariot of sight, may push toward the love of God, supported by the bodily senses. So do not give loose reins to the eyes of the flesh as if you were wanton horses, eager to turn their running away from the commandments. Subject the bodily sight to the judgment of the mind. Do not permit these eyes of ours, which God intended to be viewers and witnesses of his work, to become procurers of evil desire. *Recognitions of Clement* 7.1.37.

Disciplinary Rejection. CAESARIUS OF ARLES: If today one is cast out of the assembly of this church because of some enormity, in how much grief and tribulation will his soul be? If it causes unbearable pain to be thrown out of this church, where the one who is rejected can eat and drink and speak with others and has the hope of being called back, how much more pain will there be if, because of his sins, one is separated from that church that is in heaven, and eternally separated from the assembly of the angels and the company of all the saints? For such a person it will not be enough punishment for him to be cast away, but in addition he will be shut out into the night, to be consumed by an eternal fire. One whose impenitent behavior has warranted his being finally shut out of that heavenly Jerusalem will not only be deprived of divine fellowship but will also suffer the flames of hell, "where there is weeping and gnashing of teeth," where there will be the wailing of lamentation without any remedy, where the worm does not die and the fire is not extinguished; where death would be sought as an end to torment and not found. *Sermon* 227.4.

A Fit Pinch of Salt. EPHREM THE SYRIAN:
Glory be to God on high,
Who mixed his salt in our minds,
His leaven in our souls.
His body became bread,
To quicken our deadness.
Hymns on the Nativity 2.

⌐ CLOSING PRAYER

We beseech you, O Lord, in your compassion to increase your faith in us; because you will not deny the aid of your loving kindness to those on whom you bestow a steadfast belief in you; through Jesus Christ our Lord. *The Leonine Sacramentary*

A Blameless Life

⋇ THEME

Let us trust the Lord and live life as blamelessly as possible (Ps 26), just as Job lived a blameless life (Job 1:1; 2:1-10). Help us to be like little children in our innocence and purity (Mk 10:2-16) and in all things to follow Jesus Christ (Heb 1:1-4; 2:5-12).

⋇ OPENING PRAYER: *Proper 22*

Look mercifully, O Lord, we beseech you, on the affliction of your people; and let not our sins prevail to destroy us, but rather your abundant mercy to save us, through Jesus Christ our Lord. *The Leonine Sacramentary*

⋇ OLD TESTAMENT READING: *Job 1:1; 2:1-10*

REFLECTIONS FROM THE CHURCH FATHERS

Job Is Blessed by God. EPHREM THE SYRIAN: Even though many others lived in Uz, no one was comparable to Job with regard to piety and innocence. He was of high reputation and was celebrated in everybody's words. And so that no one might think these things had been granted to Job thanks to his human ability, God never allowed a single possession of Job's to perish. God said, "My desire is that even a single hair, a loss that would be the very slightest, may be returned and increased for Job." *Commentary on Job* 1.1.

The Duty of the Angels. CHRYSOSTOM: Why does the author describe the angels in the act of presenting themselves daily before the Lord? He does so that we might learn no actual event is overlooked by God's providence and that the angels report what happens every day. Every day they are sent to settle some question, even though we ignore all this. That is the reason why they were created; that is their task, as the blessed Paul says: "They are sent to serve for the sake of those who are to inherit salvation." "And the devil," the text says, "also came among them." You know why the angels are present. But why is the devil present? The latter is present to tempt Job; the former, in order to regulate our matters. Why is the devil questioned again before the angels themselves? Because he had said before them, "He will curse you to your face." What a shameless nature! He has dared come back! *Commentary on Job* 2.1.

Job's Likeness with Christ. GREGORY THE GREAT: How could it be that the Lord says to Satan, "You incited me against him" especially if we assume that blessed Job is an anticipation of the Redeemer in his passion? Truly the Mediator between God and man, the man Christ Jesus, came to bear the scourges of our mortal nature that he might put away the sins of our disobedience. But, seeing that he is of one and the self-same nature with the Father, how does the Father declare that he was moved by Satan against him, when it is acknowledged that no inequality of power, no diversity of will, interrupts the harmony between the Father and the Son? Yet he who is equal to the Father by the divine nature came for our sakes to be flogged in his human nature. He would have never endured these stripes if he had not taken the form of accursed human beings in the work of their redemption. *Morals on the Book of Job* 3.26.

PSALM OF RESPONSE: *Psalm 26*

NEW TESTAMENT READING: *Hebrews 1:1-4; 2:5-12*

REFLECTIONS FROM THE CHURCH FATHERS

Both Sheep and Goat. AUGUSTINE: You see, those old sacrifices of the people of God also represented in a variety of ways this single one that was to come. Christ himself, I mean, was both a sheep, because of his innocence and simplicity of soul, and a goat because of "the likeness of sinful flesh." And whatever else was foretold "in many and various ways" in the sacrifices of the old covenant refers to this single one which has been revealed in the new covenant. *Sermon* 228B.2.

The End of Labors and the Beginning of Rest. CHRYSOSTOM: He said, "in these last days," for by this he both stirs up and encourages those despairing of the future. For as he says also in another place, "The Lord is at hand; have no anxiety about anything," and again, "For salvation is nearer to us now than when we first believed." So also here. What then does he say? That whoever is spent in the conflict, hearing of the end of it, recovers his breath a little, knowing that it is the end indeed of his labors and the beginning of his rest. *On the Epistle to the Hebrews* 1.2.

Not Created as an Heir, but Appointed. SEVERIAN OF GABALA: "He spoke to us in his Son," instead of "by the Son." For he did not speak in him as an instrument but rather through him as one indwelling the flesh. . . . For when he had said, "He has spoken to us in his Son whom he appointed as an heir"—not "created as an heir"—he applied the word to his existence before the ages. And he does this intelligently, now leading us up into theology, now bringing us down into the incarnation. *Fragments on the Epistle to the Hebrews* 1.1-2.

When Our Discourse Fails Through Weakness. CHRYSOSTOM: We ought to receive all things with faith and reverence, and, when our discourse fails through weakness and is not able to set forth accurately the things that are spoken, then we ought especially to glorify God, in that we have such a God, surpassing both our thought and our conception.

For many of our conceptions about God we are unable to express, and many things we express but do not have strength to conceive. For instance, that God is everywhere we know, but how we do not understand. That there is a certain incorporeal power, the cause of all our good things, we know, but how it is or what it is, we know not. We speak and do not understand! I said that he is everywhere, but I do not understand it. I said that he is without beginning, but I do not understand it. I said that he begot from himself, and again I know not how I shall understand it. And some things there are that we may not even speak—as, for instance, that thought conceives but cannot utter. And to show you that even Paul is weak and does not put out his illustrations with exactness, and to make you tremble and refrain from searching too far, hear what he says, having called him Son and named him Creator, "who being the brightness of his glory and the express image of his person." *On the Epistle to the Hebrews* 2.1.

GOSPEL READING: *Mark 10:2-16*

REFLECTIONS FROM THE CHURCH FATHERS

Facing Deceptive Interrogation. ORIGEN: Of those who came to Jesus and interrogated him, some put questions to him simply to trick him. If our glorious Savior was tested in this way, should any of his disciples called to teach be annoyed when questioned by some who probe not from the desire to know but from the intent to trip up? *Commentary on Matthew* 14.16.

Mutual Servants, Equally Serving. TERTULLIAN: Where are we to find language adequate to express the happiness of that marriage that the church cements, the oblation confirms, the benediction signs and seals, the angels celebrate and the Father holds as approved? For all around the earth young people do not rightly and lawfully wed without their parents' consent. What kind of yoke is that of two believers who share one hope, one desire, one discipline, one service? They enjoy kinship in spirit and in flesh. They are mutual servants with no discrepancy of interests. Truly they are "two in one flesh." Where the flesh is one, the spirit is one as well. Together they pray, together bow down, together perform their fasts, mutually teaching, mutually entreating, mutually upholding. In the church of God they hold an equal place. They stand equally at the banquet of God, equally in crises, equally facing persecutions, and equally in refreshments. Neither hides anything from the other. Neither neglects the other. Neither is troublesome to the other. *To His Wife* 2.8.

When the Reception of Grace Begins. BASIL THE GREAT: The apostle praised one [Timothy] who had known the holy Scripture from infancy. He also instructed that children be reared "in the discipline and correction of the Lord." So we consider every time of life, even the very earliest, suitable for receiving persons into the community of faith. *The Long Rules* 15.

CLOSING PRAYER

O God, who desires not the death but the repentance of sinners, we beseech you, in your loving kindness, to turn your people to yourself; that when they devote themselves to you, you may remove the scourges of your anger; through Jesus Christ our Lord. *The Gelasian Sacramentary*

Hear Our Cries

⌘ THEME

Lord, hear our cries when we are in trouble (Ps 22:1-15), for we know
only you can deliver us (Job 23:1-9, 16-17). Help us to give up all we
hold dear (Mk 10:17-31) and approach you for mercy and grace in our
time of need (Heb 4:12-16).

⌘ OPENING PRAYER: *Proper 23*

O God, the life of the faithful, the joy of your servants: receive the
prayer of your people, and may the souls that thirst for your promises
be filled from your abundance; through Jesus Christ our Lord. Amen.
The Gelasian Sacramentary

⌘ OLD TESTAMENT READING: *Job 23:1-9, 16-17*

REFLECTIONS FROM THE CHURCH FATHERS

Job's Bitterness. EPHREM THE SYRIAN: "Today also my speech is
bitter," that is, my words happen to be harsh and irksome to both our
ears. In a different sense you, indeed, to use harsher speech against
you, drive me with your words. *Commentary on Job* 23.2.

No Intention to Accuse God of Injustice. CHRYSOSTOM: "Then Job
answered and said, 'Yes, I know that my accusation comes from my
hands.' " This means, I carry along with me the evidence that accuses

me. I draw from myself the demonstration of my afflictions. "His hand has been made heavy on me, and I groan over me." If it were possible, he says, to discuss my punishments with him, it would also be possible to find them out. If only I could plead my case in justice, he says, and meet him and learn what he would have answered me! See how he obtained exactly what he desired. That is, in fact, what occurs at the end of the book. I wanted to know what he would have said to me and whether he would have punished me just the same; and, by saying so, I had no intention of condemning any injustice on his part. *Commentary on Job* 23.2B.

Foreshadowing Repentance and Redemption. GREGORY THE GREAT: We bewail our sins when we begin to weigh them. We weigh them the more exactly when more anxiously we bewail them. By our lamentations it rises up more perfectly in our hearts that the severity of God threatens those who commit sin. . . .

Who else except the Mediator between God and humankind, the man Christ Jesus, is denoted by the title of "equity"? Concerning whom it is written, "Who of God is made to us wisdom and righteousness." And whereas this same righteousness came into this world against the ways of sinners, we get the better of our old enemy, by whom we were held captive. So let him say, "I do not want him to contend with me with great power or oppress me with the weight of his mightiness. Let him judge me justly, and my judgment will come to victory." In other words, for the correction of my ways let him send his incarnate Son. Then by the sentence of my absolution, I will turn out as a victor over the plotting foe. *Morals on the Book of Job* 16.36-37.

The Darkness of Dejection. CHRYSOSTOM: This unexpected disaster, he says, did not happen according to human logic. I discern that this blow comes from the hand of God. And he is right in speaking of the darkness that "covers my face," because this darkness is not ordinary darkness but is of his own dejection. *Commentary on Job* 23.16-17.

PSALM OF RESPONSE: *Psalm 22:1-15*

NEW TESTAMENT READING: *Hebrews 4:12-16*

REFLECTIONS FROM THE CHURCH FATHERS

Two Edges, Two Testaments. AUGUSTINE: He did not come "to bring peace on earth . . . but a sword," and Scripture calls the Word of God a "two-edged sword" because of the two Testaments. *City of God* 20.21.

The One in Whom Human Nature Was Innocent. LEO THE GREAT: What has been instilled in our hearts, if not that we should be "renewed" through them all "after the image" of that one who, remaining "in the form of God," condescended to become "the form of sinful flesh"? He assumed all those weaknesses of ours that come as a result of sin, though "without" any part in "sin." Consequently, he lacked none of the afflictions due to hunger and thirst, sleep and weariness, sadness and tears. He endured grievous sorrows even to the point of death. No one could be released from the fetters of mortality unless he, in whom alone the nature of all people was innocent, should allow himself to be killed by the hands of wicked persons. *Sermon* 63.

He Will Take Our Weakness into Account. THEODORET OF CYR: The believers at that time were subjected to constant billowing by trials; so he consoles them by bringing out that our high priest not only knows as God the weakness of our nature but also as man had experience of our sufferings, remaining unfamiliar with sin alone. Understanding this weakness of ours, he is saying, he both extends us appropriate help and when judging us he will take our weakness into account in delivering sentence. *Interpretation of Hebrews* 4.

GOSPEL READING: *Mark 10:17-31*

REFLECTIONS FROM THE CHURCH FATHERS

The Incomparable Goodness of the Son. ORIGEN: There is no other secondary goodness existing in the Son than that which is in the Father. So the Savior himself rightly says in the Gospel that "none is good save one, God the Father." The purpose of this statement is to make it understood that the Son is not of some other ancillary goodness, but of that alone which is in the Father; whose image he is rightly called. *On First Principles* 1.2.13.

Full Obedience. CAESARIUS OF ARLES: What that man heard, most beloved, we, too, have heard. The gospel of Christ is in heaven, but it does not cease to speak on earth. Let us not be dead to him, for he thunders. Let us not be deaf, for he shouts. If you are unwilling to commit to full obedience, do what you can. But here is the radical divine requirement: "Sell all that you have, and give to the poor; and come, follow me." The lesser road of the law says: "You shall not kill, you shall not commit adultery, you shall not seek false witness, you shall not steal, honor your father and mother, and love your neighbor as yourself." *Sermon* 153.1.

Whether One Tends to Love Wealth Inordinately. AUGUSTINE: Such, O my soul, are the miseries that attend on riches. They are gained with toil and kept with fear. They are enjoyed with danger and lost with grief. It is hard to be saved if we have them; and impossible if we love them; and scarcely can we have them, but we shall love them inordinately. Teach us, O Lord, this difficult lesson: to manage conscientiously the goods we possess, and not covetously desire more than you give to us. *Sermon* 133.

The Riches Most to Be Desired. SALVIAN THE PRESBYTER: Note what kind of riches it is that God loves. Note what wealth does he demand that we should store up for children. Note what possessions he especially orders us to guard: faith, fear of God, modesty, holiness, and discipline. Nothing earthly, nothing base, nothing perishable or transitory. *The Four Books of Timothy to the Church* 1.4.

Blessings Within of the New Family of God. JOHN CASSIAN: For he who for the sake of Christ's name distances himself from his particular beloved father or mother or child and gives himself over to the purest love of all who serve Christ, will receive a hundred times the measure of brothers and kinfolk. Instead of but one he will begin to have so many fathers and brothers bound to him by a still more fervent and admirable affection. That this is so you can prove by your own experience, since you have each left but one father and mother and home, and as you have done so you have gained without any effort or care countless fathers and mothers and brothers, as well as houses and land and most faithful servants, in any part of the world to which you go, who receive you as their own family, and welcome, and respect and take care of you with the utmost attention. *Conference* 3.24.26.

CLOSING PRAYER

Forgive us our sins, and the sins of all who are joined to us by kinship or friendship, all for whom we are desired to pray or have resolved to pray. Deliver us from the bonds of iniquity, and preserve us in that freedom wherewith you make us free; through Jesus Christ our Lord. Amen. *The Gregorian Sacramentary*

Humble Yourself

THEME

Praise the Lord, my soul (Ps 104:1-9, 24, 35c), for God laid the foundations of the earth (Job 38:1-7, 34-41). Help us to serve rather than to strive for greatness (Mk 10:35-45), just as Christ humbled himself as a sacrifice for us (Heb 5:1-10).

OPENING PRAYER: *Proper 24*

O Lord, prepare our hearts for prayer, our lips for your praise, our souls for your truth. Fill us with reverence for all that belongs to your holy name: your house, your worship, your Word; that we may benefit by these means of grace. And stretch forth, O Lord, the arms of your mercy over us and the right hand of your help toward us, that we may seek you with our whole heart and obtain what we rightly ask; through Jesus Christ our Lord. Amen. *The Gelasian Sacramentary*

OLD TESTAMENT READING: *Job 38:1-7, 34-41*

REFLECTIONS FROM THE CHURCH FATHERS

Elihu Is a Model of Arrogance. GREGORY THE GREAT: As often happens with one who incorrectly says right words and correctly bad words, so Elihu, in his arrogance, does not speak right words correctly, because in his defense of God he speaks humble sentences with an arrogant tone. So he is the perfect example of those who, in the universal church, look for vainglory. While they believe themselves to be more expert than anybody else, they are accused of being ignorant by the judgment of God, because, as the apostle says, "If one believes to know something, he still has to learn how to know." *Morals on the Book of Job* 28.11.

Symbolism of the Morning Stars. EPHREM THE SYRIAN: "And who created at the same time the morning stars?" that is, those stars that also rise and appear in the evening. But in a different sense, when we refer to these stars to the substances that are separated from our senses, their generation does not agree with the nature of angels. Therefore, we say that Christ is signified through the term *morning* and the apostles through *stars;* and the teachers, sons of the angels, are defined as participants in the angelic nature. *Commentary on Job* 38.7.

God's Divine Art. CHRYSOSTOM: Up to this point God divides the heavenly realities in terms of those through which he punishes us, as distinguished from those through which he benefits us. Notice how the lightnings answer. They do not really mean, "What do you want?" The text wants to signify that all creatures, as though they were living creatures, bend their ear to God. Every time he wants to show the difference in their formation, God talks about "begetting" and "maternal womb." Every time, on the other hand, he wants to show their docility and perfection, he depicts them as if they bent their ear to his call. Why did he present himself not only as a craftsman but as a father as well? This is because the art that presides over nature is quite superior to any manual art, for it is, so to speak, divine. *Commentary on Job* 38.35a-b.

PSALM OF RESPONSE: *Psalm 104:1-9, 24, 35c*

NEW TESTAMENT READING: *Hebrews 5:1-10*

REFLECTIONS FROM THE CHURCH FATHERS

His Petition Not to Enter Death. PHOTIUS: Now as regards the first matter we say that he did not make one petition but a twofold one. For the one petition asked to avoid death, the other petition asked for death. For he also says in the same prayer and petition, "However, not my will but yours be done." And John, showing this more clearly, says that the Son prayed by saying, "Father, glorify your Son, in order that your Son may glorify you," calling the cross and death glory, as is clear. So the excellent Paul says quite well, "He was heard." *Fragments on the Epistle to the Hebrews* 5.7-9.

Fire Is Not Harmed When Struck. CYRIL OF ALEXANDRIA: Iron or any other like material, when joined to the impact of fire, receives it and nourishes the flame. If then it happens to be struck by someone, the material receives damage, but the nature of the fire is in no way harmed by the one who strikes. In the same way, you may understand the Son can be said to suffer in the flesh but not to suffer in his divinity. *On the Unity of Christ* 776.

Salvation Accomplished. LEO THE GREAT: Our origin, corrupted right after its start, needed to be reborn with new beginnings. A victim had to be offered for reconciliation, a victim that was at one and the same time both related to our race and foreign to our defilement. In this way alone could the plan of God—wherein it pleased him that the sin of the world should be wiped away through the birth and passion of Jesus Christ—in this way alone could the plan of God be of any avail for the times of every generation. Nor would the mysteries—as they pass through various developments in time—disturb us. Instead, they would reassure us, since the faith by which we live would not have differed at any stage. *Sermon* 23.3-4.

GOSPEL READING: *Mark 10:35-45*

REFLECTIONS FROM THE CHURCH FATHERS

Their Plea Transcended. BEDE: When the sons of Zebedee were seeking from Jesus seats in his kingdom, he at once called them to drink of his chalice, that is, to pattern themselves after the struggle of his suffering. *Homily* 2.21.

The Way to Loftiness. **AUGUSTINE:** Ponder how profound this is. They were conferring with him about glory. He intended to precede loftiness with humility and, only through humility, to ready the way for loftiness itself. For, of course, even those disciples who wanted to sit, the one on his right, the other on his left, were looking to glory. They were on the lookout, but did not see by what way. In order that they might come to their homeland in due order, the Lord called them back to the narrow way. For the homeland is on high and the way to it is lowly. The homeland is life in Christ; the way is dying with Christ. The way is suffering with Christ; the goal is abiding with him eternally. Why do you seek the homeland if you are not seeking the way to it? *The Gospel of John* 28.5.2.

The Grace Offered in Baptism. **CHRYSOSTOM:** For when we immerse our heads in the water, the old humanity is buried as in a tomb below and wholly sunk forever. Then as we raise them again, the new humanity rises in its place. As it is easy for us to dip and to lift our heads again, so it is easy for God to bury the old humanity, and to lift up and display the new. And this is done three times, that you may learn that the power of the Father, the Son and the Holy Spirit fulfills all this. *Homilies on John* 25.2.

Setting Captives Free. **GREGORY OF NAZIANZUS:** He is our sanctification, as himself being purity, that the pure may be encompassed by his purity. He is our redemption, because he sets us free who were held captive under sin, giving himself as a ransom for us, the sacrifice to make expiation for the world. He is our resurrection, because he raises up, and brings to life again, those who were slain by sin. *Theological Oration* 4.20.

The Personal Relevance of Christ's Act of Ransom. **AMBROSE:** It is profitable to me to know that for my sake Christ bore my infirmities, submitted to the affections of my body, that for me and for all he was made sin and a curse, that for me and in me was he humbled and made subject, that for me he is the lamb, the vine, the rock, the servant, the Son of a handmaid, knowing not the day of judgment, for my sake ignorant of the day and the hour. *Of the Christian Faith* 2.92.

CLOSING PRAYER

Grant me, O Lord, the lamp of love that never grows dim, that it may shine in me and warm my heart, and give light to others through my love for them, and by its brightness we may have a vision of the holy city where the true and inextinguishable light shines, Jesus Christ our Lord. Amen. *Columbanus*

God's Mercy

❧ THEME

The Lord has delivered me from all my fears (Ps 34:1-8, 19-22); there is nothing he cannot do (Job 42:1-6, 10-17). His mercy, grace and power (Mk 10:46-52) are shown through his sacrifice for our sins (Heb 7:23-28).

❧ OPENING PRAYER: *Proper 25*

Let your merciful ears, O Lord, be open to the prayers of your humble servants; and that they may obtain their petitions, make them to ask such things as shall please you, through Jesus Christ our Lord. Amen.
The Gelasian Sacramentary

❧ OLD TESTAMENT READING: *Job 42:1-6, 10-17*

REFLECTIONS FROM THE CHURCH FATHERS

Job Recognizes God's Omniscience. OLYMPIODORUS: Job openly declares that he had not learned these things before but had come to know the unconquered power of God. And since God penetrates the decisions of people and understands the thoughts of all, there is nobody who can hide from his eye, which sees everything. Who is he, he says, who being sparing of words, can hide the secrets of his mind in silence, because they have not been expressed in words? *Commentary on Job* 42.1-3.

Allegorical Meaning of "Brothers and Sisters." **PHILIP THE PRIEST:** When the text says "they came," this means that they were incorporated with him through faith, so that they might be gathered into the church in a single spirit, as all those who believe in God are the limbs of the church. "Brothers and sisters" denote that entire family of Jews, from whom Christ was born. But we can also interpret "brothers and sisters" as the multitudes of all nations, because Christ assumed the flesh from the mass of humankind and through it deigned to make all human beings his brothers and sisters. *Commentary on the Book of Job* 42.

The Gathering of Souls. **GREGORY THE GREAT:** We believe that this happened in history, but we hope that this may also happen mystically. The Lord blesses the new condition of Job more than the former, because, with regard to the receiving of the people of Israel into faith—while the present world progressively moves toward its end—the Lord comforts the pain of the holy church with an abundant gathering of souls. The more clearly it appears that the time of the present life approaches its end, the more the church will be enriched with the souls [from among the Jews]. *Morals on the Book of Job* 35.35.

PSALM OF RESPONSE: *Psalm 34:1-8, 19-22*

NEW TESTAMENT READING: *Hebrews 7:23-28*

REFLECTIONS FROM THE CHURCH FATHERS

As Man Christ Intercedes. **GREGORY OF NAZIANZUS:** Petition does not imply here, as it does in popular parlance, a desire for legal satisfaction; there is something humiliating in the idea. No, it means interceding for us in his role of mediator, in the way that the Spirit too is spoken of as "making petition" on our behalf. "For there is one God, and there is one mediator between God and men, the man Christ Jesus." Even at this moment he is, as human, interceding for my salvation, until he makes me divine by the power of his incarnate humanity. "As human," I say, because he still has with him the body he assumed, though he is no longer "regarded as human," meaning the bodily experiences, which, sin aside, are ours and his. This is the "advocate" we have in Jesus—not a slave who falls prostrate before the Father on our behalf. Get rid of what is really a slavish suspicion, unworthy of the Spirit. It is not in God to make the demand, nor in the Son to submit to it; the thought is unjust to God. No, it is by what he suffered as man that he persuades us, as Word and encourager, to endure. That, for me, is the meaning of his "advocacy." *Theological Oration* 4(30).14, On the Son.

He Became Us. BASIL THE GREAT: Although we are not his brothers but have become his enemies by our transgressions, he who is not mere man, but God, after the freedom that he bestowed on us, also calls us his brothers. "I will tell of your name," he says, "to my brethren." Now, he who has redeemed us, if you examine his nature, is neither brother nor man; but if you examine his condescension to us through grace, he calls us brothers and descends to our human nature. He does not need a ransom, for he himself is the propitiation. *Homilies on the Psalms* 19.4 (Psalm 48).

The Only Son of God. AUGUSTINE: Who then is so just and holy a priest as the only Son of God, who had no need of a sacrifice for the washing away of his own sins, neither original sins nor those that are added from human life? And what could be so fittingly chosen by people to be offered for them as human flesh? And what so suitable for this immolation as mortal flesh? And what so clean for cleansing the vices of mortals as the flesh born in the womb without the contagion of carnal concupiscence, and coming from a virginal womb? And what could be so acceptably offered and received as the flesh of our sacrifice made the body of our priest? Four things are to be considered in every sacrifice: by whom it is offered, to whom it is offered, what is offered, and for whom it is offered. *On the Trinity* 4.14.19.

GOSPEL READING: *Mark 10:46-52*

REFLECTIONS FROM THE CHURCH FATHERS

The Fall from Loftiness. AUGUSTINE: Mark has recorded both the name of Bartimaeus and of his father, a circumstance that scarcely occurs in all the many cases of healing that had been performed by the Lord. . . . Consequently there can be little doubt that this Bartimaeus, the son of Timaeus, had fallen from some position of great prosperity and was now regarded as an object of the most notorious and the most remarkable wretchedness, because in addition to being blind he had also to sit begging. *Harmony of the Gospels* 2.65.

Willing the Healthy Way. CHRYSOSTOM: He will save assuredly; yet he will do so just in the way he has promised. But in what way has he promised? On our willing it, and on our hearing him. For he does not make a promise to blocks of wood. *Homily on 2 Thessalonians* 3.4.

Adoration of the Light. CLEMENT OF ALEXANDRIA: The commandment of the Lord shines clearly, enlightening the eyes. Receive Christ, receive power to see, receive your light, that you may plainly recognize both God and man. More delightful than gold and precious stones, more desirable than honey and the honeycomb is the Word that has enlightened us. How could he not be desirable, who illumined minds buried in darkness and endowed with clear vision "the light-bearing eyes" of the soul? . . . Sing his praises, then, Lord, and make known to me your Father, who is God. Your Word will save me, your song instruct me. I have gone astray in my search for God; but now that you light my path, Lord, I find God through you and receive the Father from you. I become co-heir with you, since you were not ashamed to own me as your brother. Let us, then, shake off forgetfulness of truth, shake off the mist of ignorance and darkness that dims our eyes and contemplate the true God, after first raising this song of praise to him: "All hail, O light!" For on us buried in darkness, imprisoned in the shadow of death, a heavenly light has shone, a light of a clarity surpassing the sun's and of a sweetness exceeding any this earthly life can offer. *Exhortation to the Greeks* 11.

What Following Means. AUGUSTINE: So let us follow him as our pattern: offering him for our ransom, receiving him as our Eucharistic food and waiting for him as our endless and exceeding great reward. *Harmony of the Gospels* 2.65.

CLOSING PRAYER

Grant, O Lord, we beseech you, that the course of this world may be so peaceably ordered by your governance, that your church may joyfully serve you in all godly quietness, through Jesus Christ our Lord. Amen. *The Leonine Sacramentary*

A Pure Heart

⫶ THEME

Lord, give us pure hearts (Ps 24) and let us dwell with you forever (Is 25:6-9). Christ, who has the power of life and death (Jn 11:32-44), promises us an eternity free from suffering and tears (Rev 21:1-6a).

⫶ OPENING PRAYER: *All Saints' Day*

Almighty God, you have taught us through your Son that love is the fulfilling of the law. Grant that we may love you with our whole heart and our neighbors as ourselves; through Jesus Christ our Lord. Amen.

The Leonine Sacramentary

⫶ OLD TESTAMENT READING: *Isaiah 25:6-9*

REFLECTIONS FROM THE CHURCH FATHERS

***A Shelter from the Heat.* PRIMASIUS:** They will not hunger because they will feed on living bread, for he said, "I am the living bread that came down from heaven." Neither will they thirst, because they will drink from a cup so splendid as to enact in them the truth he spoke: "Whoever believes in me will never thirst"; and again: "Whoever drinks from the water I give him will receive in himself a fountain of water springing up to eternal life." Neither will the sun strike them, nor will they be burned by the deadly fire of its heat. God made a similar promise to his church through Isaiah, saying that he would be "a shelter from the storm, a shade from the heat." *Commentary on the Apocalypse* 2.7.

Love Overcomes Death. EUSEBIUS OF CAESAREA: Now the laws of love summoned him even as far as death and the dead themselves, so that he might summon the souls of those who were long time dead. And so because he cared for the salvation of all for ages past and that "he might bring to nothing him that has the power of death," as Scripture teaches, here again he underwent the dispensation in his mingled natures: as man, he left his body to the usual burial, while as God he departed from it. For he cried with a loud cry and said to the Father, "I commend my spirit," and departed from the body free, in no way waiting for death, who was lagging as it were in fear to come to him. No, rather, he pursued him from behind and drove him on, trodden under his feet and fleeing, and he burst the eternal gates of his dark realms and made a road of return back again to life for the dead there bound with the bonds of death. Thus too, his own body was raised up, and many bodies of the sleeping saints arose and came together with him into the holy and real city of heaven, as rightly is said by the holy words: "Death has prevailed and swallowed people up; but again the Lord God has taken away every tear from every face." And the Savior of the universe, our Lord, the Christ of God, called Victor, is represented in the prophetic predictions as reviling death and releasing the souls that are bound there, by whom he raises the hymn of victory. *Proof of the Gospel* 4.12.

Christ Conquers Death. CYRIL OF ALEXANDRIA: It is appropriate and necessary that at the time the "mystery" is handed over, the "resurrection of the dead" is included. For at the time we make the confession of faith at holy baptism, we say that we expect the resurrection of the flesh. And so we believe. . . . We who come afterward will certainly follow the first fruits. He turned suffering into joy, and we cast off our sackcloth. We put on the joy given by God so that we can rejoice and say, "Where is your victory, O death?" Therefore every tear is taken away. For believing that Christ will surely raise the dead, we do not weep over them, nor are we overwhelmed by inconsolable grief like those who have no hope. Death itself is a "reproach of the people" for it had its beginning among us through sin. Corruption entered in on account of sin, and death's power ruled on earth. *Commentary on Isaiah* 3.1.25.

⁂ **PSALM OF RESPONSE:** *Psalm 24*

⁂ **NEW TESTAMENT READING:** *Revelation 21:1-6a*

REFLECTIONS FROM THE CHURCH FATHERS

When the Soul Is Restored to Its Integrity. AUGUSTINE: Every rational soul is made unhappy by its sins or happy by its well doing. Every irrational soul yields to one that is more powerful, or obeys one that is better, or is on terms of equality with its equals, exercising rivals or harming any it has overcome. Every body is obedient to its soul so far as permitted by the merits of the latter or the orderly arrangement of things. There is no evil in the universe, but in individuals there is evil due to their own fault. *Of True Religion* 23.44.

The Lord Will Reward His People with Gladness. APRINGIUS OF BEJA: The Lord gives witness to himself, for the multitude of the saints will become his temple, so that he might dwell with them forever and that he might be their Lord and they might be his people. He himself will take away all weeping and every tear from the eyes of those whom he rewards with eternal gladness and whom he makes bright with perpetual blessedness. *Tractate on the Apocalypse* 21.3-4.

The Vision of Inexpressible Gladness. ANDREW OF CAESAREA: In this tent made without hands there is no weeping or any tears, for he who supplies the joy of the eternal temple will give to all the saints the vision of inexpressible gladness. That is, it is written, "pain and sorrow

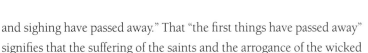
and sighing have passed away." That "the first things have passed away" signifies that the suffering of the saints and the arrogance of the wicked have ceased, for an exchange of circumstances will occur for each of these groups. *Commentary on the Apocalypse* 21.3-4.

GOSPEL READING: *John 11:32-44*

REFLECTIONS FROM THE CHURCH FATHERS

He Wept to Teach Us to Weep. AUGUSTINE: Why did Christ weep except to teach us to weep? *Tractates on the Gospel of John* 49.19.

Jesus Weeps for All Humanity. CYRIL OF ALEXANDRIA: The Jews thought that Jesus wept on account of the death of Lazarus, but in fact he wept out of compassion for all humanity, not mourning Lazarus alone but all of humanity, which is subject to death, having justly fallen under so great a penalty. *Commentary on the Gospel of John* 7.

Groaning in the Face of Death. PETER CHRYSOLOGUS: Spirit groans, so that flesh would come back to life. Life groans, so that death would be put to flight. God groans, so that humanity would rise. Pardon groans, lest the verdict be unfavorable. Christ groans as he subdues death, because one who snatches an unparalleled victory over an enemy cannot but groan. But with regard to the fact that he said that he "groaned again," he does groan again in order to provide evidence of a twofold resurrection, since at Christ's voice just as those dead in body are raised to life from their graves, so too those dead in faithfulness rise to a life of faith. *Sermon* 65.1.

Those Who Pray. ORIGEN: "I knew that you hear me always," which is reported by John as said by the Lord, makes clear that those who pray are *always* heard. *On Prayer* 13.1.

The Voice That Called Lazarus. GREGORY OF NYSSA: Here we have a man past the prime of life, a corpse, decaying, swollen, in fact, already in a state of dissolution, so that even his own relatives did not want the Lord to draw near the tomb because the decayed body enclosed there was so offensive. And yet, he is brought into life by a single call, confirming the proclamation of the resurrection, that is to say, that expectation of it as universal that we learn by a particular experience to entertain. For as in the regeneration of the universe the apostle tells us that "the Lord himself will descend with a shout, with the voice of the archangel," and by a trumpet sound raise up the dead to incorruption—so now too he who is in the tomb, at the voice of command, shakes off death as if it were only sleep. He rids himself of the corruption that had come on his condition of a corpse, leaps forth from the tomb whole and sound, not even hindered as he leaves by the bonds of the grave cloths round his feet and hands. *On the Making of Man* 25.11.

CLOSING PRAYER

O almighty and most merciful God, of your bountiful goodness keep us, we beseech you, from all things that may hurt us; that we being ready both in body and soul may cheerfully accomplish those things that you would have done, through Jesus Christ our Lord. Amen. *The Gelasian Sacramentary*

Serving God

⌇ THEME

Praise the Lord! Blessed is the maker of heaven and earth (Ps 146). Give us the faithfulness of Ruth (Ruth 1:1-18) and the strength to love you with all our hearts (Mk 12:28-34) so we may serve you, the living God (Heb 9:11-14).

⌇ OPENING PRAYER: *Proper 26*

O God, from whom all holy desires, all good counsels and all just works do proceed; give unto your servants that peace that the world cannot give, that both our hearts may be set to obey your commandments and also that, by you, we being defended from the fear of our enemies, may pass our time in rest and quietness, through the merits of Jesus Christ our Savior. Amen. *The Gelasian Sacramentary*

⌇ OLD TESTAMENT READING: *Ruth 1:1-18*

REFLECTIONS FROM THE CHURCH FATHERS

The Great Conflict. PAULINUS OF NOLA: Next pass with eager eyes to Ruth, who with one short book separates eras—the end of the period of the judges and the beginning of Samuel. It seems a short account, but it depicts the symbolism of the great conflict when the two sisters separate to go their different ways. Ruth follows after her holy mother-in-law, whereas Orpah abandons her; one daughter-in-law demonstrates faithlessness, the other fidelity. The one puts God before country, the other puts country before life. Does not such disharmony continue through the universe, one part following God and the other falling headlong through the world? If only the two groups seeking death and salvation were equal! But the broad road seduces many, and those who glide on the easy downward course are snatched off headlong by sin that cannot be revoked. *Poems* 27.511.

Ruth Prefigures the Christian Church. ISIDORE OF SEVILLE: Now let us look at Ruth, for she is a type of the church. First she is a type because she is a stranger from the Gentile people who renounced her native land and all things belonging to it. She made her way to the land of Israel. And when her mother-in-law forbade her from coming with her she persisted, saying, "Wherever you go, I shall go; your people shall be my people; and your God shall be my God. Whichever land receives you as you die, there I too shall die." This voice without doubt shows that she is a type of the church. For the church was called to God from the Gentiles in just this way: leaving her native land (which is idolatry) and giving up all earthly associations, she confessed that he in whom the saints believed is the Lord God; and that she herself will go where the flesh of Christ ascended after his passion; and that on account of his name she would suffer in this world unto death; and that she will unite with the community of the saints, that is, the patriarchs and the prophets. This company, by virtue of which she might be joined to the longed-for saints from the lineage of Abraham, Moses revealed to us in the canticle, saying, "Rejoice, you nations, with his people (that is, people of the Gentiles), pour forth what you believe; exult with those who were first chosen for eternal joy." *On Ruth.*

Merit for Solacing the Deserted. JEROME: Ruth, a foreigner, did not leave Naomi's side. See how much merit there is in standing by the deserted in solace. From her seed, Christ is born. *Letter* 39.5.

The Merits of Ruth's Faith. INCOMPLETE WORK ON MATTHEW: Boaz married Ruth on account of the merits of her faith, because she scorned her own people and land and nation and chose Israel, and because she did not despise her mother-in-law, a widow like herself, and an exile; but she was led by desire to her [Naomi's] people rather than to her [Ruth's] own. She rejected the god of her native land and chose the living God, saying to her mother-in-law, "Do not oppose me." *Homily 1.*

PSALM OF RESPONSE: *Psalm 146*

NEW TESTAMENT READING: *Hebrews 9:11-14*

REFLECTIONS FROM THE CHURCH FATHERS

The New Tabernacle of the Church. SEVERIAN OF GABALA: The tent built under Moses was to signify servitude [to the law]. Therefore, the more perfect tent is the dwelling of grace, the body of Christ whose head is Christ himself. *Fragments on the Epistle to the Hebrews 9.11.*

The Body as Tabernacle Veil in Heaven. CHRYSOSTOM: Well did he say, "greater and more perfect tent," since God the Word and all the power of the Spirit dwells therein, "for it is not by measure that he gives the Spirit." "More perfect," as being both without blame and setting right greater things. "That is, not of this creation"—see how it was greater, for it would not have been "of the Spirit," if humankind had constructed it. Nor yet is it "of this creation," that is, not of these created things, but spiritual, of the Holy Spirit. See how he calls the body tent and curtain and heaven. . . . Why then does he say this? In accordance with whether one thing or another is signified. I mean, for instance, the heaven is a curtain, for as a curtain it walls off the Holy of Holies; the flesh is a curtain hiding the Godhead; and the tent likewise holds the Godhead. Again, heaven is a tent, for the priest is there within. *On the Epistle to the Hebrews 15.4.*

For All Nations. EPHREM THE SYRIAN: Our Lord did not enter yearly like their high priest. After his coming he entered only once, not into the shrine that ceases, like their priesthood, but "into the Holy" of Holies of eternity, and he made a propitiation through his blood for all nations. *Commentary on the Epistle to the Hebrews.*

Mount Above Earthly Senses. ORIGEN: This is what the letter of the law explains to us, so that, collecting seeds of mysteries from them, we may use them as steps to climb from the lowly to a lofty place, from earthly to heavenly things. Therefore, my hearer, climb up now, if you can, and mount above earthly senses by the contemplation of your mind and by the discernment of your heart. Forget for a while earthly concerns; climb above the clouds and above heaven itself by the tread of your mind. Seek there the tabernacle of God where "Jesus has entered." *Homilies on Numbers* 3.3.

GOSPEL READING: *Mark 12:28-34*

REFLECTIONS FROM THE CHURCH FATHERS

Renouncing Other Gods. ORIGEN: When you decide to keep the command of this precept and reject all other gods and lords and have no god or lord except the one God and Lord, you have declared war on all others without treaty. When, therefore, we come to the grace of baptism, renouncing all other gods and lords, we confess the only God, Father, Son and Holy Spirit. *On Exodus,* Homily 8.4.

No Division into Parts. BASIL THE GREAT: The expression, "with the whole," admits of no division into parts. As much love as you shall have squandered on lower objects, that much will necessarily be lacking to you from the whole. *Exegetic Homilies,* Homily 17.

The Summit of Virtue. CHRYSOSTOM: This is the summit of virtue, the foundation of all God's commandments: to the love of God is joined also love of neighbor. One who loves God does not neglect his brother, nor esteem money more than a limb of his own, but shows him great generosity, mindful of him who has said, "Whoever did it to the least of my brothers did it to me." He is aware that the Lord of all considers as done to himself what is done in generosity to the poor in giving relief. He does not take into consideration the lowly appearance of the poor but the greatness of the One who has promised to accept as done to himself what is given to the poor. *Homilies on Genesis,* Homily 55.12.

Loving God Through Neighbors. **BEDE:** Neither of these two kinds of love is expressed with full maturity without the other, because God cannot be loved apart from our neighbor, nor our neighbor apart from God. Hence as many times as Peter was asked by our Lord if he loved him, and attested his love, the Lord added at the end of each inquiry, "Feed my sheep," or "Feed my lambs," as if he were clearly saying: "There is only one adequate confirmation of whole-hearted love of God—laboring steadily for the needy in your midst, exercising continuing care of them." *Exposition on the Gospel of Mark* 2.22.

⌘ CLOSING PRAYER

Almighty God, who did wonderfully create man in your own image, and did yet more wonderfully restore him: grant, we beseech you, that as your Son our Lord Jesus Christ was made in the likeness of men, so we may be made partakers of the divine nature; through the same your Son, who with you and the Holy Spirit lives and reigns, one God, world without end. Amen. *The Leonine Sacramentary*

Perfect Sacrifice

◌ THEME

All is in vain, unless it is done for the Lord (Ps 127). Even when what we are asked to do seems difficult (Ruth 3:1-5; 4:13-17), we must be willing to sacrifice everything (Mk 12:38-44) for the One who gave us his only Son as a sacrifice for our sins (Heb 9:24-28).

◌ OPENING PRAYER: *Proper 27*

O Lord, from whom all good things do come, grant to us your humble servants, that by your holy inspiration we may think those things that be good, and by your merciful guiding may perform the same, through Jesus Christ our Lord. Amen. *The Gelasian Sacramentary*

◌ OLD TESTAMENT READING: *Ruth 3:1-5; 4:13-17*

REFLECTIONS FROM THE CHURCH FATHERS

Naomi's Advice. THEODORET OF CYR: What does Naomi suggest to her daughter-in-law? When Ruth heard her mother-in-law saying, "Our neighbor is a true man," she was reminded of his great kindness and thought to want him married to her in-law, so that she might keep up the memory of the dead. Therefore, Naomi suggests to her that she sleep at Boaz's feet, not that she might sell her body (for the words of the narrative signify the opposite); rather, she trusts the man's temperance and judgment. Moreover, the actions corroborate the words. *Questions on Ruth.*

Ruth's and Boaz's Virtues. INCOMPLETE WORK ON MATTHEW:
Unless God's inspiration had been in Ruth, she would not have said
what she said or done what she did. What is praised in her first? A love
of the tribe of Israel, or obedience, or faith? She desired to have sons
out of the seed of Israel and become of the people of God. Simplicity is
praised also, because she came in under Boaz's coverlet voluntarily. She
feared neither that he would perhaps spurn her, as a just man might
spurn a lascivious woman, nor that he might deceive her and, worse,
despise a deceived woman, as many men might have done. But, obey-
ing her mother-in-law's plans, she confidently believed that God would
prosper her action, knowing her conscience, because lust did not push
her to it, but rather religion was her encouragement. What, however, is
praised in Boaz? Humility, chastity and religion. Humility indeed and
chastity, because he did not touch her as a lascivious man would touch
a girl or abhor her as a chaste man would a lascivious girl, but as soon
as he had heard her speak of the law, he ascribed her actions to religion.
Nor did he despise her as a rich man would a pauper, nor was he in
awe of her, as a mature man might be of a young woman; but, more
experienced in faith than in body, he proceeded in the morning to the
gate, calling the neighborhood together and prevailing not by the law
of kinship to her but, rather, by the favor of being the chosen one of
God. *Homily 1.*

Foreigners Not Excluded. THEOPHYLACT: And Boaz begat Obed of
Ruth. Ruth was a foreigner, but nevertheless she was married to Boaz.
So, too, the church is from among the Gentiles. For like Ruth, these
Gentiles had been foreigners and outside the covenants, yet they for-
sook their people, their idols and their father, the devil. And as Ruth
was wed to Boaz of the seed of Abraham, so too was the church taken
as bride by the Son of God. *Explanation of Matthew 1.3-4.*

PSALM OF RESPONSE: *Psalm 127*

NEW TESTAMENT READING: *Hebrews 9:24-28*

REFLECTIONS FROM THE CHURCH FATHERS

Why "At the End of the World"? CHRYSOSTOM: In this place he has also veiled over something. "But now once more in the end of the world." Why "at the end of the world"? After the many sins. If it had taken place at the beginning, then no one would have believed. He must not die a second time; otherwise all would have been useless. But since later there were many transgressions, with reason he appeared, which he expresses in another place also, "Where sin increased, grace abounded all the more." "But now once in the end of the world, he has appeared to put away sin by the sacrifice of himself." *On the Epistle to the Hebrews* 17.3.

He Put Away Sin. THEODORET OF CYR: He completely destroyed the force of sin, promising us immortality; sin is incapable of proving a problem to immortal bodies. *Interpretation of Hebrews* 9.

Christ Became As If a Sinner. OECUMENIUS: He says that "he bore the sins of many" on the cross, in order that he might quell them, paying the penalty that they deserved. Now the Father sent him, "having made him sin." For also Christ became as if a sinner, inasmuch as he took on the sins of the whole world and claimed them as his own. But then he paid the penalty that was owed, the punishment belonging to sinners. At last he will come with his Father's glory, no longer as a sinner, no longer "reckoned among the lawless." *Fragments on the Epistle to the Hebrews* 9.28.

GOSPEL READING: *Mark 12:38-44*

REFLECTIONS FROM THE CHURCH FATHERS

Measuring the Value of Gifts. JEROME: The poor widow cast only two pennies into the treasury; yet because she gave all she had it is said of her that she surpassed all the rich in offering gifts to God. Such gifts are valued not by their weight but by the good will with which they are made. *Letter,* 118 to Julian 5.

Traveling Step by Step. EVAGRIUS: It is better to begin from one's feeble state and end up strong, to progress from small things to larger, than to set your heart from the very first on the perfect way of life, then only to abandon it later—or keep to it solely out of habit, because of what others will think—in which case all this labor will be in vain. It is the same with people who travel: if they tire themselves out on the very first day by rushing along, they will end up wasting many days as a result of sickness. But if they start out walking at a gentle pace until they have got accustomed to walking, in the end they will not get tired, even though they walk great distances. Likewise anyone who wishes to embark on the labors of the virtuous life should train himself gently, until he gradually reaches the full extent of his abilities. Do not be perplexed by the many paths walked by our fathers of old, each different from the other. Do not overzealously try to imitate them all— this would only upset your way of life. Rather, choose a way of life that suits your feeble state; travel on that, and you will live, for your Lord is merciful and he will receive you, not because of your achievements, but because of your intention, just as he received the destitute woman's gift. *Admonition on Prayer.*

Invest with the Lord What He Has Given. PAULINUS OF NOLA: We have been entrusted with the administration and use of temporal wealth for the common good, not with the everlasting ownership of private property. If you accept the fact that ownership on earth is only for a time, you can earn eternal possessions in heaven. . . . Let us then invest with the Lord what he has given us, for we have nothing that does not come from him: we are dependent on him for our very existence. . . . So let us give back to the Lord the gifts he has given us. Let us give to him who receives in the person of every poor man or woman.

Let us give gladly, I say, and great joy will be ours when we receive his promised reward. *Letter* 34.2-4.

Generosity Seen in the Light of Intention. CHRYSOSTOM: When the widow put into the collection box only two small coins, the master did not give her a recompense worth only two coins. Why was that? Because he paid no attention to the amount of the money. What he did heed was the wealth of her soul. If you calculate by the value of her money, her poverty is great. If you bring her intention into the light, you will see that her store of generosity defies description. *On the Incomprehensible Nature of God* 6.12.

CLOSING PRAYER

We beseech you, almighty God, look on the hearty desires of your humble servants, and stretch forth the right hand of your majesty to be our defense against all our enemies, through Jesus Christ our Lord. Amen. *The Gregorian Sacramentary*

Confidence in Our Creator

⬧ THEME

Lord, we take refuge in you (Ps 16), for you listen to our despair (1 Sam 1:4-20) and know the future (Mk 13:1-8). Therefore, we draw near to you, holding to your promises (Heb 10:11-25).

⬧ OPENING PRAYER: *Proper 28*

O Lord God, who sees that we put not our trust in anything that we do; mercifully grant that by your power we may be defended against all adversity, through Jesus Christ our Lord. Amen. *The Gregorian Sacramentary*

⬧ OLD TESTAMENT READING: *1 Samuel 1:4-20*

REFLECTIONS FROM THE CHURCH FATHERS

Silent Prayer. CAESARIUS OF ARLES: As often as we apply ourselves to prayer, dearly beloved, we should above all pray in silence and quiet. If a man wants to pray aloud, he seems to take the fruit of prayer away from those who are standing near him. Only moans and sighs and groans should be heard. Indeed our prayer ought to be like that of holy Hannah, the mother of blessed Samuel, of whom it is written that "she prayed, shedding many tears, and only her lips moved, but her voice was not heard at all." Let everyone hear and imitate this, especially those who pray aloud without any embarrassment and in such a chattering fashion that they do not allow those near them to pray. There-fore, let us pray, as I said, with sighs and moans and groans, in accord with the words of the prophet: "I roared with the groaning of my heart." Let us pray, I repeat, not with a loud voice but with our hearts crying out to God. *Sermon 72.2.*

Conversation with God. CLEMENT OF ALEXANDRIA: Prayer is, then, to speak more boldly, a conversation with God. Though whisper-ing, consequently, and not opening the lips, we speak in silence, yet we cry inwardly. For God hears continually the whole inward conversa-tion. *Stromateis 7.7.*

Win Greater Favor from God. CHRYSOSTOM: At home, her rival mocked her. She went into the temple, and the priest's boy abused her and the priest upbraided her. She fled the storm at home, entered port and still ran into turbulence. She went to get a remedy, and not only did not get it but received an additional burden of taunts, and the wound instead was opened up again. You are aware, of course, how distressed souls are susceptible to abuse and insult: just as bad wounds cannot stand the slightest contact with the hand but become worse, so too the soul that is disturbed and upset has problems with everything and is stung by a chance remark. The woman, on the con-trary, was not like that, even in this case with the boy abusing her. Had the priest been intoxicated, the insults would not have been so sur-prising; his high rank and heavy responsibility convinced her against her will to keep her composure. But in fact she was upset with the priest's boy, and hence she won God's favor even further. Should we too be abused and suffer countless misadventures, let us put up nobly with those who insult us, and we shall thus win greater favor from God. *Homilies on Hannah 2.*

PSALM OF RESPONSE: *Psalm 16*

NEW TESTAMENT READING: *Hebrews 10:11-25*

REFLECTIONS FROM THE CHURCH FATHERS

I Will Remember Sins No More. THEODORET OF CYR: Now, this happened through the new covenant: we receive also in all-holy baptism the forgiveness of sins. In the life to come, when immortality is granted us, we shall live differently from everyone else, sin no longer capable of troubling those who have become immortal. May it be our good fortune to attain this life. We shall attain it if in the present life we embrace with enthusiasm the effort virtue involves and accept the struggles it requires. The Lord himself, who is the source of the future goods, will work with us. *Interpretation of Hebrews 10.*

The Inner Tabernacle Is Faith. EPHREM THE SYRIAN: "Therefore, brethren, we have confidence to enter the sanctuary," which is faith. In his blood he renewed for us the way of faith that the former priests had already. But since it had become obsolete among them, he renewed it for us at that time "through the curtain, that is, through his flesh." *Commentary on the Epistle to the Hebrews.*

Love Is a Highway That Leads to Virtue. CHRYSOSTOM: This then let us "confirm" toward each other. "For love is the fulfilling of the law." We have no need of labors or of sweatings if we love one another. It is a pathway leading of itself toward virtue. For on the highway, if one finds the beginning, he is guided by it and has no need of one to take him by the hand. So is it also in regard to love. Only lay hold on the beginning, and at once you are guided and directed by it. "Love does no wrong to a neighbor" and "thinks no evil." Let each person consider how he is disposed toward himself. He does not envy himself. He wishes all good things for himself. He prefers himself before all. He is willing to do all things for himself. If then we are so disposed toward others also, all grievous things are brought to an end; there is no enmity; there is no covetousness, for who would choose to overreach himself? No one. On the contrary, we shall possess all things in common and shall not cease assembling together. And if we do this, the remembrance of injuries would have no place, for who would choose to remember injuries against himself? Who would choose to be angry with himself? Do we not make allowances for ourselves most of all? If we were thus disposed toward our neighbors also, there will never be any remembrance of injuries. *On the Epistle to the Hebrews* 19.4.

GOSPEL READING: *Mark 13:1-8*

REFLECTIONS FROM THE CHURCH FATHERS

The Temple in Ruins. CYRIL OF JERUSALEM: Antichrist will come at such a time as there shall not be let of the temple of the Jews "one stone on another," to quote the sentence pronounced by the Savior. For it is not until all the stones are overthrown whether by the decay of age or through being pulled down for building material or in consequence of this or that other happening, and I do not mean merely the stones of the outer walls, but the floor of the inner temple where the cherubim were, that Antichrist will come "with all signs and lying wonders" treating all the idols with disdain. *Catechetical Lectures* 15.15.

The Common Condition of Nations. AUGUSTINE: As to wars, when has the earth not been scourged by them at different periods and places? To pass over remote history, when the barbarians were everywhere invading Roman provinces in the reign of Gallienus, how many of our brothers who were then alive do we think could have believed that the end was near, since this happened long after the ascension of the Lord! Thus, we do not know what the nature of those signs will be when the end is really near at hand, if those present ones have not been so foretold that they should at least be understood in the church. Certainly, there are two nations and two kingdoms, namely, one of Christ, the other of the devil. *Letter,* 199 to Hesychius 35.

Ecological Crisis. ORIGEN: Just as bodies become sick before their death if they do not suffer violence from without, and in all cases the way of separation of soul from body comes through weakness, so it happens with the whole course of the world creation. When the creation begins to decay, having as it has both beginning and end, it must grow weak before its dissolution. At this point the earth may be frequently shaken with earthquakes. The air having received some diseased contagion may become overrun with pestilence. Moreover the vital energies of the earth itself may suddenly fail and strangle its fruits. These destructive forces may pollute the regenerative capacity of all trees. *Commentary on Matthew* 34.

⌗ CLOSING PRAYER

Almighty and merciful God . . . grant, we beseech you, that we may so faithfully serve you in this life that we fail not finally to attain your heavenly promises, through the merits of Jesus Christ our Lord. Amen. *The Leonine Sacramentary*

Christic Will Come Again

THEME

We call to the Lord (Ps 132:1-18), who has made a covenant with us (2 Sam 23:1-7) through his only son, Jesus Christ (Jn 18:33-37), that he will free us from our sins and come again (Rev 1:4b-8).

OPENING PRAYER: *Proper 29, Reign of Christ the King*

Look down, O Lord, from your heavenly throne, illumine the darkness of this night with your celestial brightness, and from the children of light, banish the deeds of darkness; through Jesus Christ our Lord. Amen. *The Ambrosian Sacramentary*

OLD TESTAMENT READING: *2 Samuel 23:1-7*

REFLECTIONS FROM THE CHURCH FATHERS

The Grace Will Come. CYRIL OF JERUSALEM: In Moses' day the Spirit was given by the imposition of hands; and Peter imparted the Spirit by the imposition of hands. On you also, who are to be baptized, the grace will come. In what manner I do not say, for I do not anticipate the proper time. . . . We learn clearly in the book of Kings [Samuel], of Samuel and David, how by the Holy Spirit they prophesied and were leaders of the prophets. Samuel in fact was called the "seer." David says plainly, "The spirit of the Lord has spoken by me"; and in the psalms, "and do not take your holy spirit from me"; and again, "May your good

spirit guide me on level ground." *Catechetical Lectures* 16.26, 28.

PSALM OF RESPONSE: *Psalm 132:1-18*

NEW TESTAMENT READING: *Revelation 1:4b-8*

REFLECTIONS FROM THE CHURCH FATHERS

Through the Spirit the Apostles Bring Grace. CAESARIUS OF ARLES: Asia means "elevated," by which the human race is indicated. These seven churches and the lampstands are to be seriously considered because it is the sevenfold grace that is given by God through Jesus Christ, our Lord, to us of the human race who have believed. For he himself promised to send to us the Spirit Paraclete from heaven, whom he also sent to the apostles who were seen to be in Asia, that is, in the prideful world, where he also gave the sevenfold grace to the seven churches, that is to us, through his servant John. *Exposition on the Apocalypse* 1.4, Homily 1.

Christ Is the Pattern of Our Salvation. ATHANASIUS: Although it was after us that he was made man for us and became our brother by likeness of body, still he is called and is the firstborn of us. Since all people were lost through the transgression of Adam, Christ's flesh was saved first of all and was liberated, because it was the Word's body. Henceforth also we, having become joined together with his body, are saved through it. For in his body the Lord becomes our guide to the kingdom of heaven and to his own Father, saying, "I am the way" and "the door," and "through me all must enter." Wherefore he is also said to be "firstborn from the dead," not because he died before us, since we died first, but because he suffered death for us and abolished it, and therefore, as man, was the first to rise, raising his own body for our sakes. Therefore, since he has risen, we too shall rise from the dead from him and through him. *Discourses Against the Arians* 2.61.

Christ Will Return in the Flesh. FULGENTIUS OF RUSPE: Hold most firmly and never doubt that the Word made flesh always has the same truly human flesh with which God the Word was born of the Virgin, with which he was crucified and died, with which he rose and ascended to heaven and sits at the right hand of God, with which he will come again to judge the living and the dead. For this reason, the apostles heard from the angels, "He . . . will return in the same way as you have seen him going into heaven," and the blessed John says, "Behold, he will come amid the clouds, and every eye will see him, even those who pierced him; and all the tribes of the earth will see him." *Letter to Peter on the Faith* 20.63.

GOSPEL READING: *John 18:33-37*

REFLECTIONS FROM THE CHURCH FATHERS

Pilate Worried That Caesar's Rule Is Endangered. CYRIL OF ALEXANDRIA: For, as the inhabitants of Judea were always moved to riots and civil strife and were easily provoked to revolt, Caesar's officers were proportionally vigilant in this respect and were more careful guardians of order. To this end, they inflicted the most summary penalties on people who had this charge brought against them, sometimes groundlessly. The Jews, therefore, make it a charge against Christ that he ruled over Israel. . . . Pilate, then, speaks out plainly what he heard the Jews muttering and bids Jesus answer him, whether he was in truth the King of the Jews. Pilate was full of anxiety, it would appear, and thought Caesar's rule was endangered. Therefore he was anxious to learn the truth in order to meet what had been done with appropriate retribution and acquit of blame the office entrusted to him by the Romans. *Commentary on the Gospel of John* 12.

In the World, but Not of It. AUGUSTINE: Listen, everyone, Jews and Gentiles, circumcised and uncircumcised. Listen, all kings of the earth.

I am no hindrance to your rule in this world, for "my kingdom is not of this world." . . . What in fact is Christ's kingdom? It is simply those who believe in him, those to whom he said, "You are not of this world, even as I am not of this world." He willed, nevertheless, that they should be in the world, which is why he prayed to the Father, "I ask you not to take them out of the world but to protect them from the evil one." . . . Indeed, his kingdom is here until the end of time, and until the harvest it will contain weeds. . . . For God has snatched us from the powers of darkness and brought us into the kingdom of his beloved Son. That is that kingdom of which he said, "My kingdom is not of this world; my kingly power does not come from here." *Tractates on the Gospel of John* 155.2.

Jesus Rejects Dignity and Power. TERTULLIAN: If he exercised no right of power even over his own followers, to whom he discharged menial tasks—if, in short, though conscious of his own kingdom, he shrank back from being made a king—he in the fullest way possible gave his own as an example for turning coldly from all the pride and outward trappings, as well of dignity as of power. *On Idolatry* 18.

Jesus' Kingdom Continues. EUSEBIUS OF CAESAREA: The throne of the kingdom conferred on Jesus is nothing mortal or temporal. Rather, it truly extended throughout the whole world like light shining as the moon established forever, enlightening understanding souls through his divine and heavenly teaching. *To Stephanus* 15.4.

⌘ CLOSING PRAYER

Almighty and everlasting God, mercifully look on our infirmities, and in all our dangers and necessities stretch forth your right hand to help and defend us, through Jesus Christ our Lord. Amen. *The Gregorian Sacramentary*

Ancient Christian Commentary on Scripture
CITATIONS

The following volumes from the Ancient Christian Commentary on Scripture, Thomas C. Oden, general editor (Downers Grove, Ill.: InterVarsity Press), were cited in this book.

Genesis 1–11, ed. Andrew Louth, Old Testament volume 1, ©2001.

Exodus, Leviticus, Numbers, Deuteronomy, ed. Joseph T. Lienhard, Old Testament volume 3, ©2001.

Joshua, Judges, Ruth, 1–2 Samuel, ed. John R. Franke, Old Testament volume 4, ©2005.

1–2 Kings, 1–2 Chronicles, Ezra, Nehemiah, Esther, ed. Mario Conti, Old Testament volume 5, ©2008.

Job, ed. Manlio Simonetti and Marco Conti, Old Testament volume 6, ©2003.

Psalms 1–50, ed. Craig A. Blaising and Carmen S. Hardin, Old Testament volume 7, ©2008.

Psalms 51–150, ed. Quentin F. Wesselschmidt, Old Testament volume 8

Proverbs, Ecclesiastes, Song of Solomon, ed. J. Robert Wright, Old Testament volume 9, ©2005.

Isaiah 1–39, ed. Steven A. McKinion, Old Testament volume 10, ©2004.

Isaiah 40–66, ed. Mark W. Elliott, Old Testament volume 11, ©2007.

Jeremiah, Lamentations, ed. Dean O. Wenthe, Old Testament volume 12, ©2009.

Ezekiel, Daniel, ed. Kenneth Stevenson and Donald McCullough, Old Testament volume 13, ©2008.

The Twelve Prophets, ed. Alberto Ferreiro, Old Testament volume 14, ©2003.

Matthew 1–13, ed. Manlio Simonetti, New Testament volume 1a, ©2001.

Mark, ed. Thomas C. Oden and Christopher A. Hall, New Testament volume 2 (2nd ed.), ©2005.

Luke, ed. Arthur A. Just Jr., New Testament volume 3, ©2003.

John 1–10, ed. Joel C. Elowsky, New Testament volume 4a, ©2006.

John 11–21, ed. Joel C. Elowsky, New Testament volume 4b, ©2007.

Acts, ed. Francis Martin, New Testament volume 5, ©2006.

Romans, ed. Gerald L. Bray, New Testament volume 6, ©2005.

1–2 Corinthians, ed. Gerald L. Bray, New Testament volume 7, ©2006.

Galatians, Ephesians, Philippians, ed. Mark J. Edwards, New Testament volume 8, ©2005.

Colossians, 1–2 Thessalonians, 1–2 Timothy, Titus, Philemon, ed. Peter Gorday, New Testament volume 9, ©2000.

Hebrews, ed. Erik M. Heen and Philip D. W. Krey, New Testament volume 10, ©2005.

James, 1–2 Peter, 1–3 John, Jude, ed. Gerald L. Bray, New Testament volume 11, ©2000.

Revelation, ed. William C. Weinrich, New Testament volume 12, ©2005.

PRAYER CITATIONS

WEEK 1

Opening Prayer: The Gelasian Sacramentary, *A Chain of Prayer Across the Ages,* arranged by Selina Fitzherbert Fox (New York: E. P. Dutton, 1943), p. 6.

Closing Prayer: The Gregorian Sacramentary, *A Chain of Prayer Across the Ages,* p. 35.

WEEK 2

Opening Prayer: Bede, *The Westminster Collection of Christian Prayers,* compiled by Dorothy M. Stewart (Louisville, Ky.: Westminster John Knox Press, 2002), p. 15.

Closing Prayer: Ambrose, *The Westminster Collection of Christian Prayers,* p. 173.

WEEK 3

Opening Prayer: Rabbula of Edessa, *Two Thousand Years of Prayer,* compiled by Michael Counsell (Harrisburg, Penn.: Morehouse, 1999), p. 59.

Closing Prayer: Ephrem the Syrian, *The Westminster Collection of Christian Prayers,* p. 249.

WEEK 4

Opening Prayer: Clement of Rome, *The Westminster Collection of Christian Prayers,* p. 337.

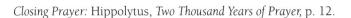
Closing Prayer: Hippolytus, *Two Thousand Years of Prayer,* p. 12.

WEEK 5

Opening Prayer: The Gregorian Sacramentary, *Two Thousand Years of Prayer,* p. 103.

Closing Prayer: The Ambrosian Sacramentary, *Two Thousand Years of Prayer,* p. 102.

WEEK 6

Opening Prayer: The Gelasian Sacramentary, printed in the Book of Common Prayer, 1549, *A Chain of Prayer Across the Ages,* p. 55.

Closing Prayer: The Leonine Sacramentary, *A Chain of Prayer Across the Ages,* p. 126.

WEEK 7

Opening Prayer: The Leonine Sacramentary, printed in the Book of Common Prayer, 1549, *A Chain of Prayer Across the Ages,* p. 61.

Closing Prayer: Synesius, *The Macmillan Book of Earliest Christian Hymns,* edited by F. Forrester Church and Terrence J. Mulry (New York: Macmillan, 1986), p. 165.

WEEK 8

Opening Prayer: The Leonine Sacramentary, *Ancient Collects and Other Prayers,* compiled by William Bright (Oxford: James Parker, 1908), p. 85.

Closing Prayer: Augustine, *Readings for the Daily Office from the Early Church,* compiled by J. Robert Wright (New York: Church Hymnal Corporation, 1991), p. 109.

WEEK 9

Opening Prayer: Augustine, *The Westminster Collection of Christian Prayers,* p. 273.

Closing Prayer: The Leonine Sacramentary, *A Chain of Prayer Across the Ages,* p. 265.

WEEK 10

Opening Prayer: The Gregorian Sacramentary, *Book of English Collects,* no. 13, Roger Geffen, *The Handbook of Public Prayer* (New York: Macmillan, 1963), p. 75.

Closing Prayer: The Gelasian Sacramentary, *Two Thousand Years of Prayer,* p. 98.

WEEK 11

Opening Prayer: The Gelasian Sacramentary, printed in the Book of Common Prayer, 1549, *A Chain of Prayer Across the Ages,* p. 121.

Closing Prayer: Clement of Rome, *The Westminster Collection of Christian Prayers,* p. 242.

WEEK 12

Opening Prayer: The Gregorian Sacramentary, *Two Thousand Years of Prayer,* p. 103.

Closing Prayer: Augustine, *The Westminster Collection of Christian Prayers,* p. 351.

WEEK 13

Opening Prayer: The Gelasian Sacramentary, *The Westminster Collection of Christian Prayers,* p. 197.

Closing Prayer: The Leonine Sacramentary, *Two Thousand Years of Prayer,* p. 108.

WEEK 14

Opening Prayer: The Gelasian Sacramentary, *Prayers for Public Worship,* compiled and edited by James Ferguson (New York: Harper & Brothers, 1958), p. 84.

Closing Prayer: Clement of Rome, *The Westminster Collection of Christian Prayers,* p. 262.

WEEK 15

Opening Prayer: Augustine, *The Fellowship of the Saints,* compiled by Thomas S. Kepler (New York: Abingdon-Cokesbury, 1948), p. 77.

Closing Prayer: Hilary of Poitiers, *Two Thousand Years of Prayer,* p. 28.

WEEK 16

Opening Prayer: The Gelasian Sacramentary, *Two Thousand Years of Prayer,* pp. 99-100.

Closing Prayer: The Liturgy of St. Mark, *Prayers for Public Worship,* p. 43.

WEEK 17

Opening Prayer: The Leonine Sacramentary, *Ancient Collects and Other Prayers,* p. 79.

Closing Prayer: Bede, *Prayers for Public Worship,* no. 373, *The Handbook of Public Prayer,* p. 154.

WEEK 18

Opening Prayer: The Gregorian Sacramentary, *Book of English Collects,* no. 40, *The Handbook of Public Prayer,* p. 81.

Closing Prayer: The Gelasian Sacramentary, *A Chain of Prayer Across the Ages,* p. 188.

WEEK 19

Opening Prayer: The Gelasian Sacramentary, *A Chain of Prayer Across the Ages,* p. 140.

Closing Prayer: The Gregorian Sacramentary, printed in the Book of Common Prayer, *A Chain of Prayer Across the Ages,* p. 131.

WEEK 20

Opening Prayer: Irenaeus, in the Old Gallican Sacramentary, *A Chain of Prayer Across the Ages,* p. 135.

Closing Prayer: The Gelasian Sacramentary, *A Chain of Prayer Across the Ages,* p. 178.

WEEK 21

Opening Prayer: Didache, in *Prayers for Public Worship,* p. 40.

Closing Prayer: The Liturgy of St. Basil, *The Handbook of Public Prayer,* p. 199.

WEEK 22

Opening Prayer: The Gelasian Sacramentary, *A Chain of Prayer Across the Ages,* p. 66.

Closing Prayer: The Leonine Sacramentary, *A Chain of Prayer Across the Ages,* p. 117.

WEEK 23

Opening Prayer: Bede, *The Westminster Collection of Christian Prayers,* p. 138.

Closing Prayer: The Leonine Sacramentary, *The Westminster Collection of Christian Prayers,* p. 331.

WEEK 24

Opening Prayer: Rerum Deus Tenax Vigor, Ambrose, *The Macmillan Book of Earliest Christian Hymns,* p. 208.

Closing Prayer: The Gelasian Sacramentary, *Two Thousand Years of Prayer,* p. 99.

WEEK 25

Opening Prayer: The Leonine Sacramentary, *Ancient Collects and Other Prayers,* p. 3.

Closing Prayer: The Gelasian Sacramentary, *A Chain of Prayer Across the Ages,* p. 100.

WEEK 26

Opening Prayer: The Leonine Sacramentary, *A Chain of Prayer Across the Ages,* p. 175.

Closing Prayer: The Gregorian Sacramentary, *A Chain of Prayer Across the Ages,* p. 177.

WEEK 27

Opening Prayer: The Gelasian Sacramentary, *A Chain of Prayer Across the Ages,* p. 237.

Closing Prayer: The Leonine Sacramentary, *A Chain of Prayer Across the Ages,* p. 238.

WEEK 28

Opening Prayer: The Gelasian Sacramentary, *Prayers for Public Worship,* p. 135.

Closing Prayer: Irenaeus, *The Westminster Collection of Christian Prayers,* p. 98.

WEEK 29

Opening Prayer: Polycarp, *The Westminster Collection of Christian Prayers,* p. 44.

Closing Prayer: The Gelasian Sacramentary, *Ancient Collects and Other Prayers,* p. 124.

WEEK 30

Opening Prayer: The Leonine Sacramentary, *Ancient Collects and Other Prayers,* p. 84.

Closing Prayer: The Gelasian Sacramentary, *Ancient Collects and Other Prayers,* p. 85.

WEEK 31

Opening Prayer: The Gelasian Sacramentary, *A Chain of Prayer Across the Ages,* p. 24.

Closing Prayer: The Gallican Sacramentary, *A Chain of Prayer Across the Ages,* p. 20.

WEEK 32

Opening Prayer: The Leonine Sacramentary, *A Chain of Prayer Across the Ages,* p. 160.

Closing Prayer: The Gelasian Sacramentary, *A Chain of Prayer Across the Ages,* p. 70.

WEEK 33

Opening Prayer: The Gallican Sacramentary, *A Chain of Prayer Across the Ages,* p. 175.

Closing Prayer: The Leonine Sacramentary, *Ancient Collects and Other Prayers,* p. 174.

WEEK 34

Opening Prayer: The Gelasian Sacramentary, *A Chain of Prayer Across the Ages,* p. 115.

Closing Prayer: The Leonine Sacramentary, *A Chain of Prayer Across the Ages,* p. 177.

WEEK 35

Opening Prayer: From an Ancient Collect, *A Chain of Prayer Across the Ages,* p. 198.

Closing Prayer: The Gelasian Sacramentary, printed in the Book of Common Prayer, 1549, *A Chain of Prayer Across the Ages,* p. 208.

WEEK 36

Opening Prayer: The Gelasian Sacramentary, *A Chain of Prayer Across the Ages,* p. 209.

Closing Prayer: The Leonine Sacramentary, *A Chain of Prayer Across the Ages,* p. 220.

WEEK 37

Opening Prayer: The Gregorian Sacramentary, *A Chain of Prayer Across the Ages,* p. 221.

Closing Prayer: Ephrem the Syrian, *The Westminster Collection of Christian Prayers,* p. 283.

WEEK 38

Opening Prayer: The Gregorian Sacramentary, Prayer Book version, in *Book of English Collects,* no. 11, *The Handbook of Public Prayer,* p. 74.

Closing Prayer: The Gelasian Sacramentary, *A Chain of Prayer Across the Ages,* p. 71.

WEEK 39

Opening Prayer: The Gregorian Sacramentary, in *Book of English Collects,* no. 27, *The Handbook of Public Prayer,* p. 78.

Closing Prayer: Columbanus, *Two Thousand Years of Prayer,* p. 76.

WEEK 40

Opening Prayer: Bede, *Two Thousand Years of Prayer,* p. 87.

Closing Prayer: The Gelasian Sacramentary, *Prayers for Public Worship,* p. 10.

WEEK 41

Opening Prayer: The Gelasian Sacramentary, *Prayers for Public Worship,* p. 54.

Closing Prayer: Augustine, *Readings for the Daily Office from the Early Church,* p. 114.

WEEK 42

Opening Prayer: The Gelasian Sacramentary, *Ancient Collects and Other Prayers*, p. 16.

Closing Prayer: The Leonine Sacramentary, *Ancient Collects and Other Prayers*, p. 83.

WEEK 43

Opening Prayer: The Gelasian Sacramentary, *Prayers for Public Worship*, p. 67.

Closing Prayer: The Leonine Sacramentary, *Ancient Collects and Other Prayers*, p. 74.

WEEK 44

Opening Prayer: The Leonine Sacramentary, *Ancient Collects and Other Prayers*, p. 168.

Closing Prayer: The Gelasian Sacramentary, *Ancient Collects and Other Prayers*, p. 168.

WEEK 45

Opening Prayer: The Gelasian Sacramentary, *Prayers for Public Worship*, p. 241.

Closing Prayer: The Gregorian Sacramentary, *Prayers for Public Worship*, p. 245.

WEEK 46

Opening Prayer: The Gelasian Sacramentary, *Prayers for Public Worship*, p. 77.

Closing Prayer: Columbanus, *Two Thousand Years of Prayer*, p. 76.

WEEK 47

Opening Prayer: The Gelasian Sacramentary, *Two Thousand Years of Prayer*, p. 99.

Closing Prayer: The Leonine Sacramentary, *Two Thousand Years of Prayer,* p. 108.

WEEK 48

Opening Prayer: The Leonine Sacramentary, *Two Thousand Years of Prayer,* p. 107.

Closing Prayer: The Gelasian Sacramentary, *Two Thousand Years of Prayer,* p. 99.

WEEK 49

Opening Prayer: The Gelasian Sacramentary, *Two Thousand Years of Prayer,* p. 100.

Closing Prayer: The Leonine Sacramentary, *Two Thousand Years of Prayer,* p. 107.

WEEK 50

Opening Prayer: The Gelasian Sacramentary, *Two Thousand Years of Prayer,* p. 101.

Closing Prayer: The Gregorian Sacramentary, *Two Thousand Years of Prayer,* p. 106.

WEEK 51

Opening Prayer: The Gregorian Sacramentary, *Two Thousand Years of Prayer,* p. 105.

Closing Prayer: The Leonine Sacramentary, *Two Thousand Years of Prayer,* p. 106.

WEEK 52

Opening Prayer: The Ambrosian Sacramentary, *Two Thousand Years of Prayer,* p. 102.

Closing Prayer: The Gregorian Sacramentary, *Two Thousand Years of Prayer,* p. 102.

BIOGRAPHICAL SKETCHES

Ambrose of Milan (c. 333-397). Bishop of Milan and teacher of Augustine who defended the divinity of the Holy Spirit and the perpetual virginity of Mary. He was known as a pastor of souls as well as a scholar, a good listener and counselor. Among his chief works are *On the Gospel of Luke, On the Holy Spirit and Mysteries.*

Ambrosian Sacramentary. One of three surviving distinct liturgical rites regularly used in the Latin Church, and attributed to St. Ambrose for the first time in the eighth century.

Ambrosiaster (fl. c. 366-384). Name given by Erasmus to the author of a work once thought to have been composed by Ambrose.

Ammonius (c. fifth century). An Aristotelian commentator and teacher in Alexandria, where he was born and of whose school he became head. Also an exegete of Plato, he enjoyed fame among his contemporaries and successors, although modern critics accuse him of pedantry and banality.

Andreas (c. seventh century). Monk who collected commentary from earlier writers to form a catena on various biblical books.

Andrew of Caesarea (early sixth century). Bishop of Caesarea in Cappadocia. He produced one of the earliest Greek commentaries on Revelation and defended the divine inspiration of its author.

Aphrahat (c. 270-350; fl. 337-345). "The Persian Sage" and first major

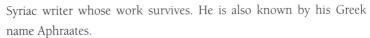

Syriac writer whose work survives. He is also known by his Greek name Aphraates.

Apostolic Constitutions (c. 381-394). Also known as *Constitutions of the Holy Apostles* and thought to be redacted by Julian of Neapolis. The work is divided into eight books and is primarily a collection of and expansion on previous works such as the *Didache* (c. 140) and the *Apostolic Traditions*. Book 8 ends with 85 canons from various sources and is elsewhere known as the Apostolic Canons.

Apringius of Beja (middle sixth century). Iberian bishop and exegete. Heavily influenced by Tyconius, he wrote a commentary on Revelation in Latin, of which two large fragments survive.

Arator (490-550). Latin poet and orator, perhaps of Milan. He is known for his epic *On the Acts of the Apostles,* which he composed in Rome for Pope Vigilius, who ordained him a subdeacon. It is the only Western writing on Acts before Bede. The epic, favored by Bede and popular during medieval times, is marked by Arator's allegorical and mystical exegesis.

Athanasius (c. 295-373). A native of Alexandria and secretary/deacon to his bishop at the Council of Nicaea (325), Athanasius was elevated to the Episcopal See of Alexandria. He was exiled more than four times. He was a prolific writer whose works include *Three Discourses Against the Arians* and *Life of St. Anthony.*

Augustine of Hippo (354-430). Bishop of Hippo and a voluminous writer on philosophical, exegetical, theological and ecclesiological topics. He formulated the Western doctrines of predestination and original sin in his writings against the Pelagians. He was very involved in the theological controversies of the time period.

Basil of Seleucia (fl. 444-468). Bishop of Seleucia in Isauria and ecclesiastical writer. He took part in the Synod of Constantinople in 448 for the condemnation of the Eutychian errors and the deposition of their great champion, Dioscurus of Alexandria.

Basil the Great (b. c. 330; fl. 357-379). One of the Cappadocian fathers, bishop of Caesarea and champion of the teaching on the Trinity propounded at Nicaea in 325. He was a great administrator and founded a monastic rule. His devotion to the cause of the poor earned him the title of "Great."

Bede the Venerable (c. 672/673-735). Born in Northumbria, he was put under the care of Benedictine monks at the age of seven and received a broad classical education in the monastic tradition. Considered one of the most learned men of his age, he is the author of *An Ecclesiastical History of the English People.*

Braulio of Saragossa (c. 585-651). Bishop of Saragossa (631-651) and noted writer of the Visigothic renaissance. His *Life* of St. Aemilianus is his crowning literary achievement.

Caesarius of Arles (c. 470-543). Bishop of Arles renowned for his attention to his pastoral duties. Among his surviving works, the most important is a collection of some 238 sermons that display an ability to preach Christian doctrine to a variety of audiences.

Cassiodorus (c. 485-580). Founder of the monastery of Vivarium, Calabria, where monks transcribed classic sacred and profane texts, Greek and Latin, preserving them for the Western tradition.

Chromatius of Aquileia (fl. 400). Bishop of Aquileia, friend of Rufinus and Jerome, and author of tracts and sermons.

Chrysostom (John Chrysostom) (344/354-407; fl. 386-407). Bishop of Constantinople who was noted for his orthodoxy, his eloquence (hence his nickname Chrysostom = "Golden-tongued") and his attacks on Christian laxity in high places.

Clement of Alexandria (c. 150-215). Born to pagan parents, Clement is sometimes called "the first Christian scholar." A highly educated Christian convert from paganism, head of the catechetical school in Alexandria and pioneer of Christian scholarship. His major works, *Protrepticus, Paedagogus* and the *Stromata,* bring Christian doctrine face to face with the ideas and achievements of his time.

Clement of Rome (fl. c. 92-101). Pope whose *Epistle to the Corinthians*

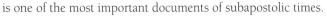

is one of the most important documents of subapostolic times.

Clementina (Pseudo-Clementines) (third-fourth century). A series of apocryphal writings pertaining to a conjured life of Clement of Rome. Written in a form of popular legend, the stories from Clement's life, including his opposition to Simon Magus, illustrate and promote articles of Christian teaching. It is likely that the corpus is a derivative of a number of Gnostic and Judeo-Christian writings. Dating the corpus is a complicated issue.

Columbanus (Columban) (543-615). A teacher, missionary, and founder of monasteries who fought against corruption in the church. His Irish Latin poetry, rules and letters were formational for the culture of the time period.

Cyprian (fl. 248-258). Martyred bishop of Carthage who maintained that those baptized by schismatics and heretics had no share in the blessings of the church. He was generous with his wealth and dedicated to chastity.

Cyril of Alexandria (375-444; fl. 412-444). Patriarch of Alexandria whose extensive exegesis, characterized especially by a strong espousal of the unity of Christ, led to the condemnation of Nestorius in 431.

Cyril of Jerusalem (c. 315-386; fl. c. 348). Bishop of Jerusalem after 350 and author of Catechetical Homilies, which were important for sacramental theology and baptism.

Didache (c. 140). Of unknown authorship, this text intertwines Jewish ethics with Christian liturgical practice to form a whole discourse on the "way of life." It exerted an enormous amount of influence in the patristic period and was especially used in the training of catechumen.

Didymus the Blind (c. 313-398). Blind from the age of four or five, this Alexandrian exegete was much influenced by Origen and admired by Jerome, who considered him his master.

Ephrem the Syrian (b. c. 306; fl. 363-373). A Syrian writer of commentaries and devotional hymns that are sometimes regarded as the greatest specimens of Christian poetry prior to Dante.

Eusebius of Caesarea (c. 260/263-340). Bishop of Caesarea, partisan of the Emperor Constantine and first historian of the Christian church. He argued that the truth of the gospel had been foreshadowed in pagan writings but had to defend his own doctrine against suspicion of Arian sympathies.

Euthymius (377-473). A native of Melitene and influential monk. He was educated by Bishop Otreius of Melitene, who ordained him priest and placed him in charge of all the monasteries in his diocese. When the Council of Chalcedon (451) condemned the errors of Eutyches, it was greatly due to the authority of Euthymius that most of the Eastern recluses accepted its decrees. The empress Eudoxia returned to Chalcedonian orthodoxy through his efforts.

Evagrius of Pontus (c. 345-399). Disciple and teacher of ascetic life who astutely absorbed and creatively transmitted the spirituality of Egyptian and Palestinian monasticism of the late fourth century. Although Origenist elements of his writings were formally condemned by the Fifth Ecumenical Council (Constantinople II, A.D. 553), his literary corpus continued to influence the tradition of the church.

Fulgentius of Ruspe (c. 467-532). Bishop of Ruspe and author of many orthodox sermons and tracts under the influence of Augustine.

Gallican Sacramentary. From the fifth century to the ninth century, these were chants of the ancient liturgies as practiced in French Gaul.

Gaudentius of Brescia (fl. 395). Successor of Filastrius as bishop of Brescia and author of twenty-one Eucharistic sermons.

Gelasian Sacramentary. The most complete and oldest extant manuscript of the Roman Sacramentary. Its ancestry is believed to date back to between 628 and 715. Trium Magorum ("Three Magi") refers to the prayers associated with the Feast of the Epiphany.

Gregorian Sacramentary. A service book with a complex history, whose date and authenticity are still debated. It has been suggested it dates back to 593. It received its definitive form under Gregory II.

Gregory of Elvira (fl. 359-385). Bishop of Elvira who wrote allegorical

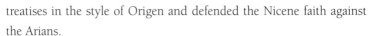

treatises in the style of Origen and defended the Nicene faith against the Arians.

Gregory of Nazianzus (b. 329/330; fl. 372-389). Cappadocian father, bishop of Constantinople, friend of Basil the Great and Gregory of Nyssa, and author of theological orations, sermons and poetry.

Gregory of Nyssa (c. 335-394). Bishop of Nyssa and brother of Basil the Great. A Cappadocian father and author of catechetical orations, he was a philosophical theologian of great originality.

Gregory the Great (c. 540-604). Pope from 590, the fourth and last of the Latin "Doctors of the Church." He was a prolific author and a powerful unifying force within the Latin Church, initiating the liturgical reform that brought about the Gregorian Sacramentary and Gregorian chant.

Hilary of Arles (c. 401-449). Archbishop of Arles and leader of the Semi-Pelagian party. Hilary incurred the wrath of Pope Leo I when he removed a bishop from his see and appointed a new bishop. Leo demoted Arles from a metropolitan see to a bishopric to assert papal power over the church in Gaul.

Hilary of Poitiers (c. 315-367). Bishop of Poitiers and called the "Athanasius of the West" because of his defense (against the Arians) of the common nature of Father and Son.

Hippolytus (fl. 222-245). Recent scholarship places Hippolytus in a Palestinian context, personally familiar with Origen. Though he is known chiefly for *The Refutation of All Heresies,* he was primarily a commentator on Scripture (especially the Old Testament) employing typological exegesis.

Ignatius of Antioch (c. 35-107/112). Bishop of Antioch who wrote several letters to local churches while being taken from Antioch to Rome to be martyred. In the letters, which warn against heresy, he stresses orthodox Christology, the centrality of the Eucharist and unique role of the bishop in preserving the unity of the church.

Incomplete Work on Matthew. A widely disseminated commentary on the Gospel of Matthew, once thought to be the work of John Chrysostom, containing 54 homilies. It lacks comment, however, on Matthew 8:11–10:15 and 13:14–18:35; hence the attribution "incomplete."

Irenaeus (c. 135-c. 202). Bishop of Lyons who published the most famous and influential refutation of Gnostic thought.

Isaac of Nineveh (d. c. 700). Also known as Isaac the Syrian or Isaac Syrus, this monastic writer served for a short while as bishop of Nineveh before retiring to live a secluded monastic life. His writings on ascetic subjects survive in the form of numerous homilies.

Isho'dad of Merv (fl. c. 850). Nestorian bishop of Hedatta. He wrote commentaries on parts of the Old Testament and all of the New Testament, frequently quoting Syriac fathers.

Isidore of Seville (c. 560-636). Youngest of a family of monks and clerics, including sister Florentina and brothers Leander and Fulgentius. He was an erudite author of comprehensive scale in matters both religious and sacred, including his encyclopedic *Etymologies*.

Jerome (c. 347-420). Gifted exegete and exponent of a classical Latin style, now best known as the translator of the Latin Vulgate. He defended the perpetual virginity of Mary, attacked Origen and Pelagius, and supported extreme ascetic practices.

John Cassian (360-432). Author of the *Institutes* and the *Conferences*, works purporting to relay the teachings of the Egyptian monastic fathers on the nature of the spiritual life which were highly influential in the development of Western monasticism.

John of Carpathus (c. seventh/eighth century). Perhaps John the bishop from the island of Carpathus, situated between Crete and Rhodes, who attended the Synod of 680/81. He wrote two "centuries" (a literary genre in Eastern spirituality consisting of 100 short sections, or chapters). These were entitled *Chapters of Encouragement to the Monks of India* and *Chapters on Theology and Knowledge* which are included in the *Philokalia*.

John of Damascus (c. 650-750). Arab monastic and theologian whose writings enjoyed great influence in both the Eastern and Western Churches. His most influential writing was the *Orthodox Faith*.

John the Monk. Traditional name found in *The Festal Menaion*, believed to refer to John of Damascus. *See* John of Damascus.

Justin Martyr (c. 100/110-165; fl. c. 148-161). Palestinian philosopher who was converted to Christianity, "the only sure and worthy philosophy." He traveled to Rome where he wrote several apologies against both pagans and Jews, combining Greek philosophy and Christian theology; he was eventually martyred.

Lactantius (c. 260-c. 330). Christian apologist removed from his post as teacher of rhetoric at Nicomedia upon his conversion to Christianity. He was tutor to the son of Constantine and author of *The Divine Institutes*.

Leo the Great (regn. 440-461). Bishop of Rome whose Tome to Flavian helped to strike a balance between Nestorian and Cyrilline positions at the Council of Chalcedon in 451.

Leonine Sacramentary. Mass prayer formularies with a Roman origin, which have been variously attributed, including to Leo I. It was likely written in the seventh century.

Liturgy of St. Basil (fourth century and onward). The liturgical collections of the Byzantine liturgy containing an anaphora attributed to Basil the Great. The liturgy has evolved considerably over the centuries.

Liturgy of St. Mark. The traditional main liturgy of the Orthodox Church of Alexandria.

Marius Victorinus (b. c. 280/285; fl. c. 355-363). Grammarian of African origin who taught rhetoric at Rome and translated works of Platonists. After his conversion (c. 355), he wrote against the Arians, and also wrote commentaries on Paul's letters.

Methodius (d. 311). Bishop of Olympus who celebrated virginity in a *Symposium* partly modeled on Plato's dialogue of that name.

Novatian (fl. 235-258). Roman theologian, otherwise orthodox, who formed a schismatic church after failing to become pope. His treatise on the Trinity states the classic Western doctrine.

Oecumenius (sixth century). Called the Rhetor or the Philosopher, Oecumenius wrote the earliest extant Greek commentary on Revelation. Scholia by Oecumenius on some of John Chrysostom's commentaries on the Pauline Epistles are still extant.

Olympiodorus (early sixth century). Exegete and deacon of Alexandria, known for his commentaries that come to us mostly in catenae.

Origen (b. 185; fl. c. 200-254). Influential exegete and systematic theologian. He was condemned (perhaps unfairly) for maintaining the preexistence of souls while purportedly denying the resurrection of the body. His extensive works of exegesis focus on the spiritual meaning of the text.

Paulinus of Nola (355-431). Roman senator and distinguished Latin poet whose frequent encounters with Ambrose of Milan (c. 333-397) led to his eventual conversion and baptism in 389. He eventually renounced his wealth and influential position and took up his pen to write poetry in service of Christ. He also wrote many letters to, among others, Augustine, Jerome and Rufinus.

Peter Chrysologus (c. 380-450). Latin archbishop of Ravenna whose teachings included arguments for adherence in matters of faith to the Roman see, and the relationship between grace and Christian living.

Philip the Priest (d. 455/56) Acknowledged by Gennadius as a disciple of Jerome. In his *Commentary on the Book of Job,* Philip utilizes Jerome's Vulgate, providing an important witness to the transmission of that translation. A few of his letters are extant.

Photius (c. 820-891). An important Byzantine churchman and university professor of philosophy, mathematics and theology. He was twice the patriarch of Constantinople. First he succeeded Ignatius in 858, but was deposed in 863 when Ignatius was reinstated. Again he followed Ignatius in 878 and remained the patriarch until 886, at which time he was removed by Leo VI. His most important theological work is *Address on the Mystagogy of the Holy Spirit,* in which he articulates his opposition to the Western filioque, i.e., the procession of the Holy Spirit from the Father and the Son. He is also known for his Amphilochia and Library (Bibliotheca).

Polycarp (of Smyrna) (c. 69-155). Bishop of Smyrna who vigorously fought heretics such as the Marcionites and Valentinians. He was the leading Christian figure in Roman Asia in the middle of the second century.

Primasius (fl. 550-560). Bishop of Hadrumetum in North Africa (modern Tunisia) and one of the few Africans to support the condemnation of the Three Chapters. Drawing on Augustine and Tyconius, he wrote a commentary on the apocalypse, which in allegorizing fashion views the work as referring to the history of the church.

Proclus of Constantinople (c. 390-446). Patriarch of Constantinople (434-446). His patriarchate dealt with the Nestorian controversy, rebutting, in his *Tome to the Armenian Bishops,* Theodore of Mopsuestia's Christology where Theodore was thought to have overly separated the two natures of Christ. Proclus stressed the unity of Christ in his formula "One of the Trinity suffered," which was later taken up and spread by the Scythian monks of the sixth century, resulting in the theopaschite controversy. Proclus was known as a gifted preacher and church politician, extending and expanding Constantinople's influence while avoiding conflict with Antioch, Rome and Alexandria.

Prosper of Aquitaine (c. 390-c. 463). Probably a lay monk and supporter of the theology of Augustine on grace and predestination. He collaborated closely with Pope Leo I in his doctrinal statements.

Prudentius (c. 348-c. 410). Latin poet and hymn-writer who devoted his later life to Christian writing. He wrote didactic theological poetry.

Pseudo-Clementines (third-fourth century). A series of apocryphal writings pertaining to a conjured life of Clement of Rome. Written in a form of popular legend, the stories from Clement's life, including his opposition to Simon Magus, illustrate and promote articles of Christian teaching. It is likely that the corpus is a derivative of a number of Gnostic and Judeo-Christian writings. Dating the corpus is a complicated issue.

Rabanus (Hrabanus) Maurus (c. 780-856). Frankish monk, theologian and teacher, student of Alcuin of York, then Abbot of Fulda from 822 to 842 and Archbishop of Mainz from 848 until his death in 856.

The author of poetry, homilies, treatises on education, grammar, and doctrine, and an encyclopedia titled *On the Nature of Things,* he also wrote commentaries on Scripture, including the books of Kings and Esther. Though he is technically an early medieval writer, his works are included as they reflect earlier thought.

Romanus the Melodist (fl. c. 536-556). A Jewish convert to Christianity, who may have written as many as eighty metrical sermons, which were sung rather than preached.

Sahdona (fl. 635-640). Known in Greek as Martyrius, this Syriac author was bishop of Beth Garmai. He studied in Nisibis and was exiled for his christological ideas. His most important work is the deeply scriptural "Book of Perfection," which ranks as one of the masterpieces of Syriac monastic literature.

Salvian the Presbyter (c. 400-c. 480). An important author for the history of his own time. He saw the fall of Roman civilization to the barbarians as a consequence of the reprehensible conduct of Roman Christians. In *The Governance of God* he developed the theme of divine providence.

Severian of Gabala (fl. c. 400). A contemporary of John Chrysostom, he was a highly regarded preacher in Constantinople, particularly at the imperial court, and ultimately sided with Chrysostom's accusers. He wrote homilies on Genesis.

Severus of Antioch (fl. 488-538). A monophysite theologian, consecrated bishop of Antioch in 522. Born in Pisidia, he studied in Alexandria and Beirut, taught in Constantinople and was exiled to Egypt.

Shepherd of Hermas (second century). Divided into five *Visions,* twelve *Mandates* and ten *Similitudes,* this Christian apocalypse was written by a former slave and named for the form of the second angel said to have granted him his visions. This work was highly esteemed for its moral value and was used as a textbook for catechumens in the early church.

Symeon the New Theologian (c. 949-1022). Compassionate spiritual leader known for his strict rule. He believed that the divine light could be perceived and received through the practice of mental prayer.

Synesius (c. 370-c. 413). Bishop of Ptolemais elected in 410. Born of a noble pagan family, Synesius studied in Alexandria under the neoplatonist philosopher Hypatia. His work includes nine hymns that present a complex trinitarian theology with neoplatonic influences.

Tertullian (c. 155/160-225/250; fl. c. 197-222). Brilliant Carthaginian apologist and polemicist who laid the foundations of Christology and trinitarian orthodoxy in the West, though he himself was later estranged from the catholic tradition due to its laxity.

Theodore of Heraclea (d. c. 355). An anti-Nicene bishop of Thrace. He was part of a team seeking reconciliation between Eastern and Western Christianity. In 343 he was excommunicated at the council of Sardica. His writings focus on literal interpretations of Scripture.

Theodore of Mopsuestia (c. 350-428). Bishop of Mopsuestia, founder of the Antiochene, or literalistic, school of exegesis. A great man in his day, he was later condemned as a precursor of Nestorius.

Theodoret of Cyr (c. 393-466). Bishop of Cyr (Cyrrhus), he was an opponent of Cyril who commented extensively on Old Testament texts as a lucid exponent of Antiochene exegesis.

Theophylact (c. 1050-c. 1108). Byzantine archbishop of Ohrid (or Achrida) in what is now Bulgaria. Drawing on earlier works, he wrote commentaries on several Old Testament books and all of the New Testament except for Revelation.

Valerian of Cimiez (fl. c. 422-439). Bishop of Cimiez. He participated in the councils of Riez (439) and Vaison (422) with a view to strengthening church discipline. He supported Hilary of Arles in quarrels with Pope Leo I.

Index of Names and Sources

Scripture Index

THE ANCIENT CHRISTIAN COMMENTARY ON SCRIPTURE is a twenty-nine-volume series offering contemporary readers the opportunity to study for themselves the key writings of the early church fathers. Each portion of the commentary allows the living voices of the church in its formative centuries to speak as they engage the sacred pages of Scripture.

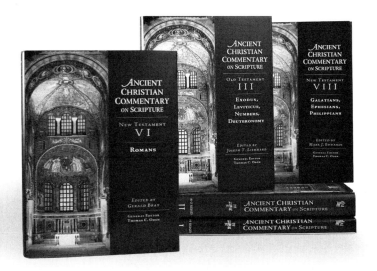

Also available:
ANCIENT CHRISTIAN COMMENTARY ON SCRIPTURE
CD-ROM COMPLETE SET

www.ivpress.com/accs